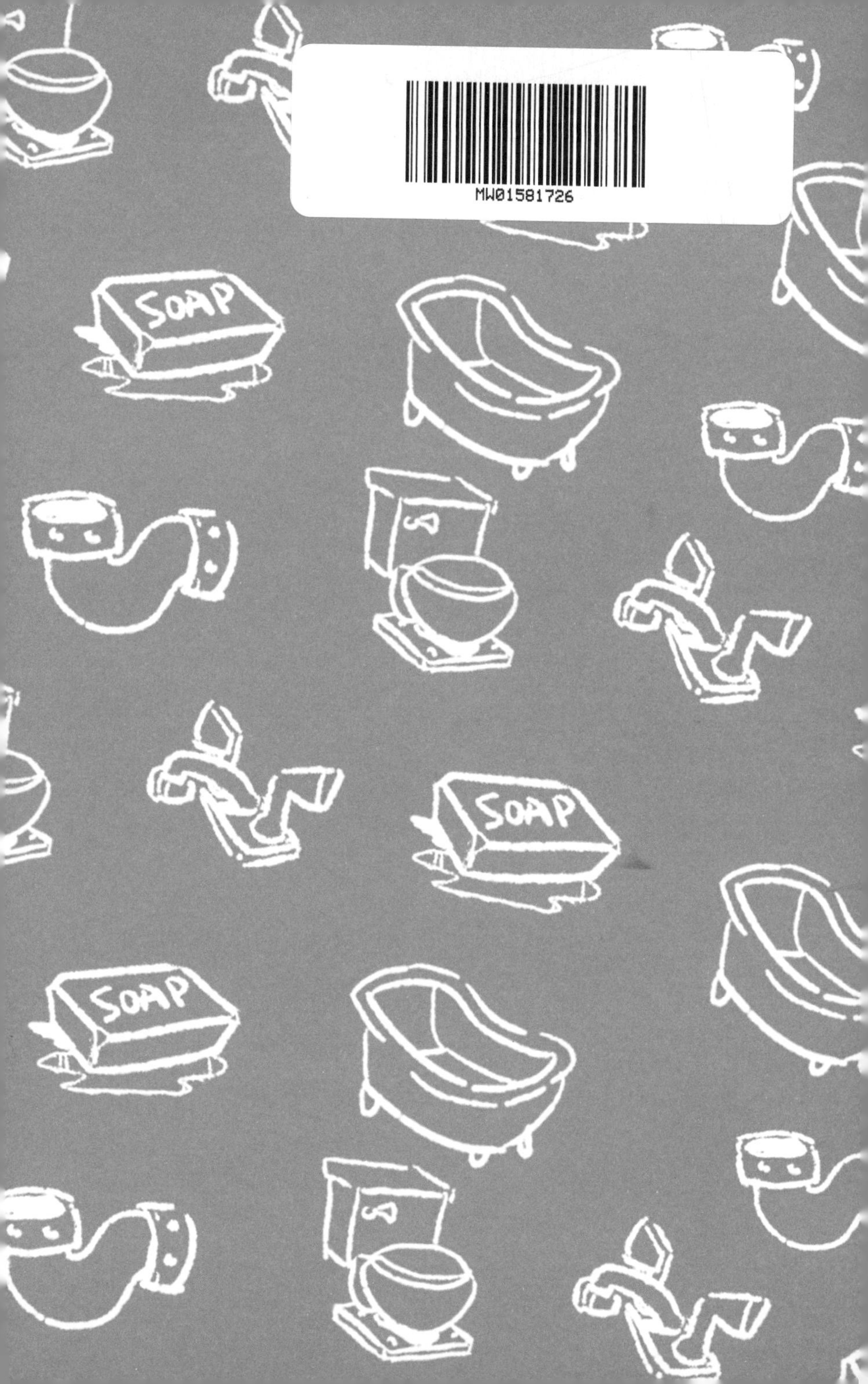
SOAP
SOAP
SOAP

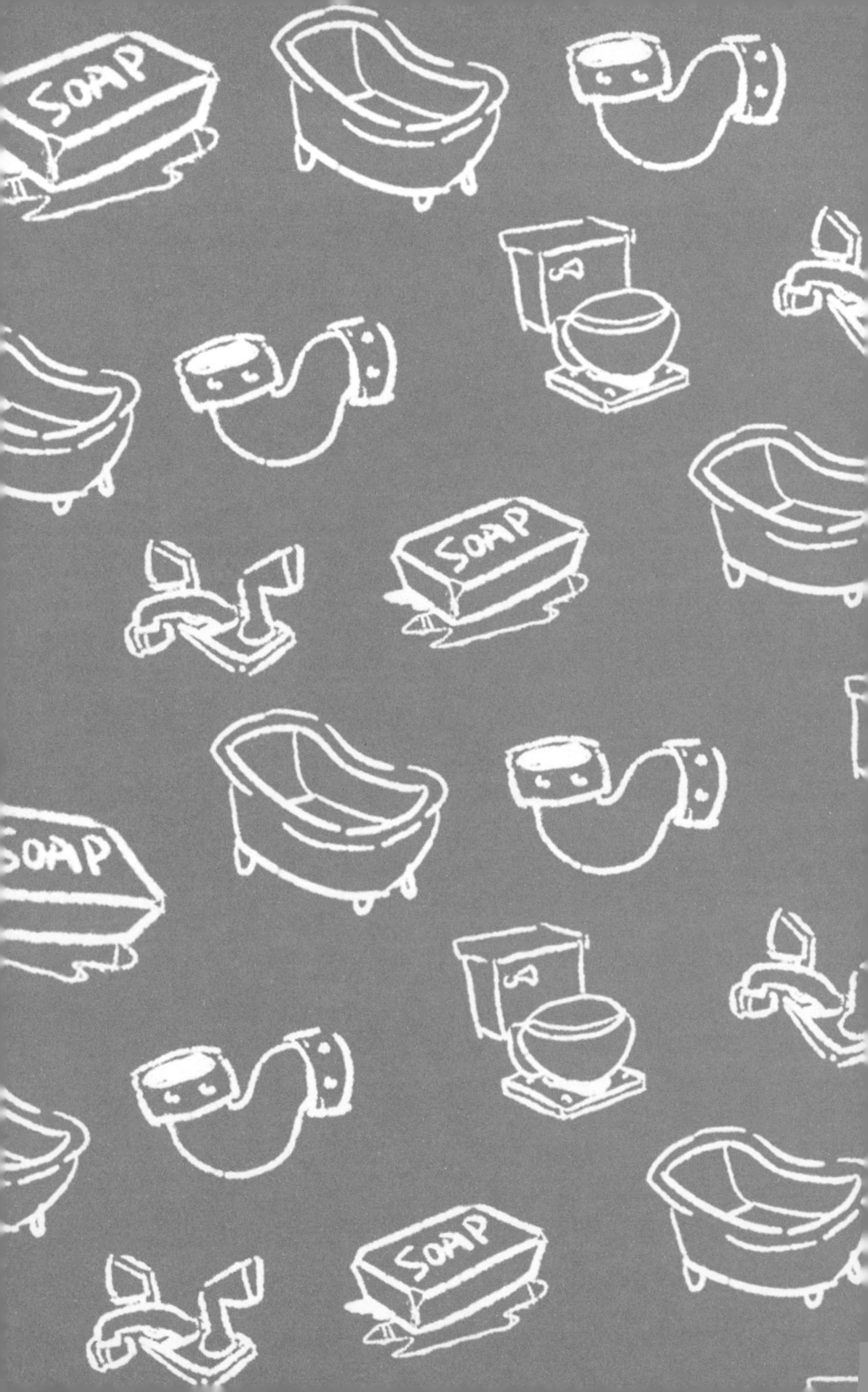
SOAP
SOAP
SOAP

BIG IDEAS THAT CHANGED THE WORLD
KEEP IT CLEAN!
DON BROWN

ABRAMS FANFARE • NEW YORK

The artwork for this book was created digitally.

Cataloging-in-Publication Data has been applied for and may be obtained from the Library of Congress.

Hardcover ISBN 978-1-4197-7996-1
eISBN 979-8-88707-578-5

Text and illustrations © 2025 Don Brown
Photograph of George E. Waring Jr. on page 112 taken by Frederick Gutekunst; courtesy of US Library of Congress Prints and Photographs Division

Editor: Howard W. Reeves
Designer: Celina Carvalho
Design Manager: Deena Micah Fleming
Managing Editor: Krista Keplinger
Production Manager: Katie Gaffney

Published in 2025 by Abrams Fanfare, an imprint of ABRAMS. All rights reserved. No portion of this book may be reproduced, stored in a retrieval system, or transmitted in any form or by any means, mechanical, electronic, photocopying, recording, or otherwise, without written permission from the publisher.

Printed and bound in China
10 9 8 7 6 5 4 3 2 1

Abrams Fanfare books are available at special discounts when purchased in quantity for premiums and promotions as well as fundraising or educational use. Special editions can also be created to specification. For details, contact specialsales@abramsbooks.com or the address below.

Abrams Fanfare™ and the Abrams Fanfare logo are trademarks of
Harry N. Abrams, Inc.

ABRAMS The Art of Books
195 Broadway, New York, NY 10007
abramsbooks.com

Dedicated to Andy and Cody . . . unironically.

Note to Reader: Unless otherwise noted, quotation marks signal actual quotes.

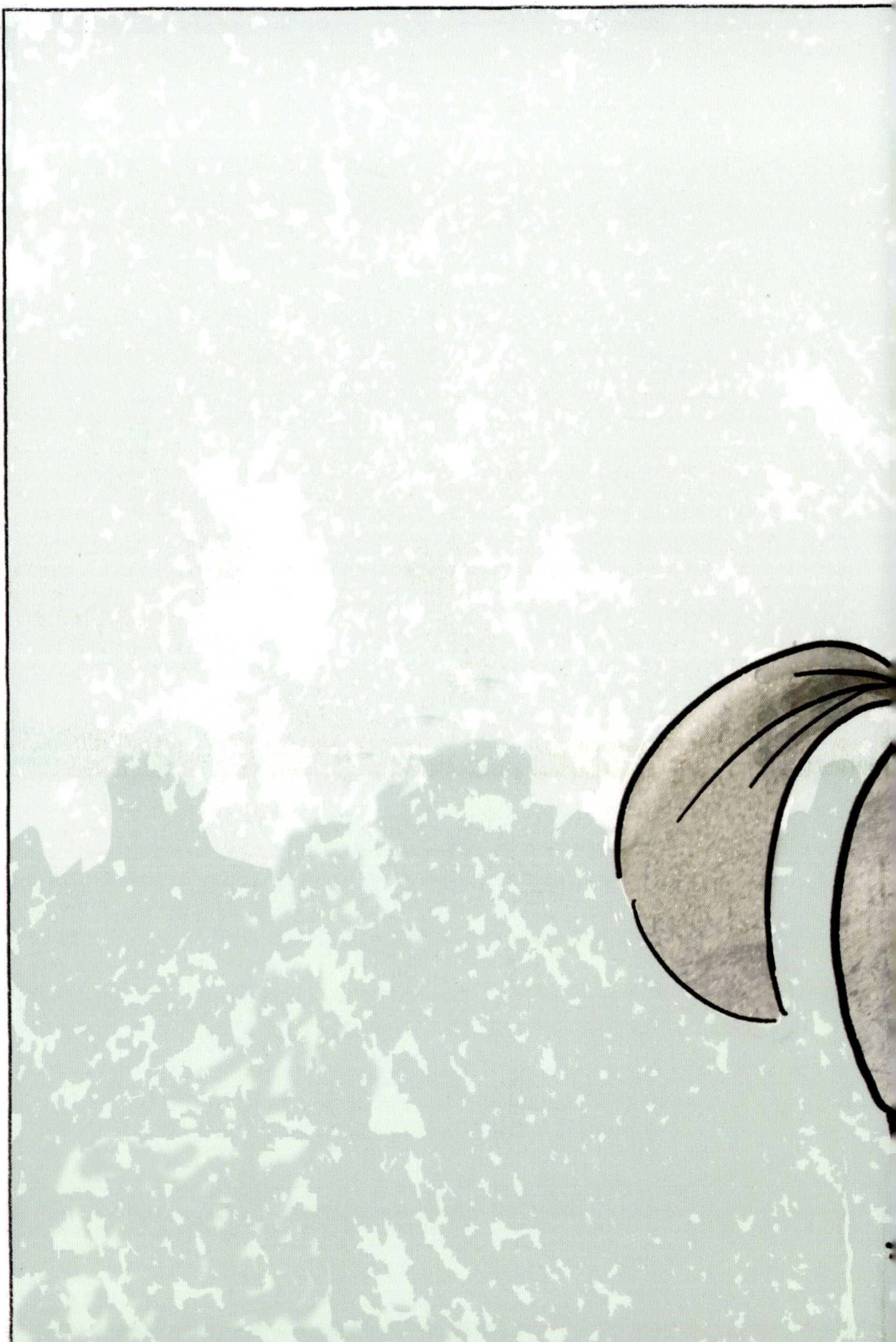

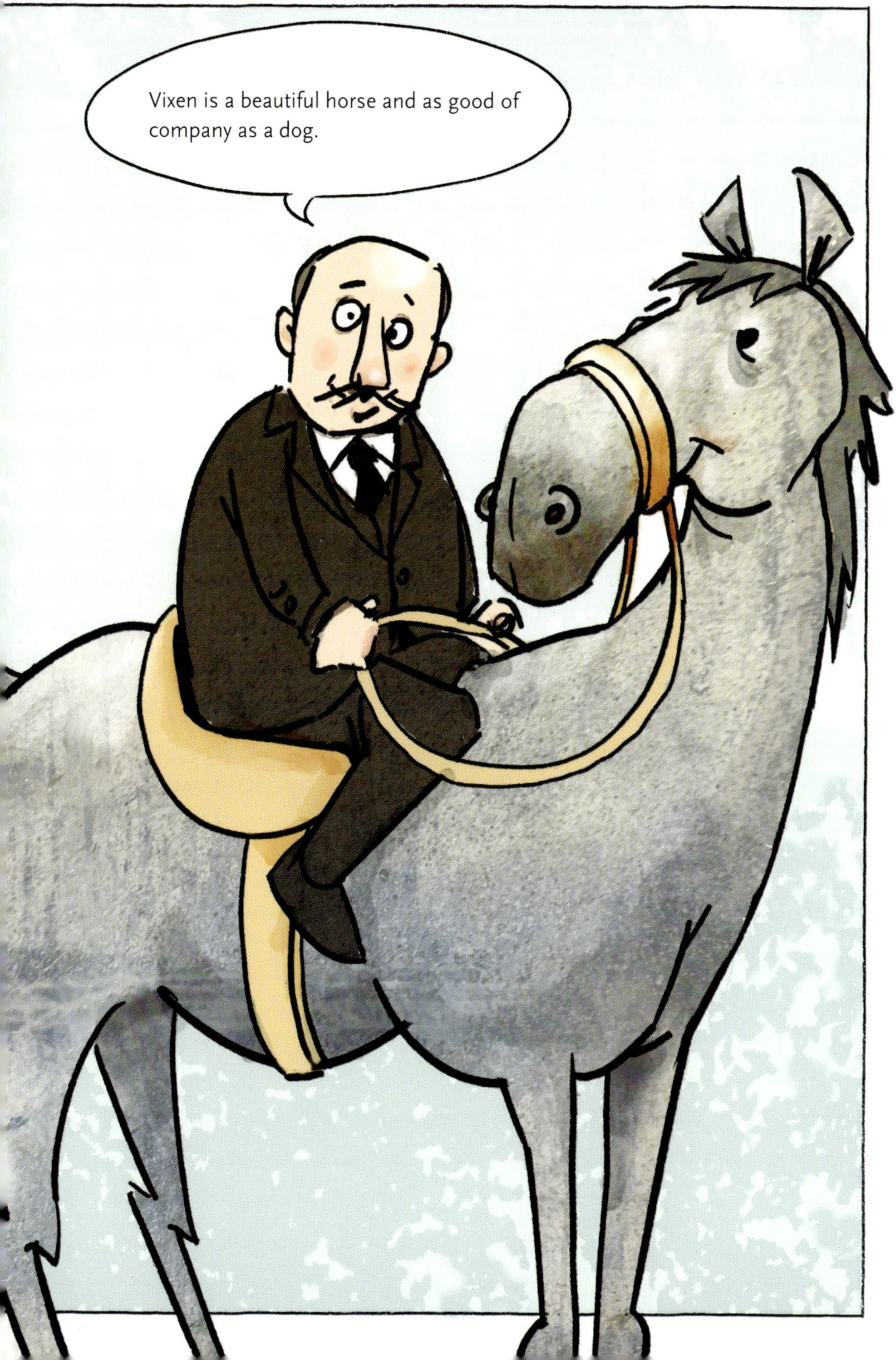
Vixen is a beautiful horse and as good of company as a dog.

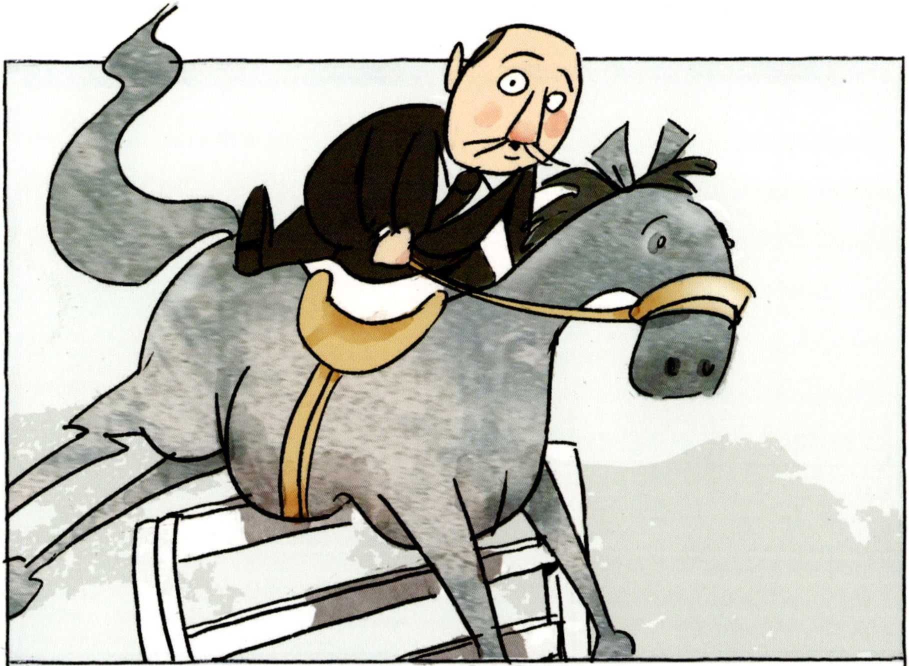

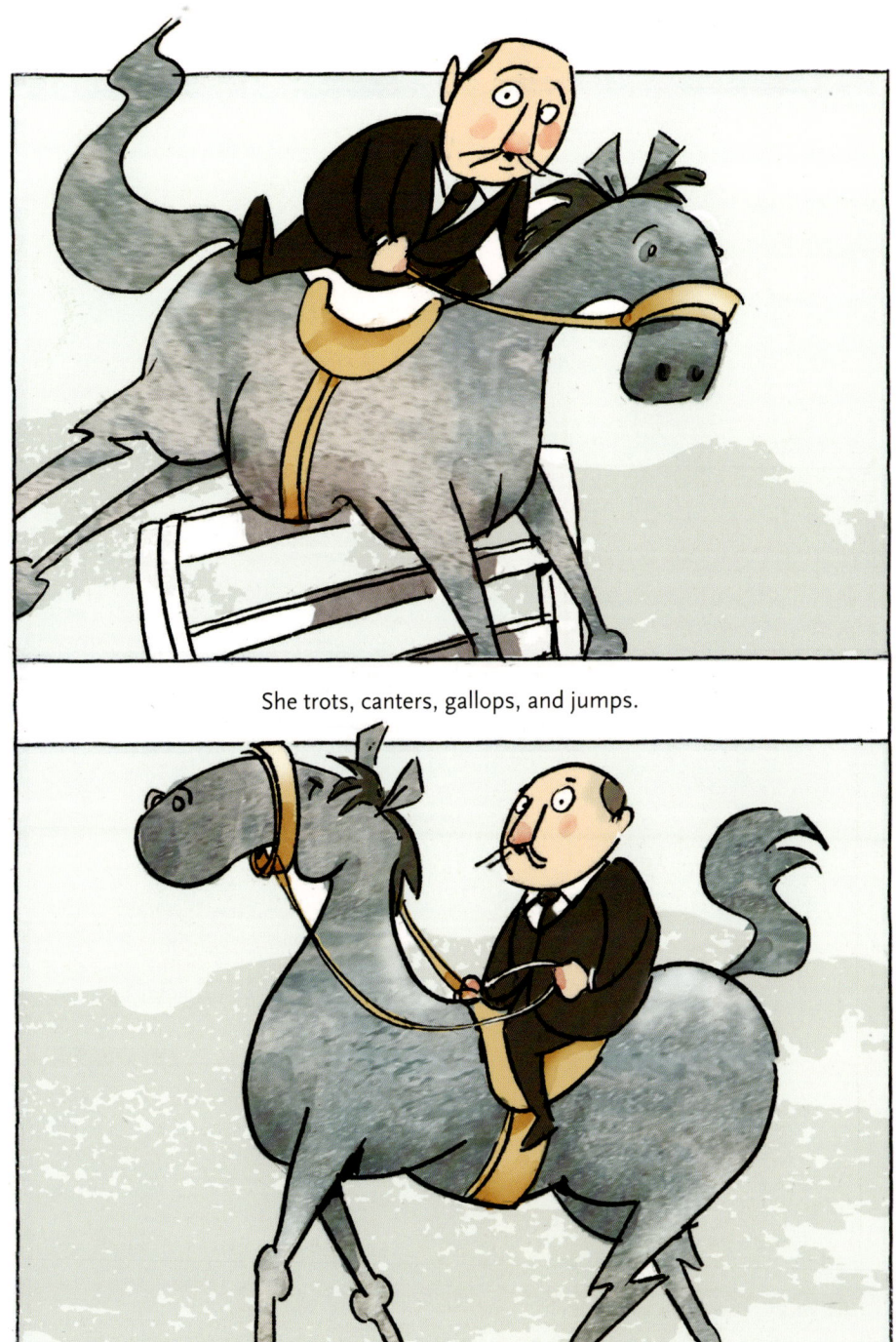

She trots, canters, gallops, and jumps.

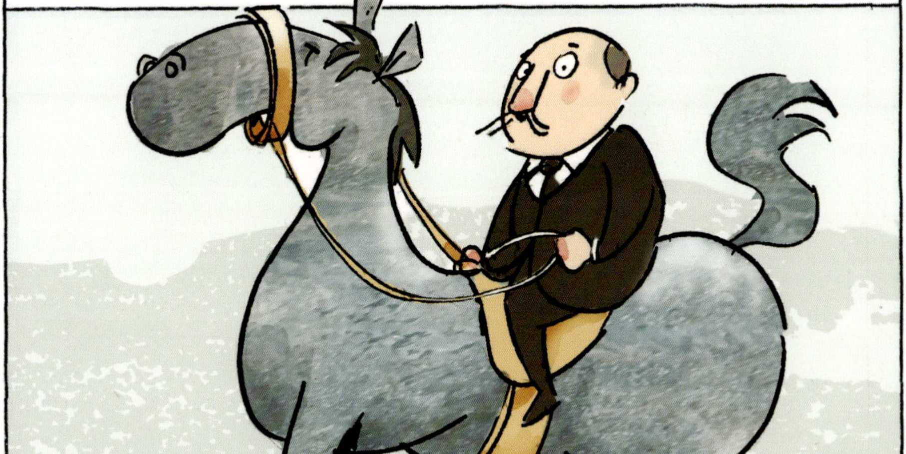

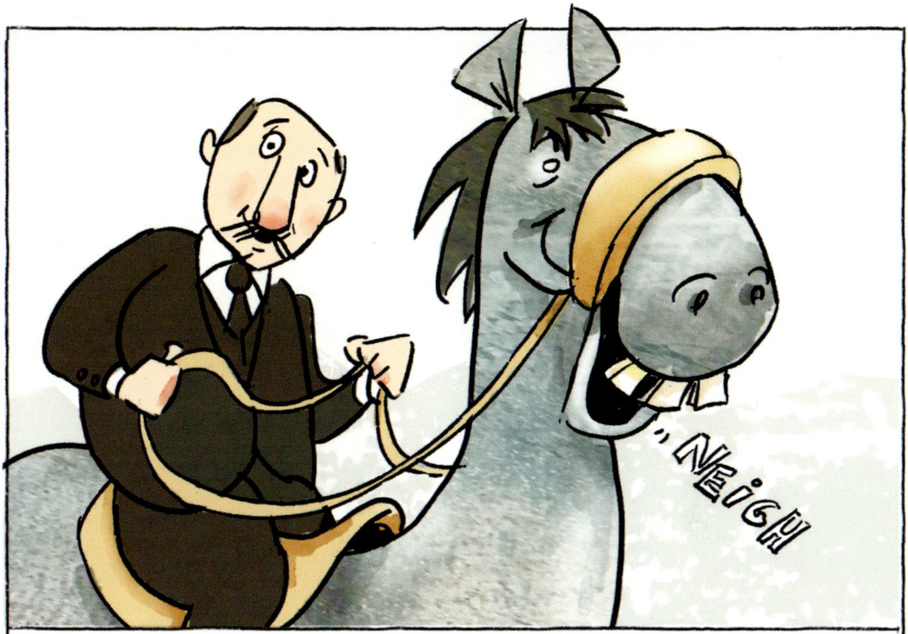
NEIGH

She neighs and whinnies. She eats. She drinks. She sleeps.

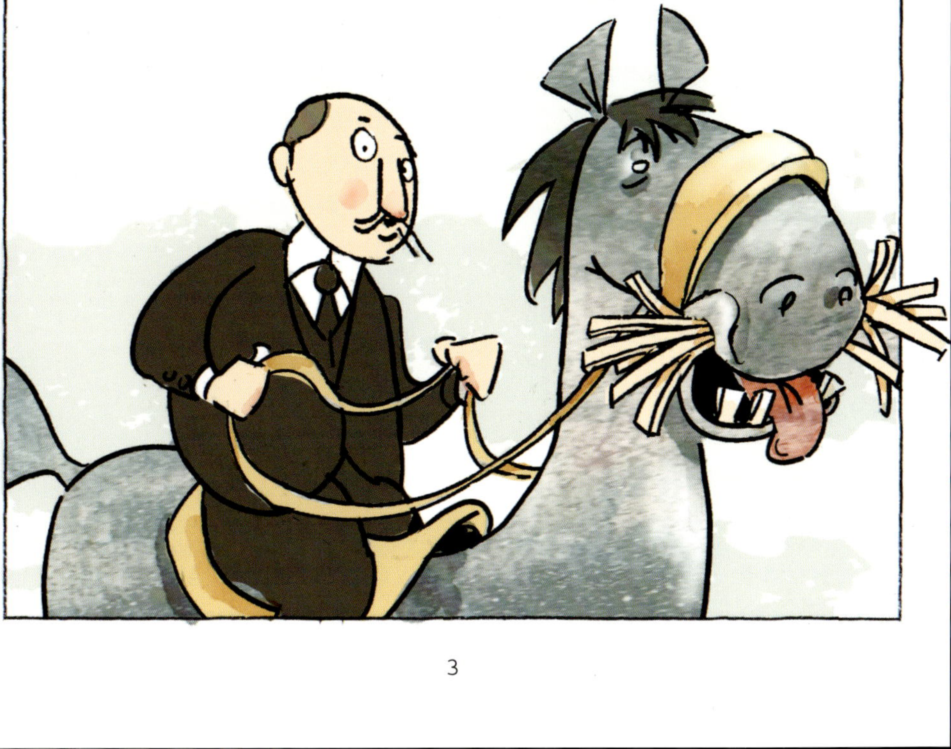

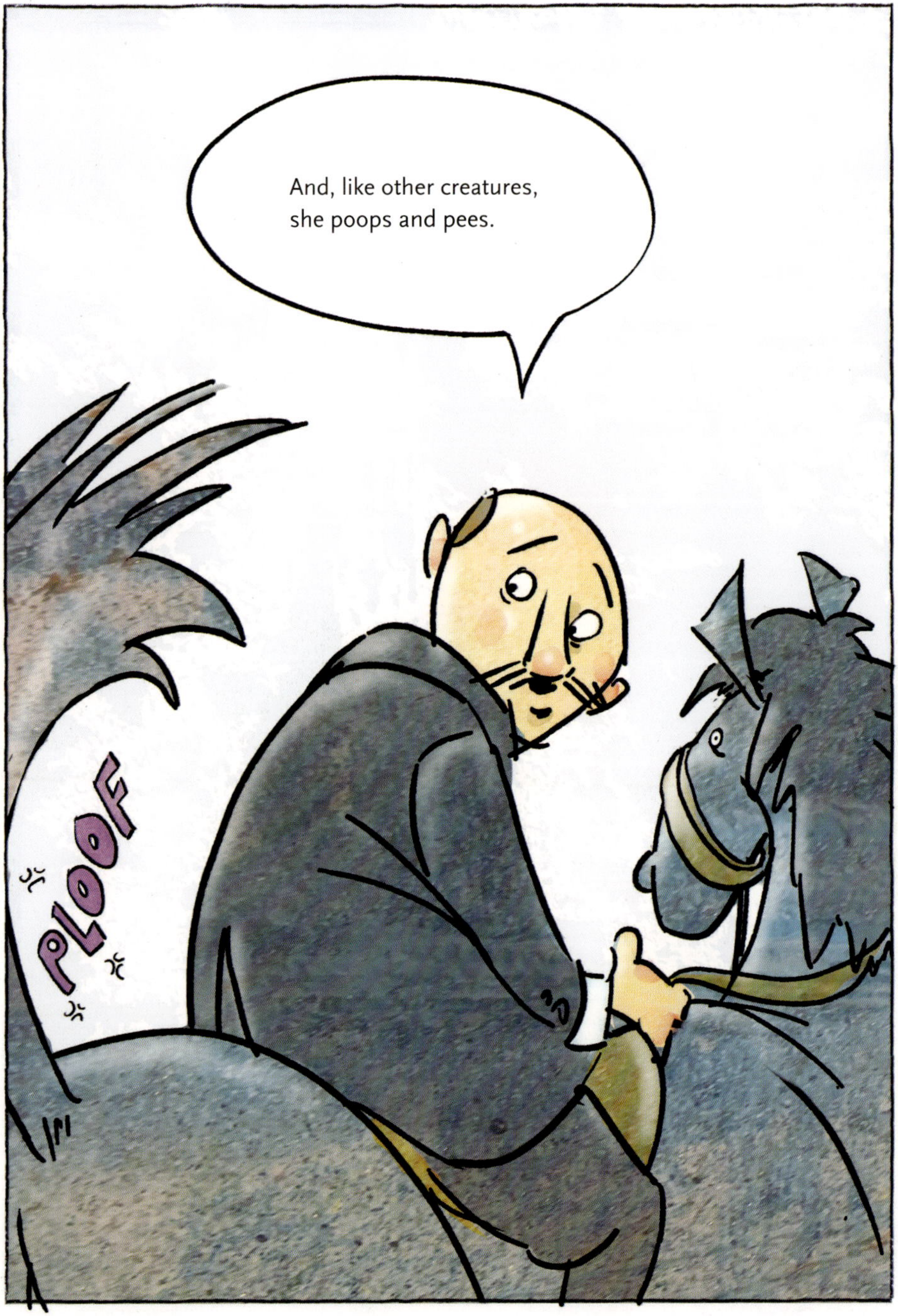
And, like other creatures,
she poops and pees.
PLOOF

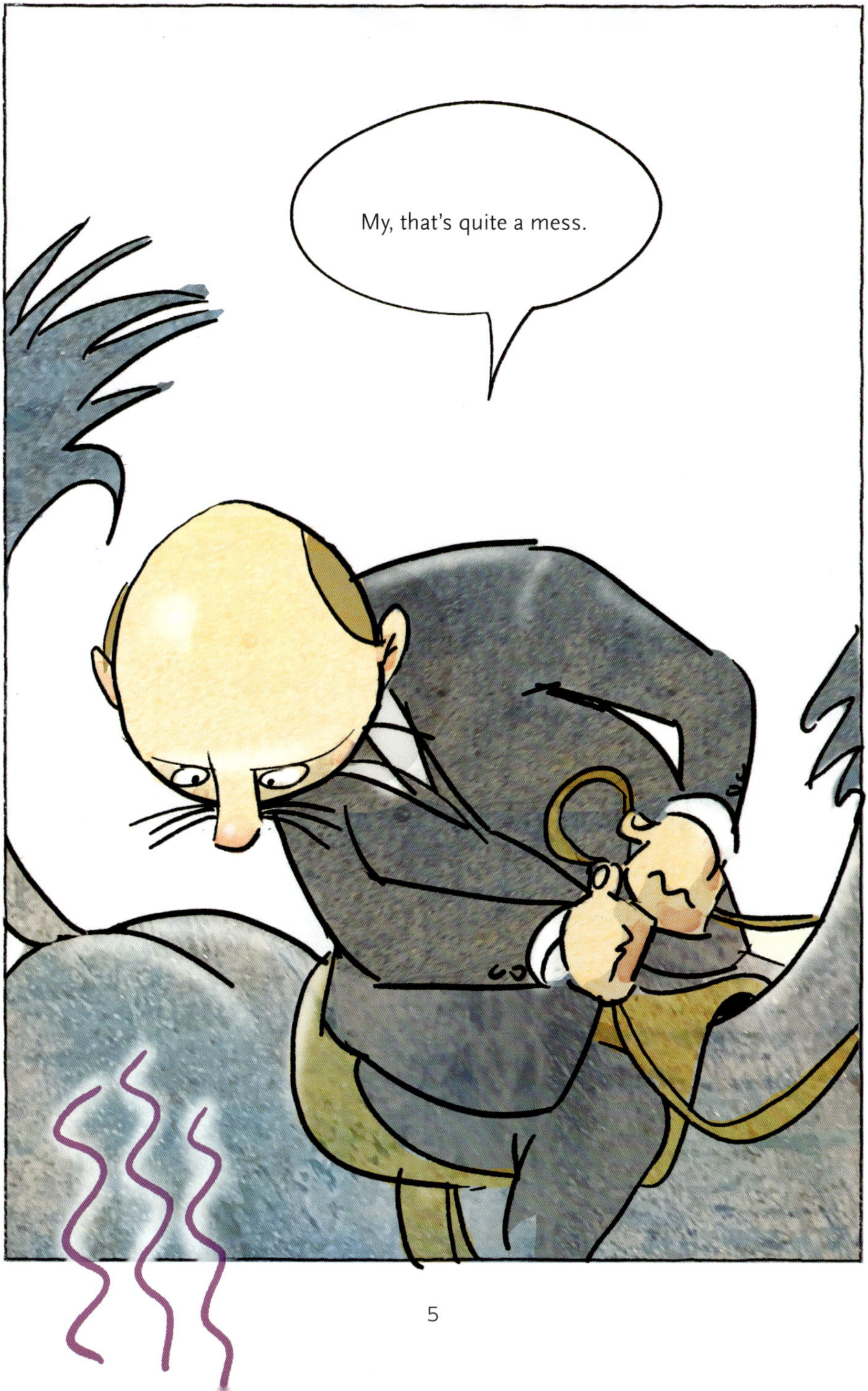
My, that's quite a mess.

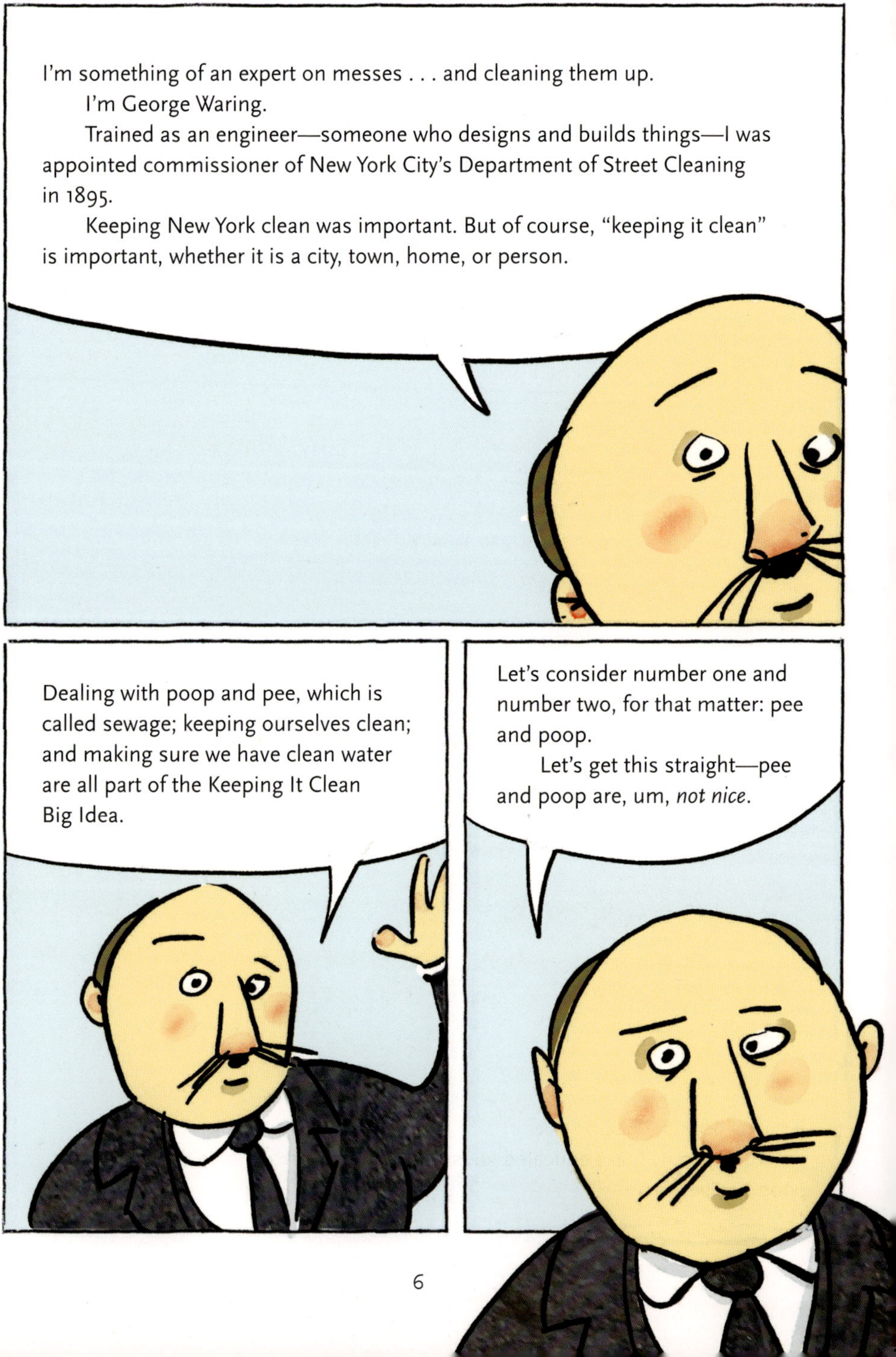
I'm something of an expert on messes . . . and cleaning them up.
I'm George Waring.
Trained as an engineer—someone who designs and builds things—I was appointed commissioner of New York City's Department of Street Cleaning in 1895.
Keeping New York clean was important. But of course, "keeping it clean" is important, whether it is a city, town, home, or person.
Dealing with poop and pee, which is called sewage; keeping ourselves clean; and making sure we have clean water are all part of the Keeping It Clean Big Idea.
Let's consider number one and number two, for that matter: pee and poop.
Let's get this straight—pee and poop are, um, *not nice*.

Most everyone has had that feeling about poop and pee for just about forever . . . right back to the very first people.

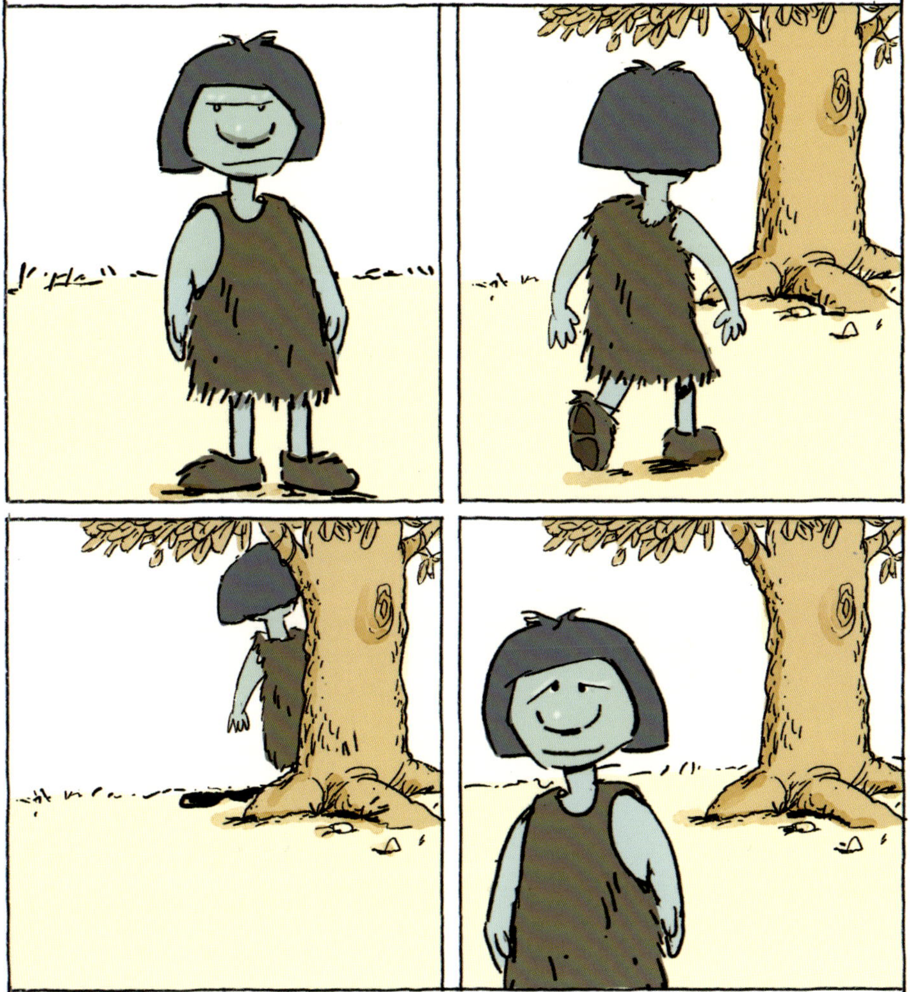

Perhaps behind a nearby tree?

We can only make educated guesses about how early people dealt with their poop and pee.

But as people began to assemble in permanent settlements, they had Big Ideas.

More than eight thousand years ago in Scotland, people's stone huts had indoor toilets that drained into a village trough, making for a nifty way to discard waste.

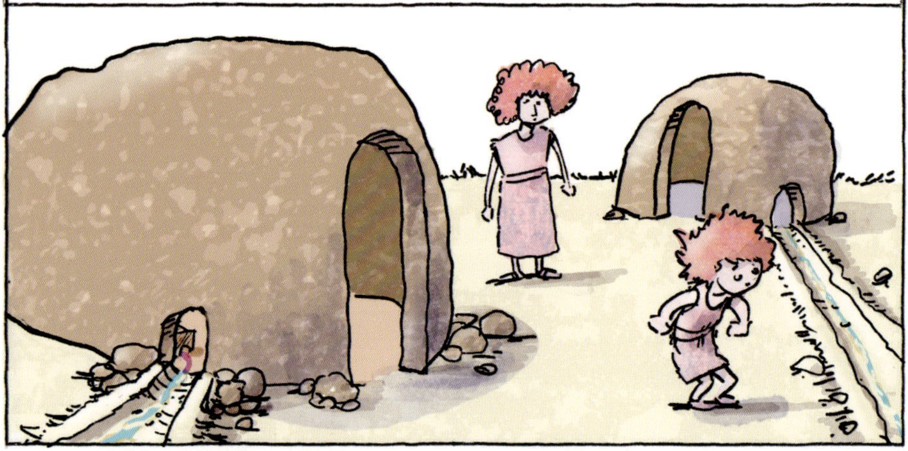

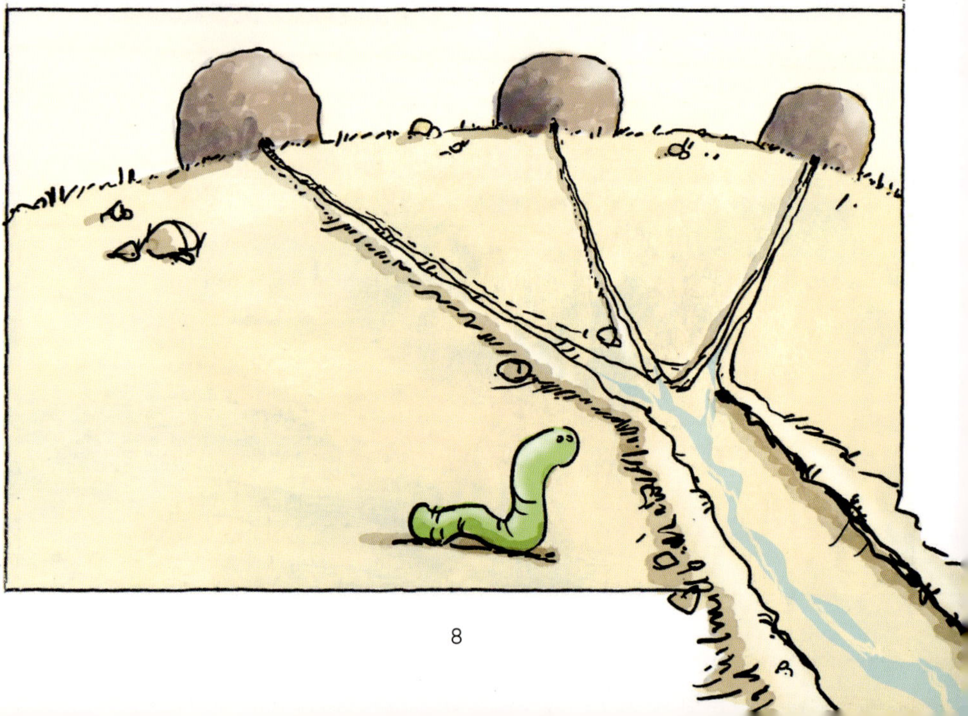

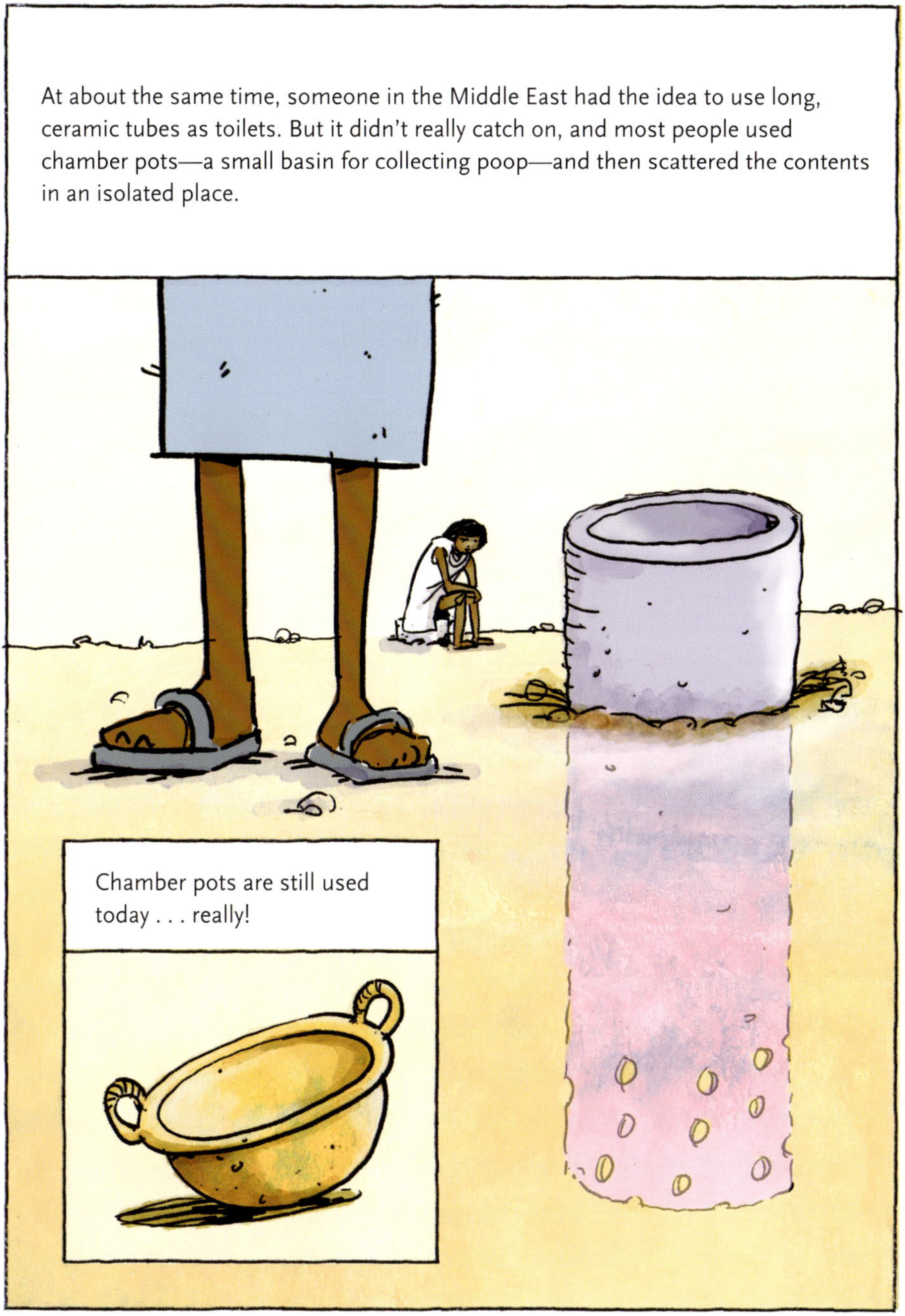
At about the same time, someone in the Middle East had the idea to use long, ceramic tubes as toilets. But it didn't really catch on, and most people used chamber pots—a small basin for collecting poop—and then scattered the contents in an isolated place.
Chamber pots are still used today . . . really!

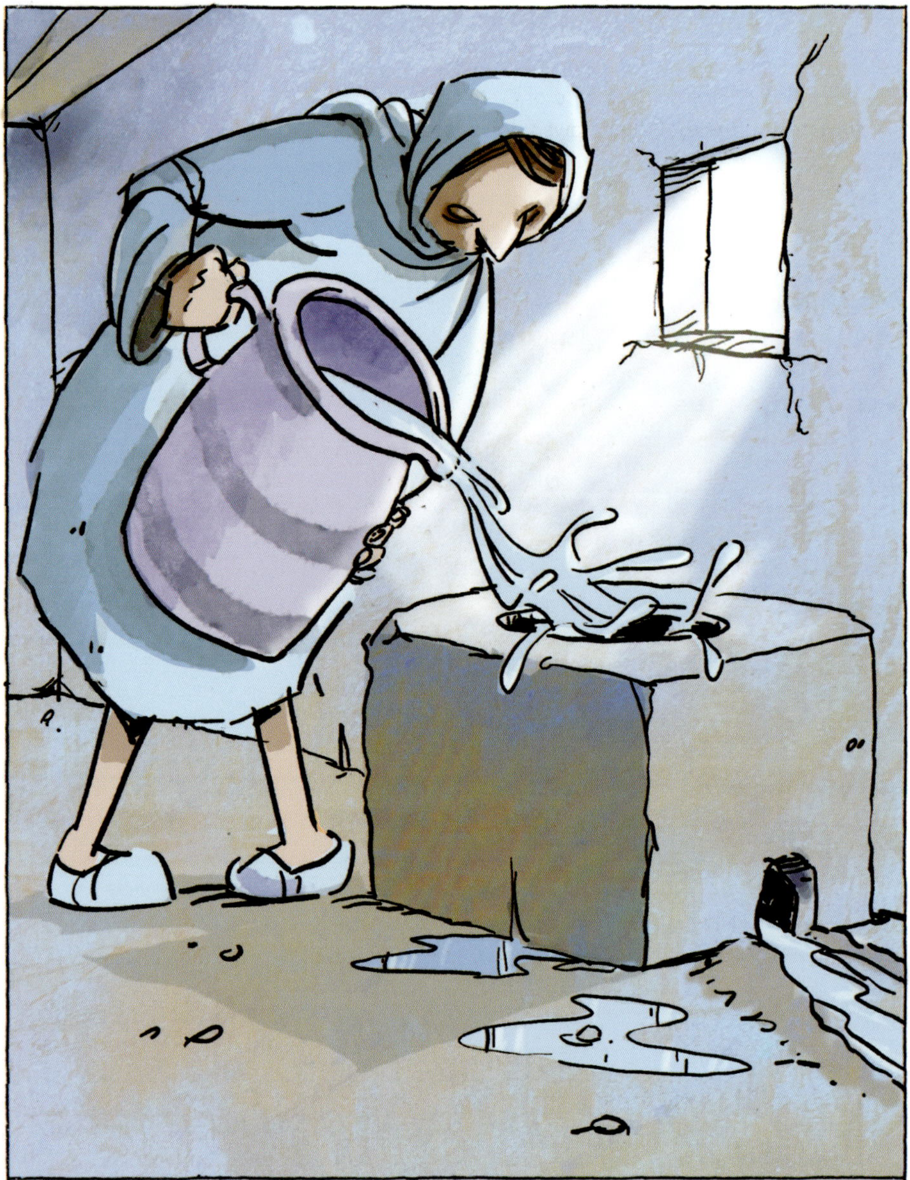

About four thousand years ago, people in Greece and the Indus Valley—modern-day India and Pakistan—used water to clear, or flush, toilets.

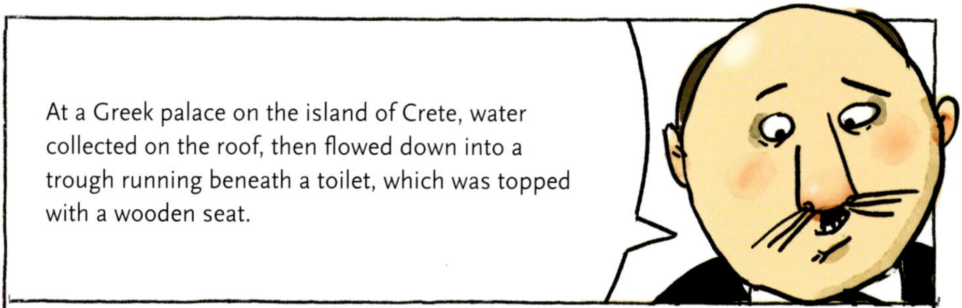
At a Greek palace on the island of Crete, water collected on the roof, then flowed down into a trough running beneath a toilet, which was topped with a wooden seat.

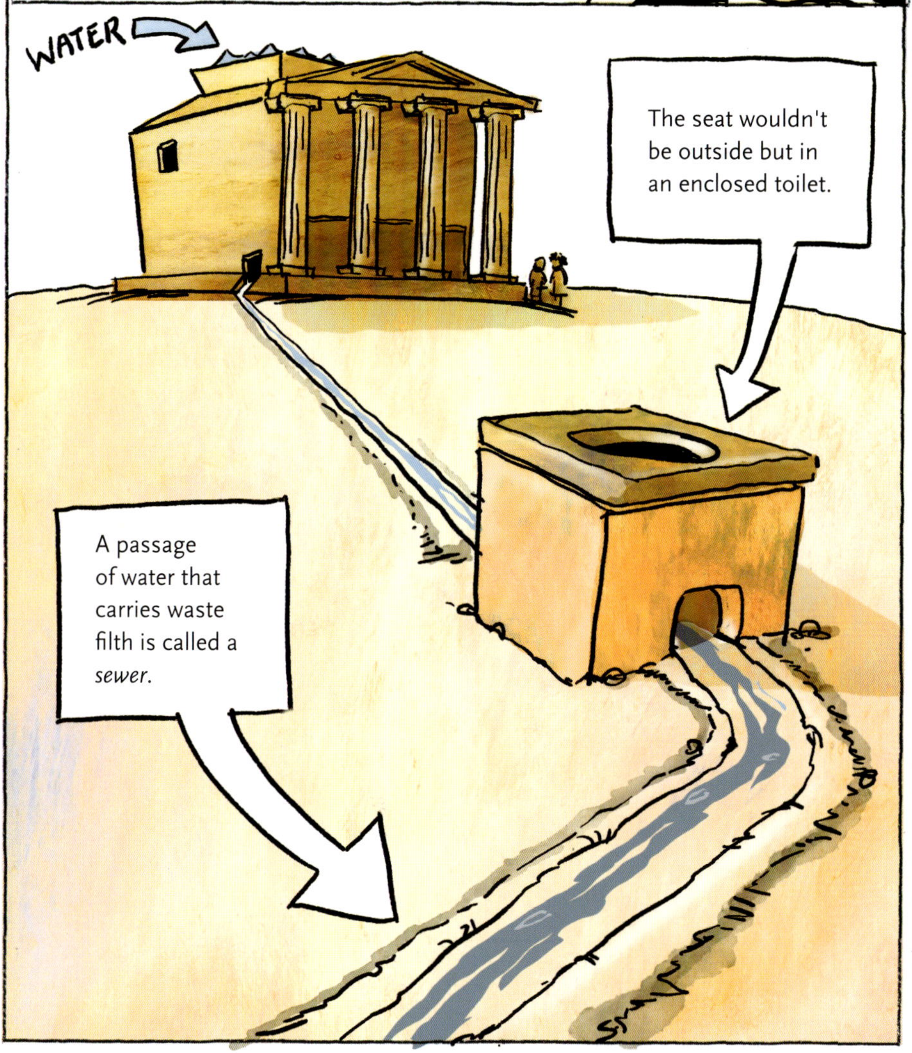
WATER
The seat wouldn't be outside but in an enclosed toilet.
A passage of water that carries waste filth is called a *sewer*.

The ancient Greeks constructed public toilets of large rooms and bench seats.

But it was the Romans who really threw themselves into toilets!

Err . . . threw themselves into toilet . . . construction.

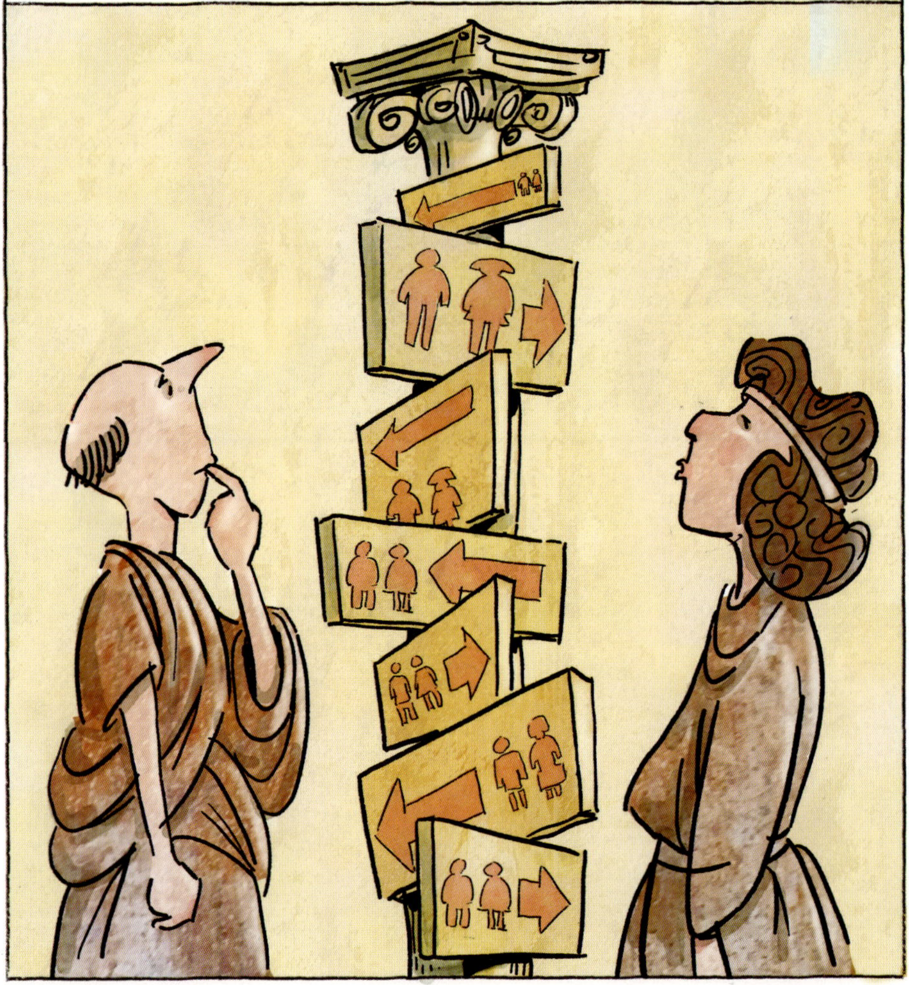

They built public toilets just about everywhere they went. The city of Rome boasted 144 large rooms of wooden or stone seats above flowing water sewers. No partitions separated the seats. Instead, users counted on their flowing togas to protect their privacy.

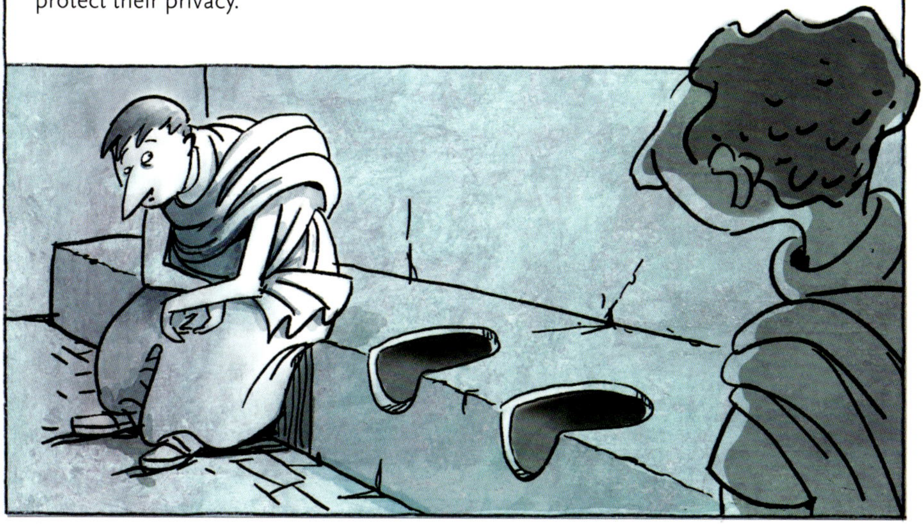

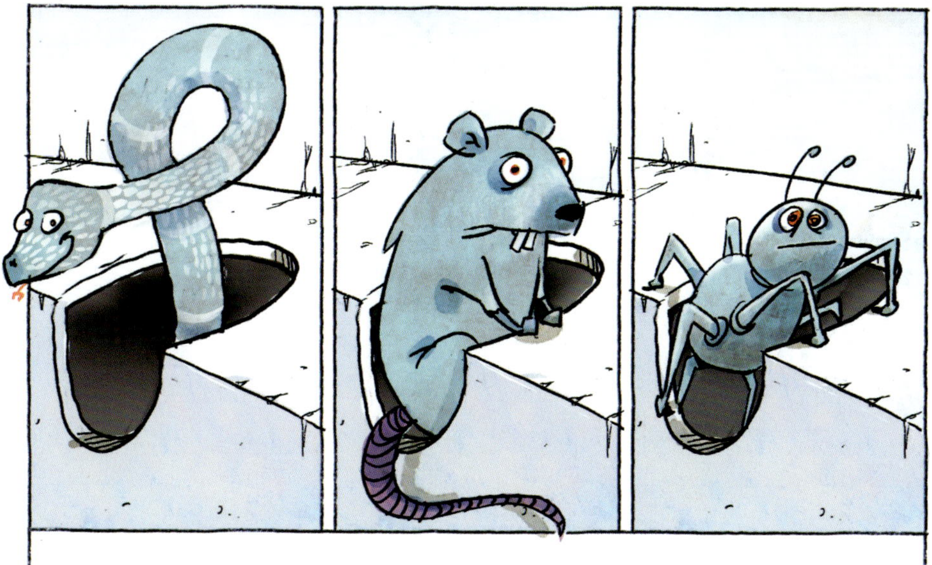

Snakes, rats, and spiders might crawl up through the seats.

Still, people lined up to use them, sometimes entertaining themselves as they waited by scratching graffiti into the walls.

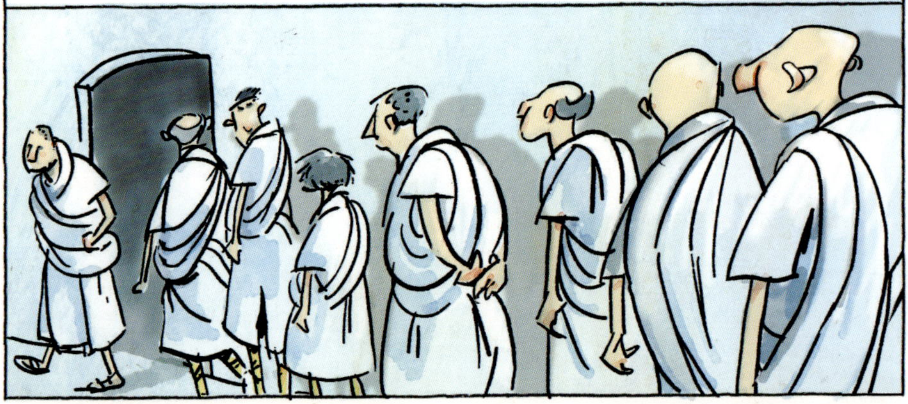

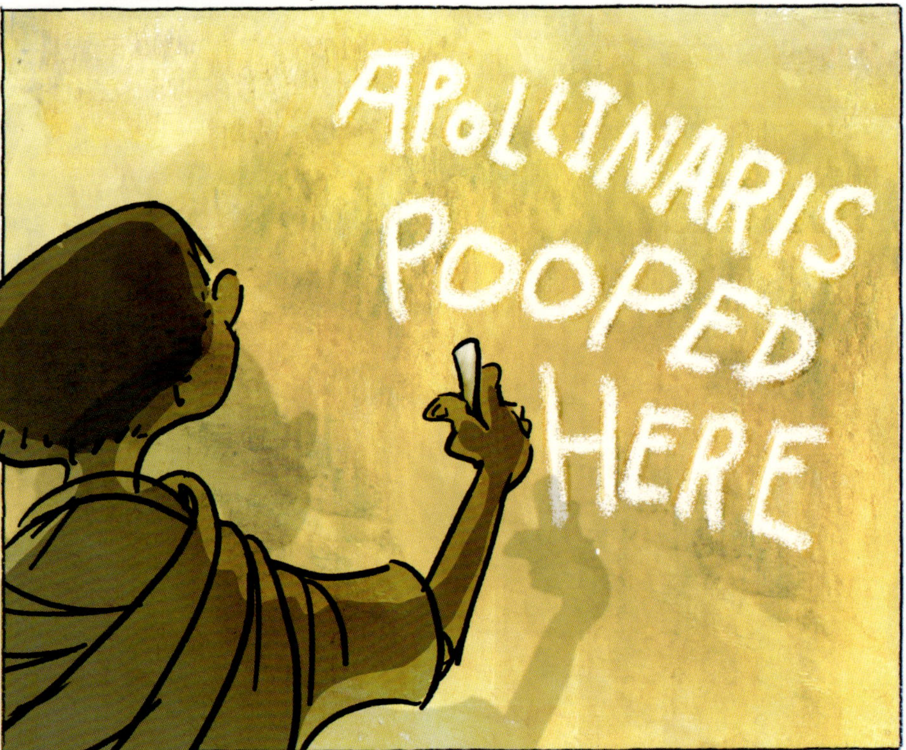
APOLLINARIS POOPED HERE

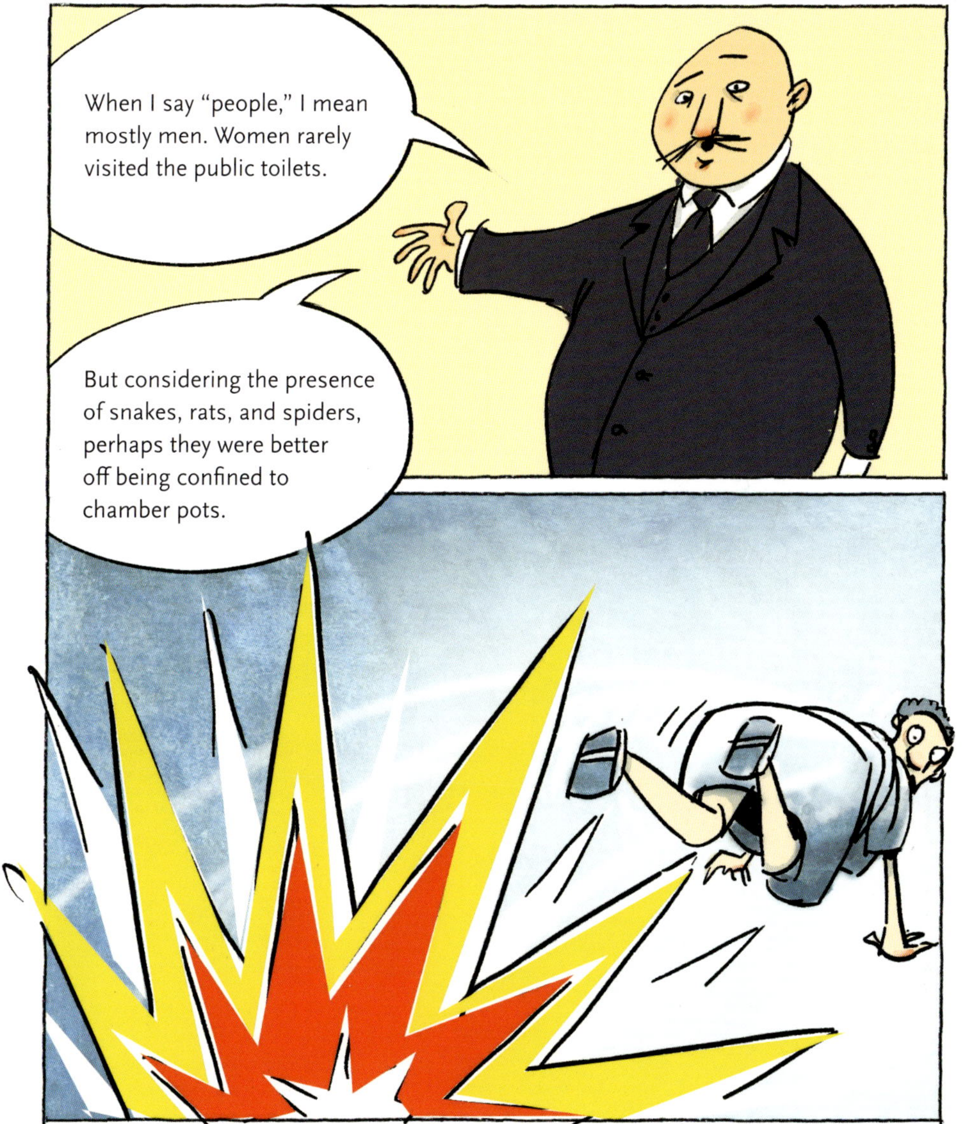
When I say "people," I mean mostly men. Women rarely visited the public toilets.
But considering the presence of snakes, rats, and spiders, perhaps they were better off being confined to chamber pots.

The sewers running beneath the toilets sometimes clogged, making a revolting stench and attracting flies. The waste sometimes created explosive gases that ignited from heat or a stray spark and sent flames licking through the seats.

Oh, my!

Toilets could also be found in private Roman homes, set right beside the kitchen so that food scraps could be thrown into them . . . which isn't very healthy, if you think about it . . .

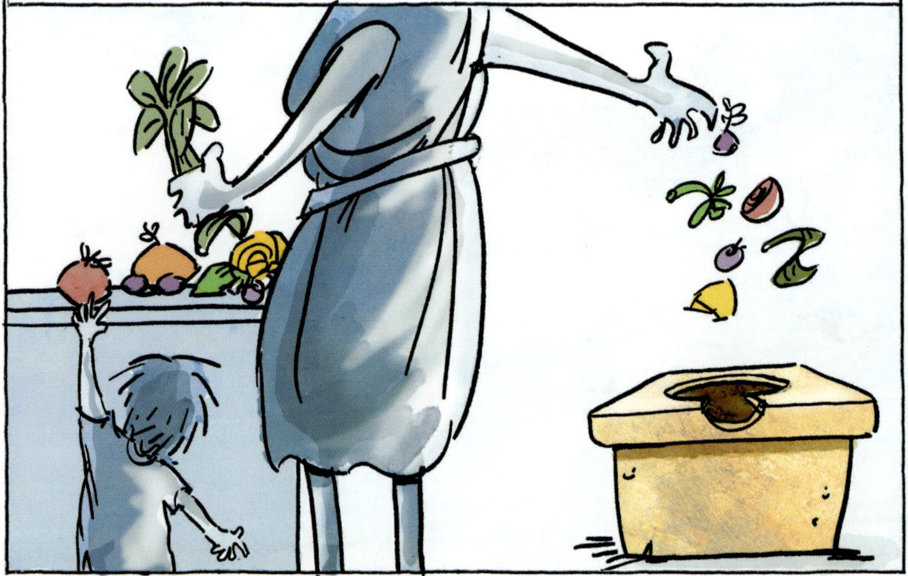

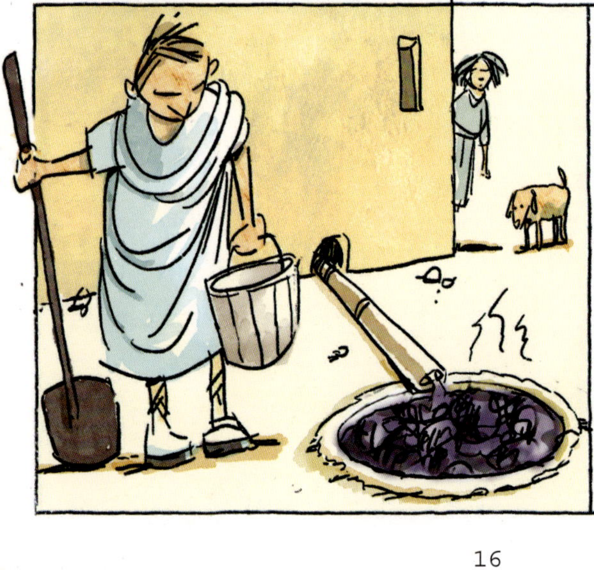

And the home toilets lacked sewers, with the product of the toilets collecting in a pit, which needed regular emptying.

I'm not sure if there was a special Roman plumber whose job was to remove pit poop.

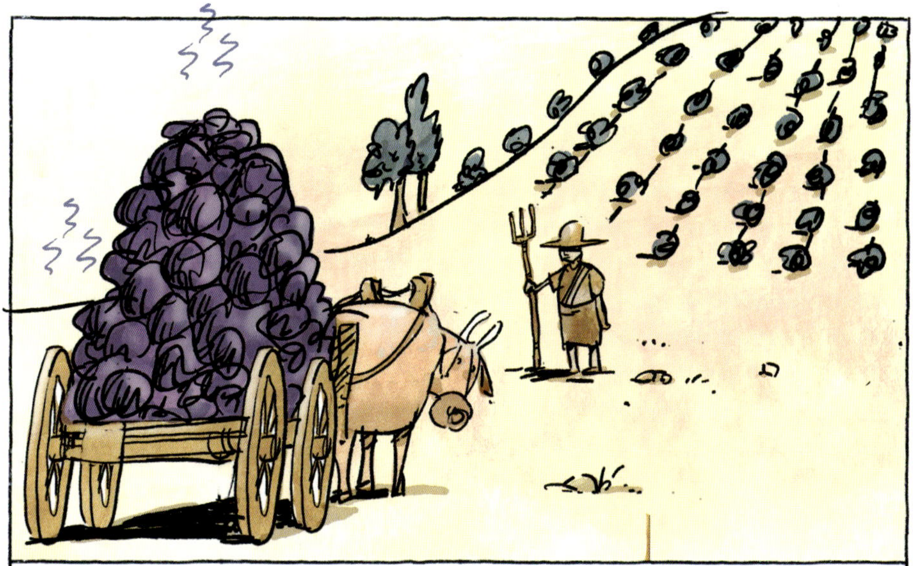

Where were the pit's contents taken?

To nearby farms to be used as fertilizer. The risk of raw human sewage carrying parasites and disease-causing germs wasn't known to the Romans.

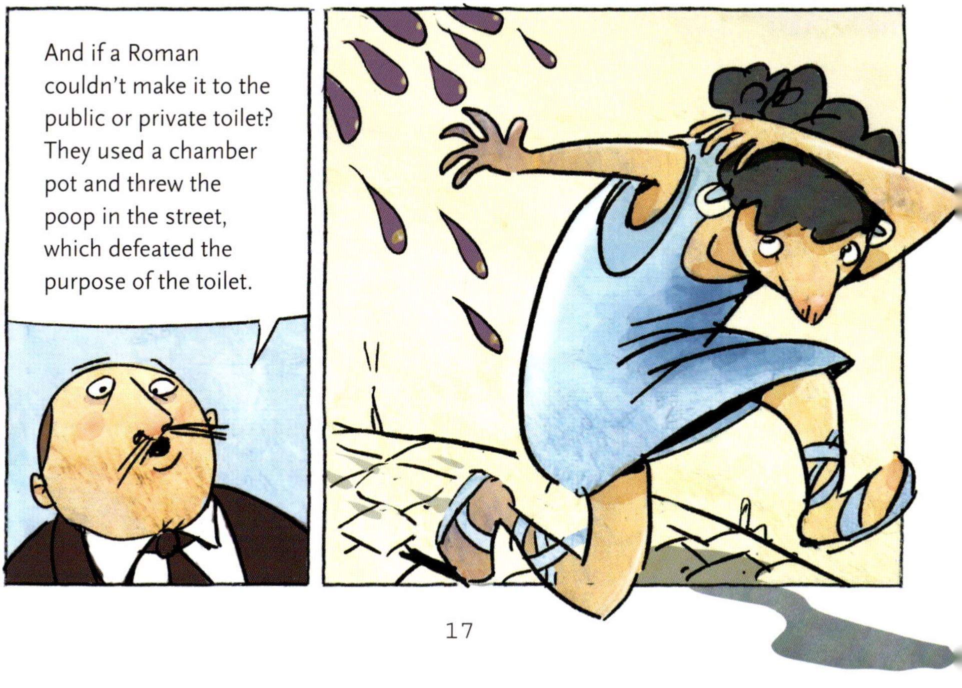
And if a Roman couldn't make it to the public or private toilet? They used a chamber pot and threw the poop in the street, which defeated the purpose of the toilet.

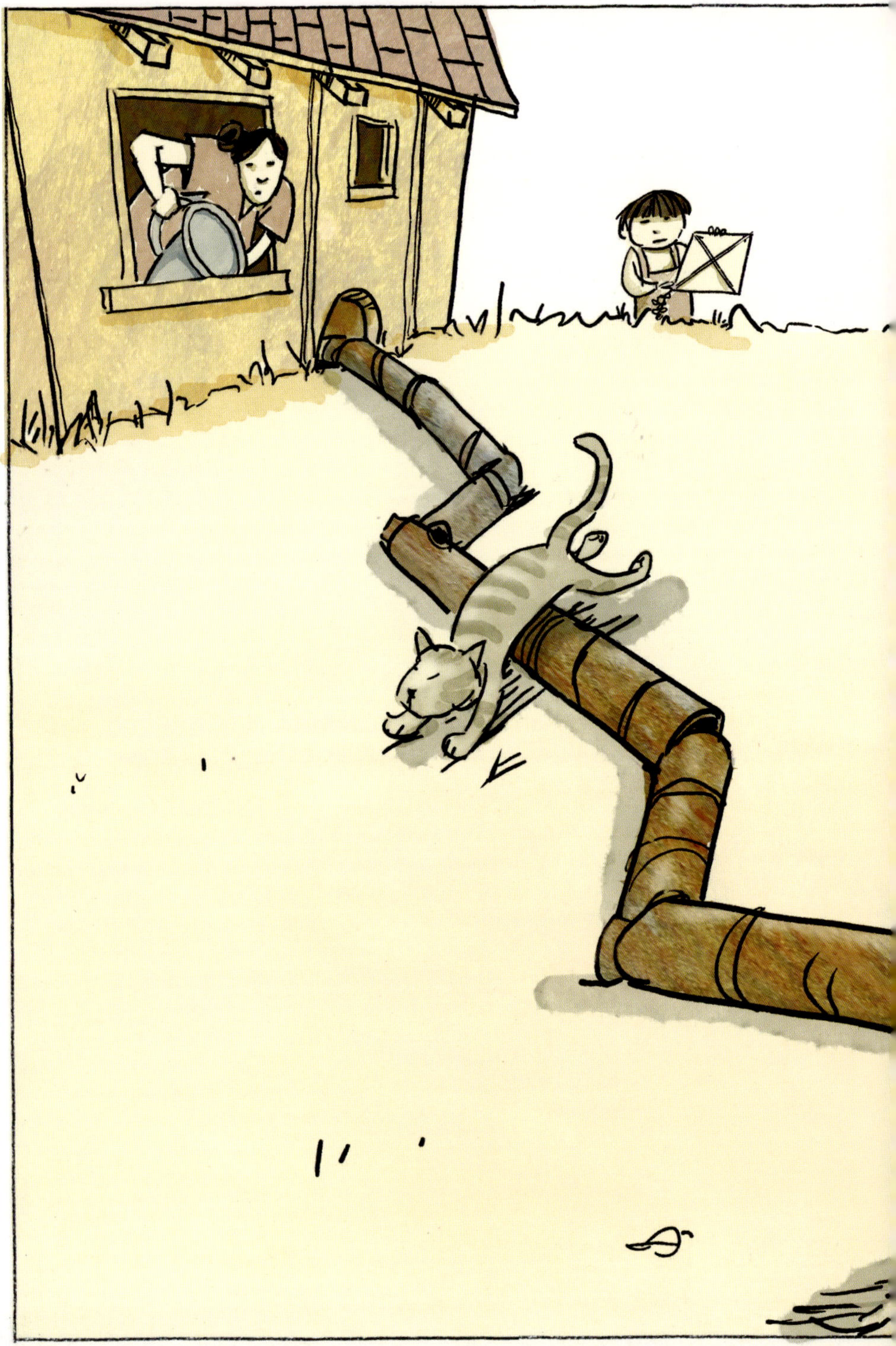

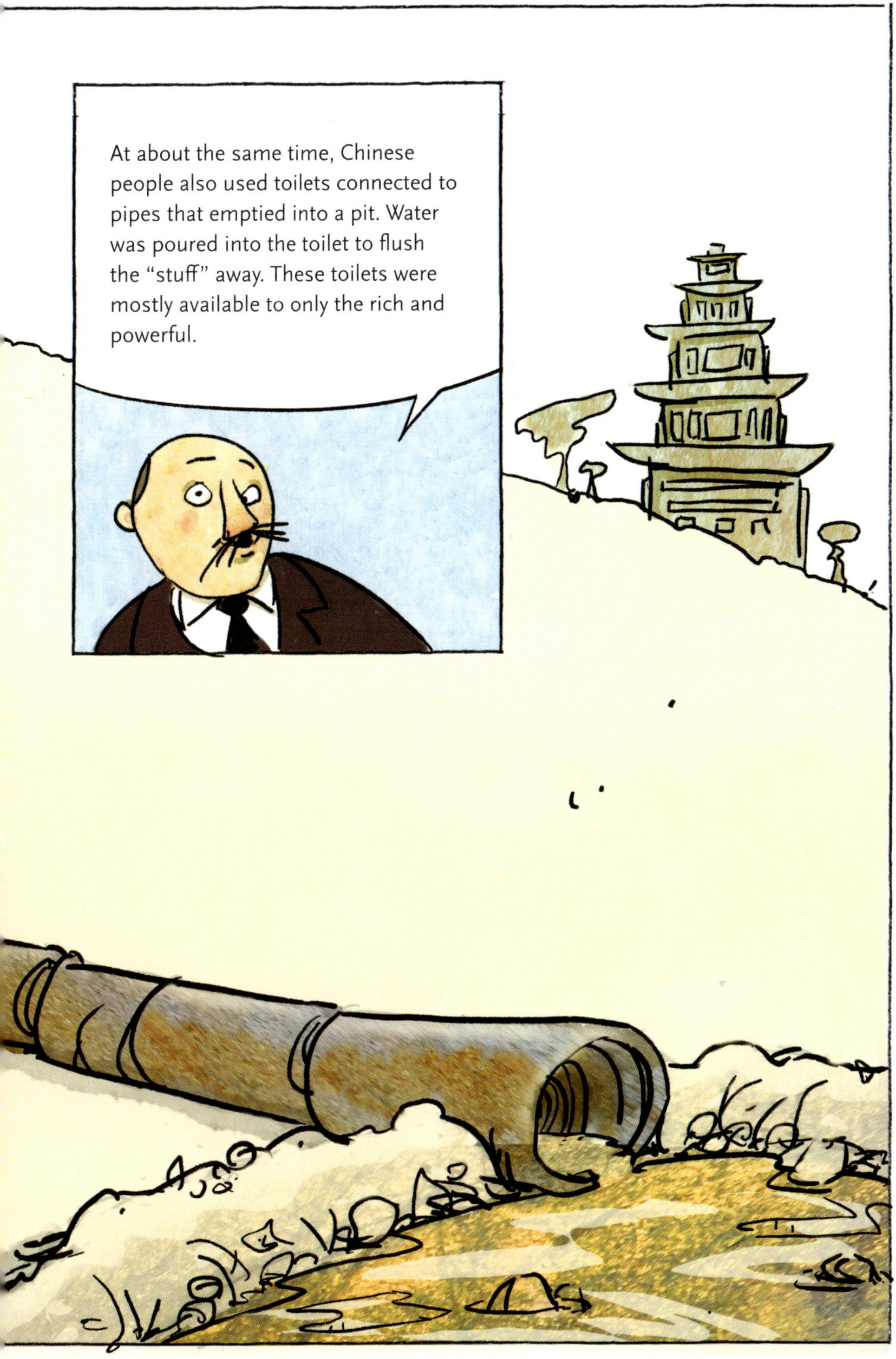
At about the same time, Chinese people also used toilets connected to pipes that emptied into a pit. Water was poured into the toilet to flush the "stuff" away. These toilets were mostly available to only the rich and powerful.

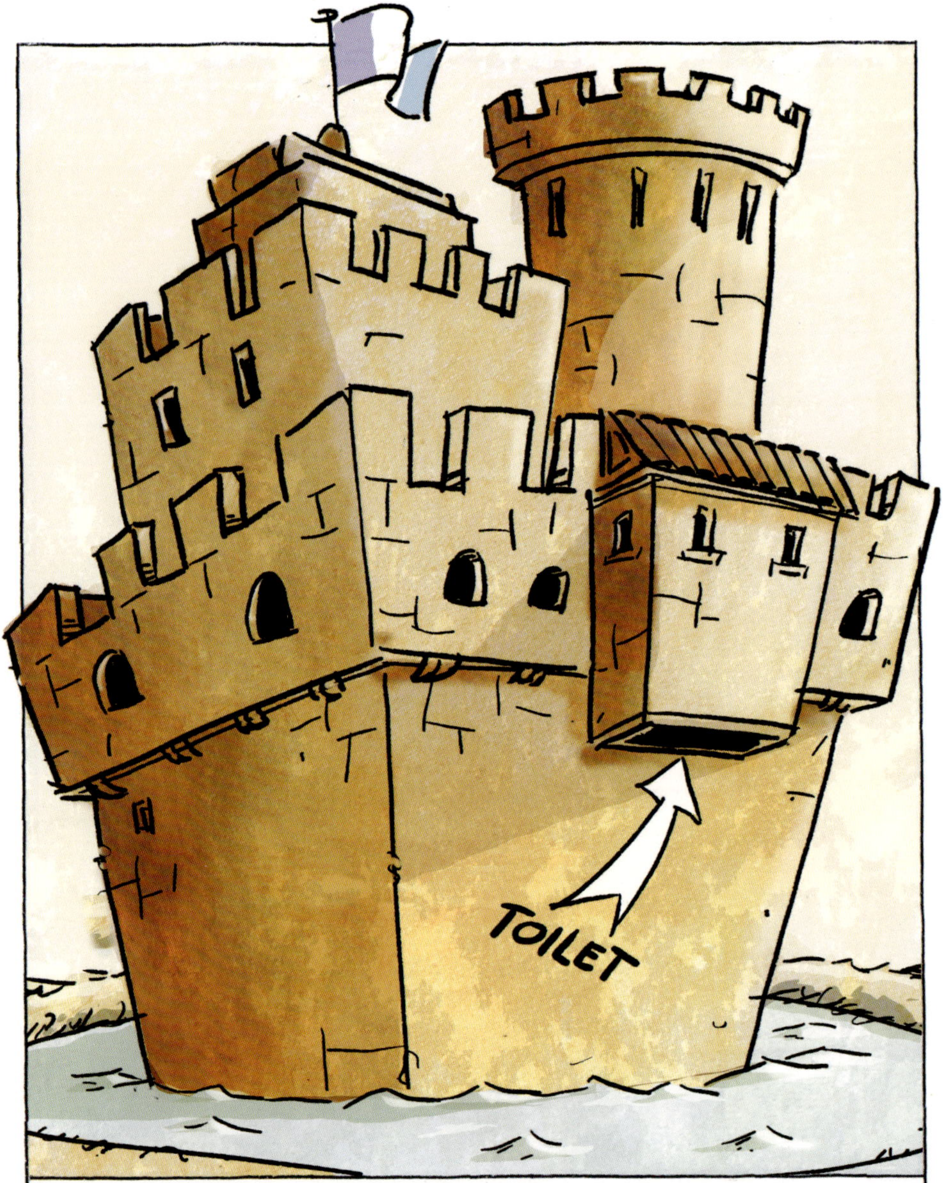
TOILET

By the Middle Ages in Europe, castle toilets were built into rooms projecting outside the stone walls so that poop would fall into the surrounding moat.

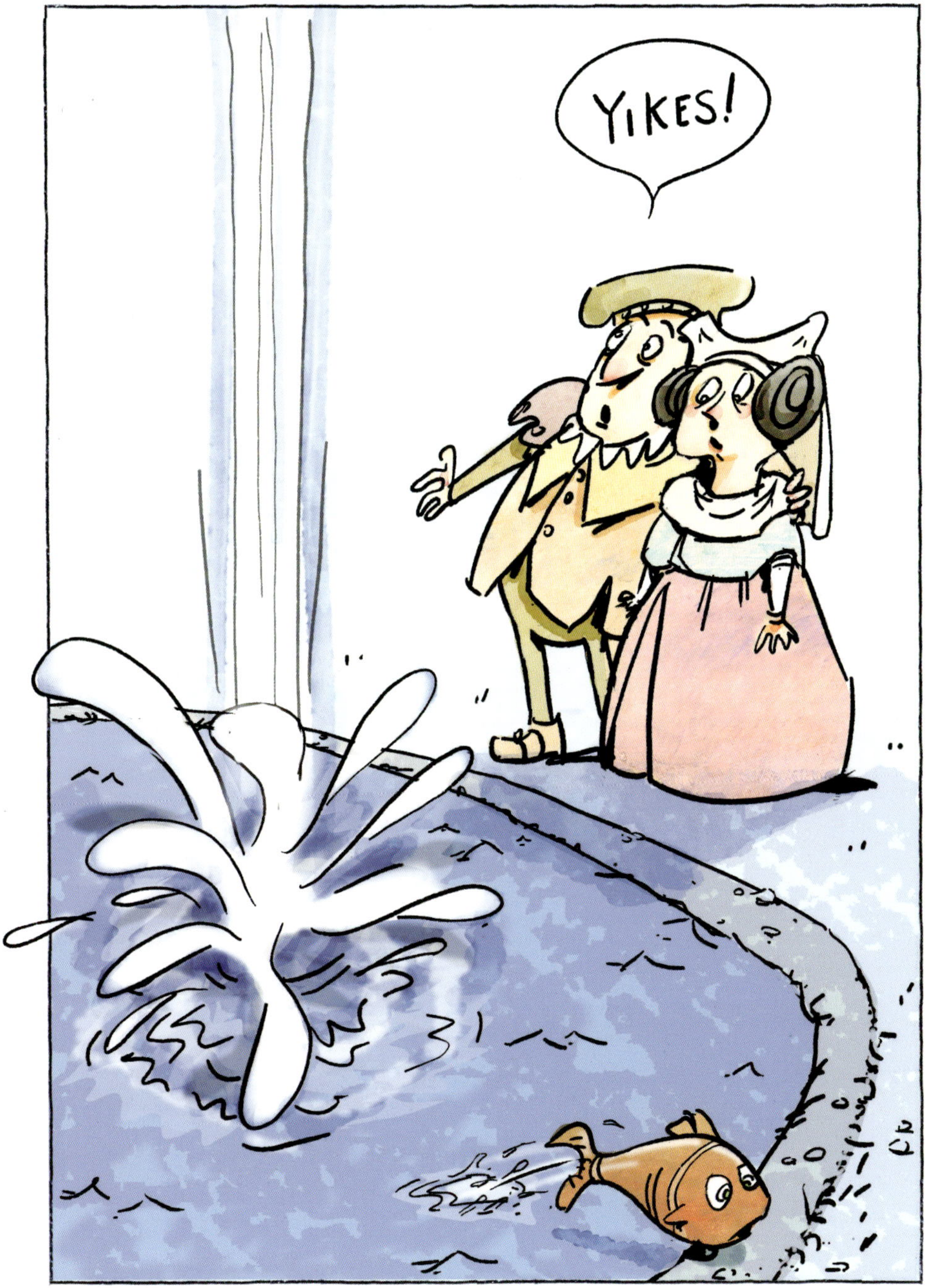
YIKES!

A poop-filled moat might be bad, but it's still better than a poop-filled basement in your giant mansion, which was the bad idea of German king Henry VI.

You'd think the stink would have persuaded him otherwise.

In any case, the king's second bad idea was in 1184, when he threw an enormous royal get-together.

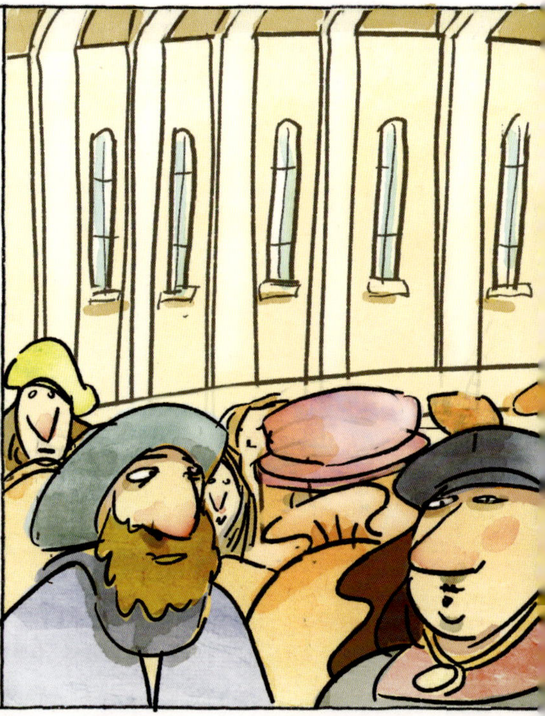

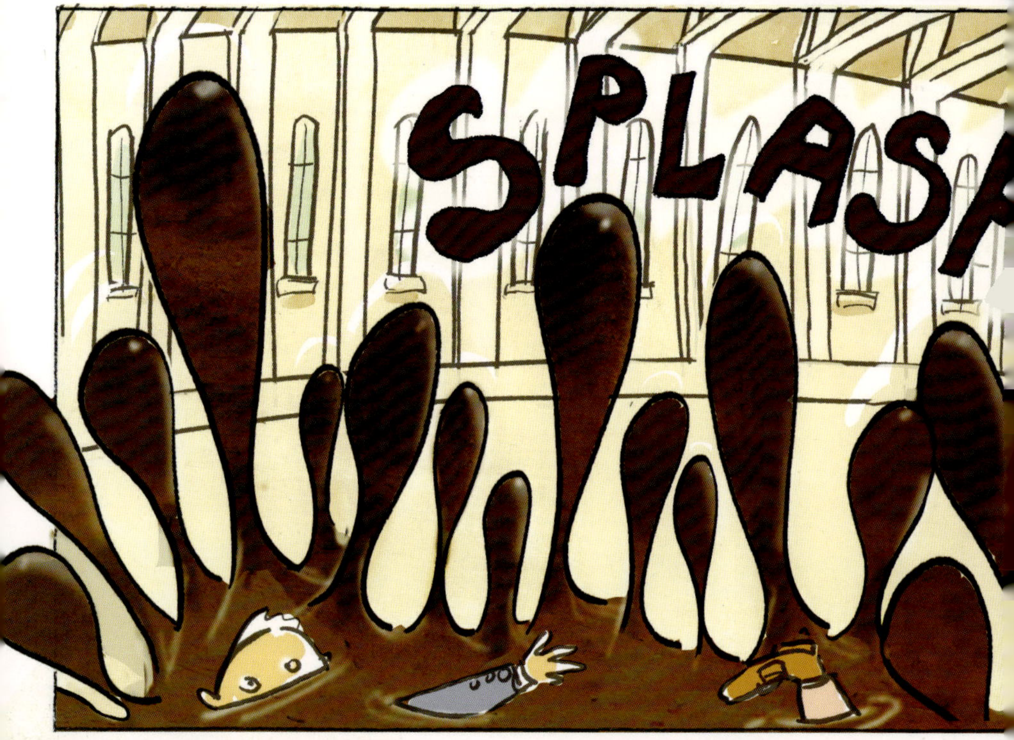
SPLASH

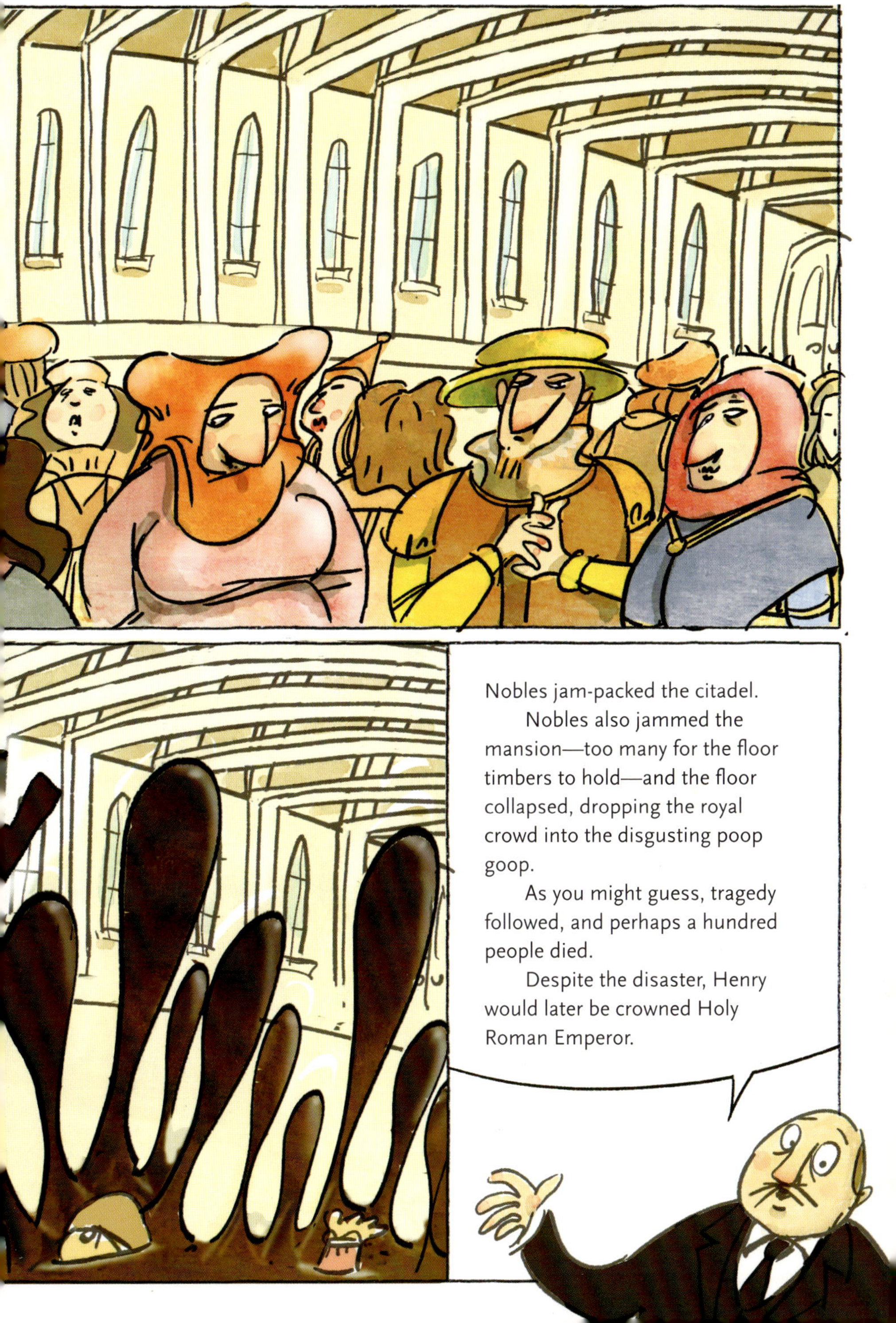
Nobles jam-packed the citadel.
Nobles also jammed the mansion—too many for the floor timbers to hold—and the floor collapsed, dropping the royal crowd into the disgusting poop goop.
As you might guess, tragedy followed, and perhaps a hundred people died.
Despite the disaster, Henry would later be crowned Holy Roman Emperor.

In 1423, the mayor of London, England, built a 128-seat toilet, divided equally between men and women. It hung over the river Thames with the idea the poop would drop into the water and wash away.

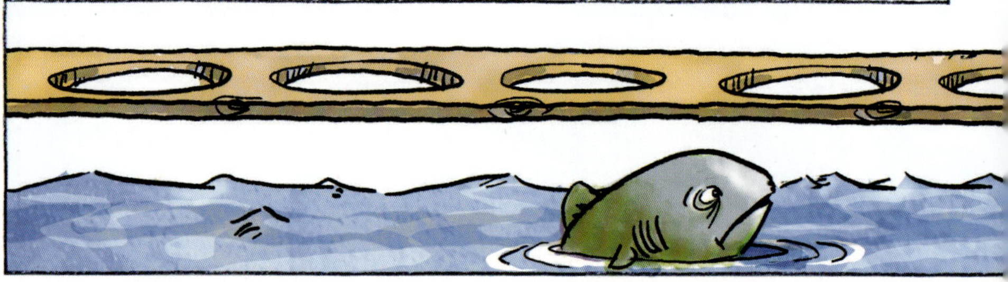

In the fifteenth century, England's Henry VII created the royal position of Groom of the Stool. The groom was responsible for the king's toilet needs, which meant tending to a cushioned, velvet and gold, braided box containing a chamber pot.

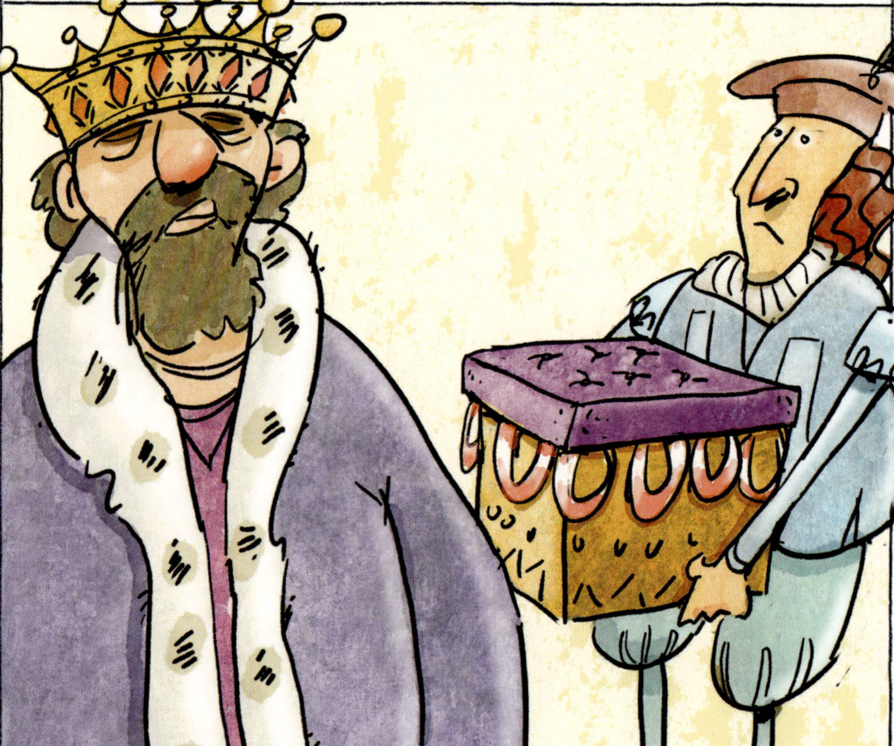

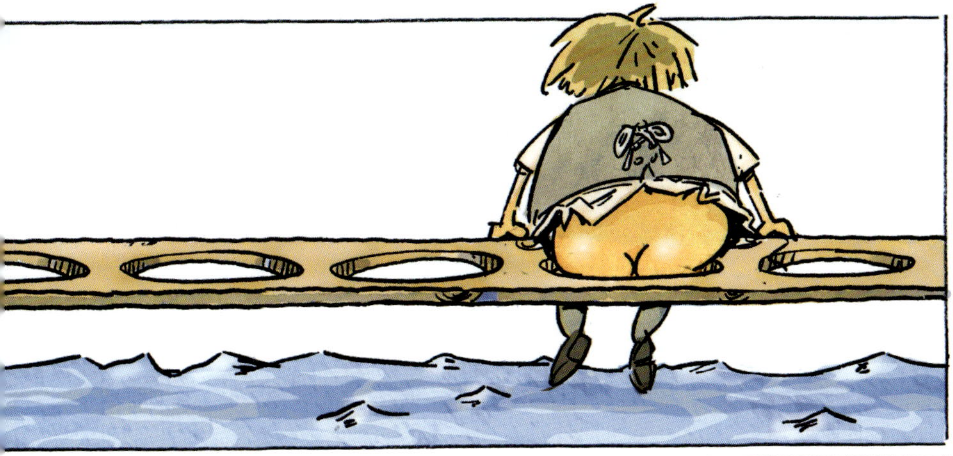

Yes, it seems to be an icky job, but being in charge of the king's rear end also gave the groom access to the king's ear, which made the groom a powerful and influential advisor. One managed to become prime minister.

The position of Groom of the Stool continued until 1901.

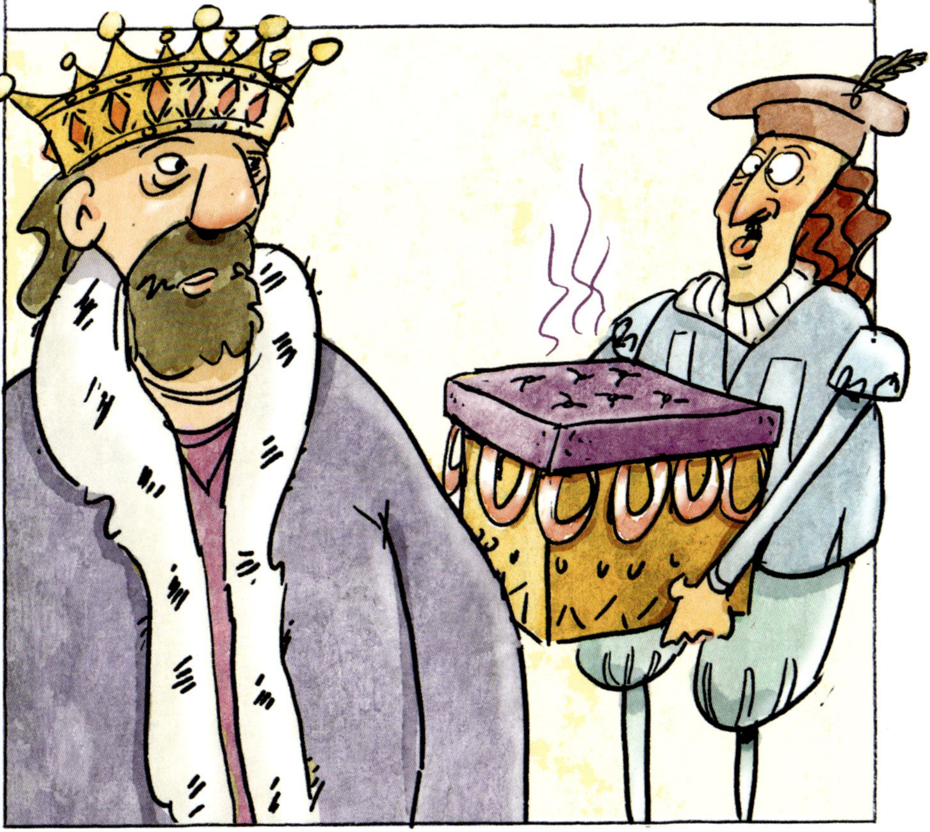

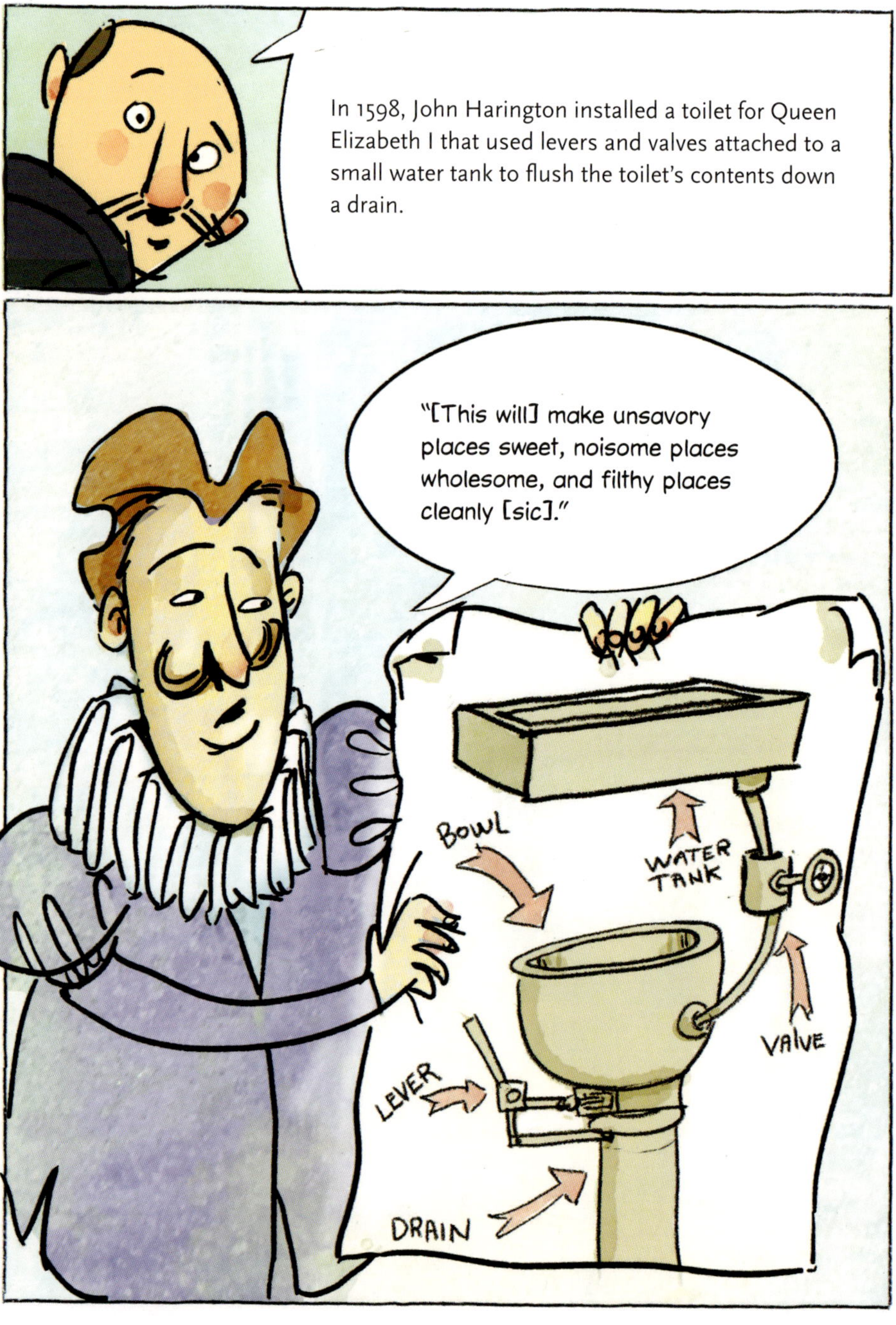
In 1598, John Harington installed a toilet for Queen Elizabeth I that used levers and valves attached to a small water tank to flush the toilet's contents down a drain.
"[This will] make unsavory places sweet, noisome places wholesome, and filthy places cleanly [sic]."
BOWL
WATER TANK
VALVE
LEVER
DRAIN

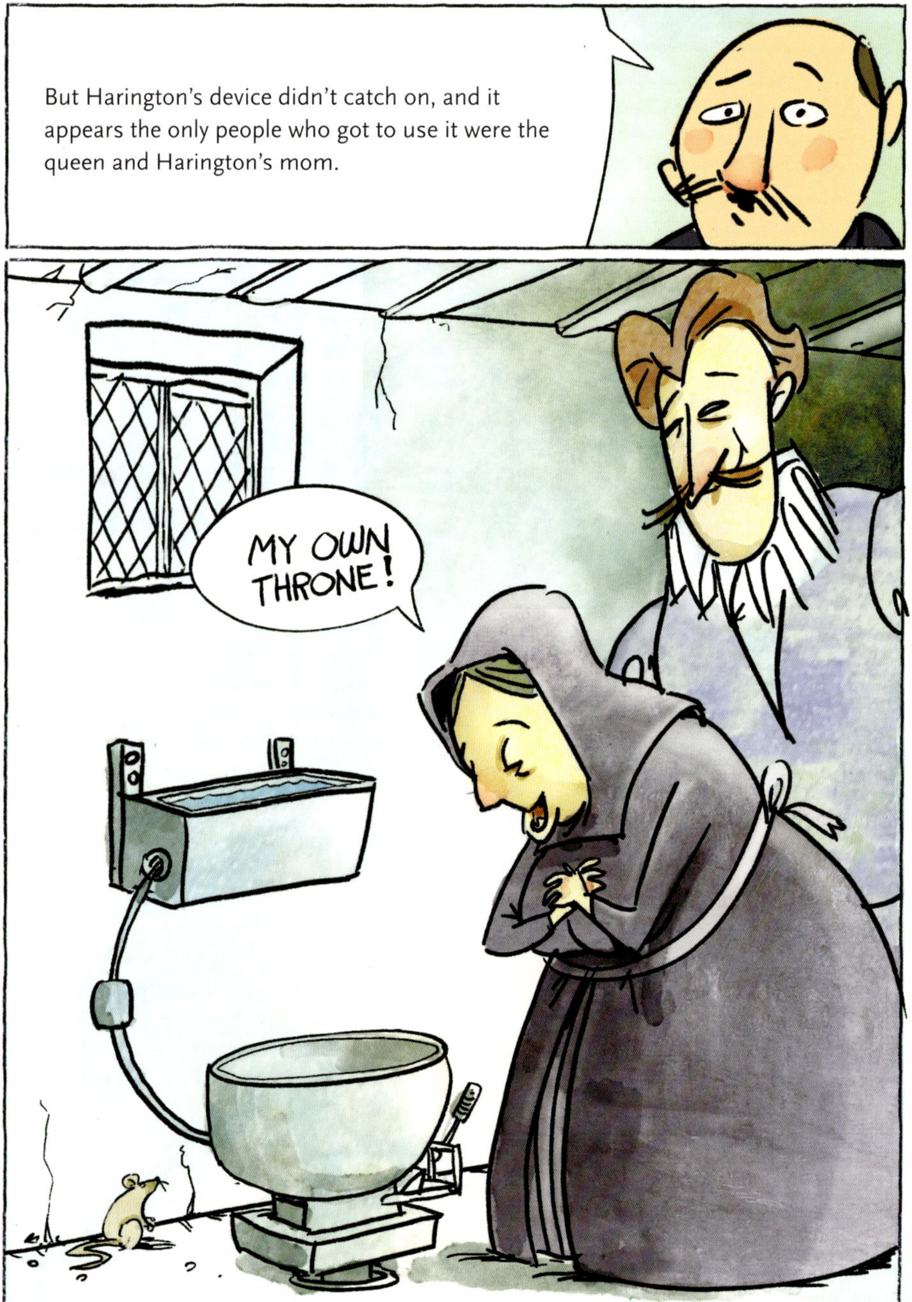
But Harington's device didn't catch on, and it appears the only people who got to use it were the queen and Harington's mom.
MY OWN THRONE!

Nearly two hundred years passed until Scottish watchmaker Alexander Cumming had a Big Idea to improve on Harington's design. He included an *S*-shaped pipe directly below the toilet bowl. When clean water is flushed into the toilet, it can't rise higher in the S-shaped pipe than the water in the bowl.

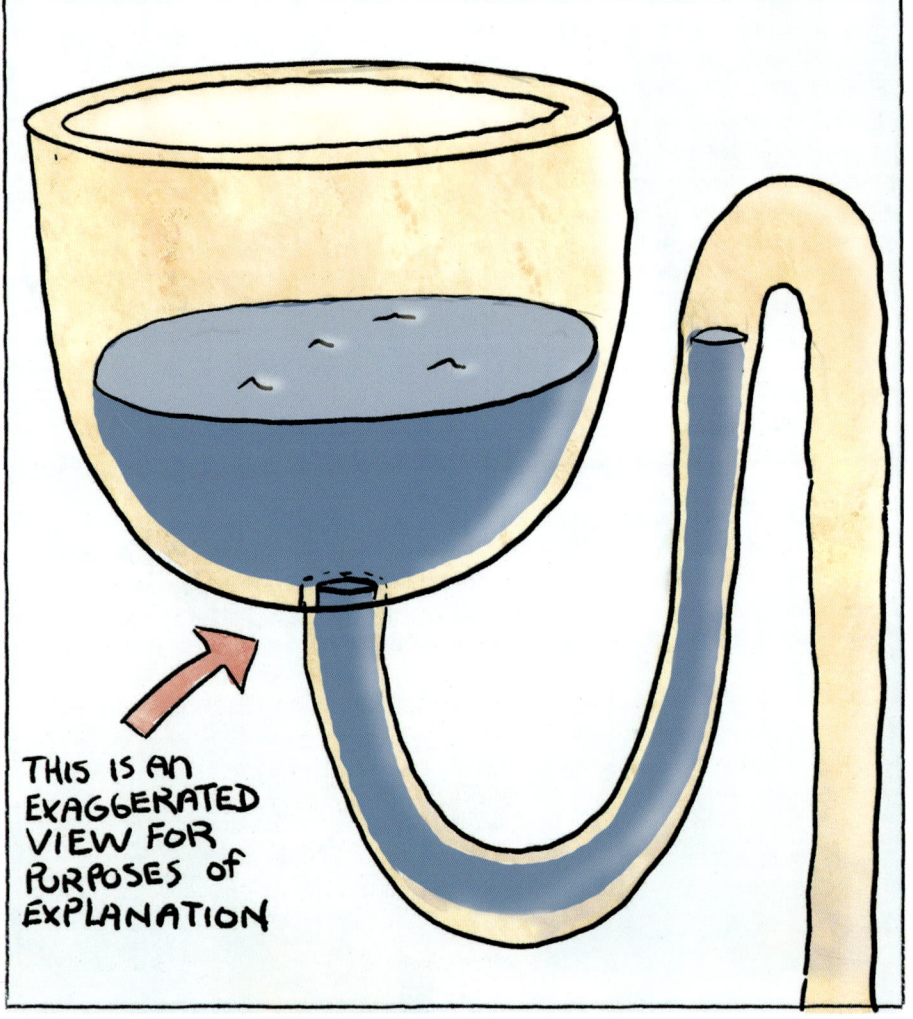

THIS IS AN EXAGGERATED VIEW FOR PURPOSES OF EXPLANATION

The resulting standing water seals off stinky smells from below and discouraged bugs.

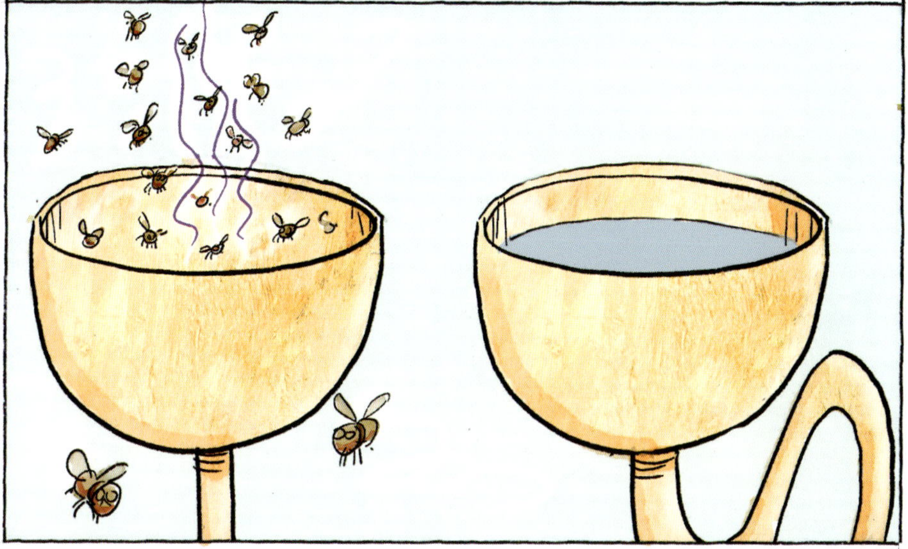

Nevertheless, popular interest in Cumming's device wasn't greater than Harington's.

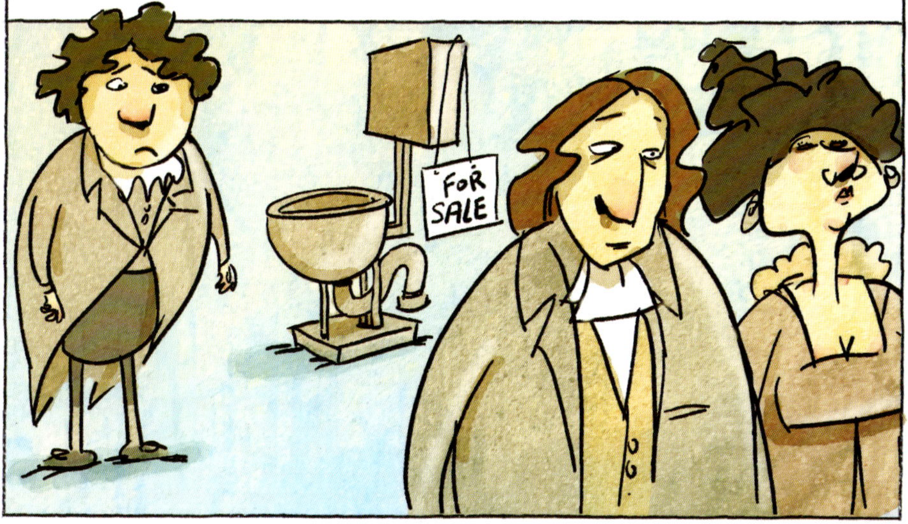
FOR SALE

Then, in 1851, the first public flush toilets based on Harington's and Cumming's designs were installed at the Great Exhibition, a giant fair celebrating British technical and manufacturing wonders. As it turned out, the public considered the toilets to be one of the exhibition's wonders. Eight hundred thousand people used them, forking over a penny per use for the privilege.

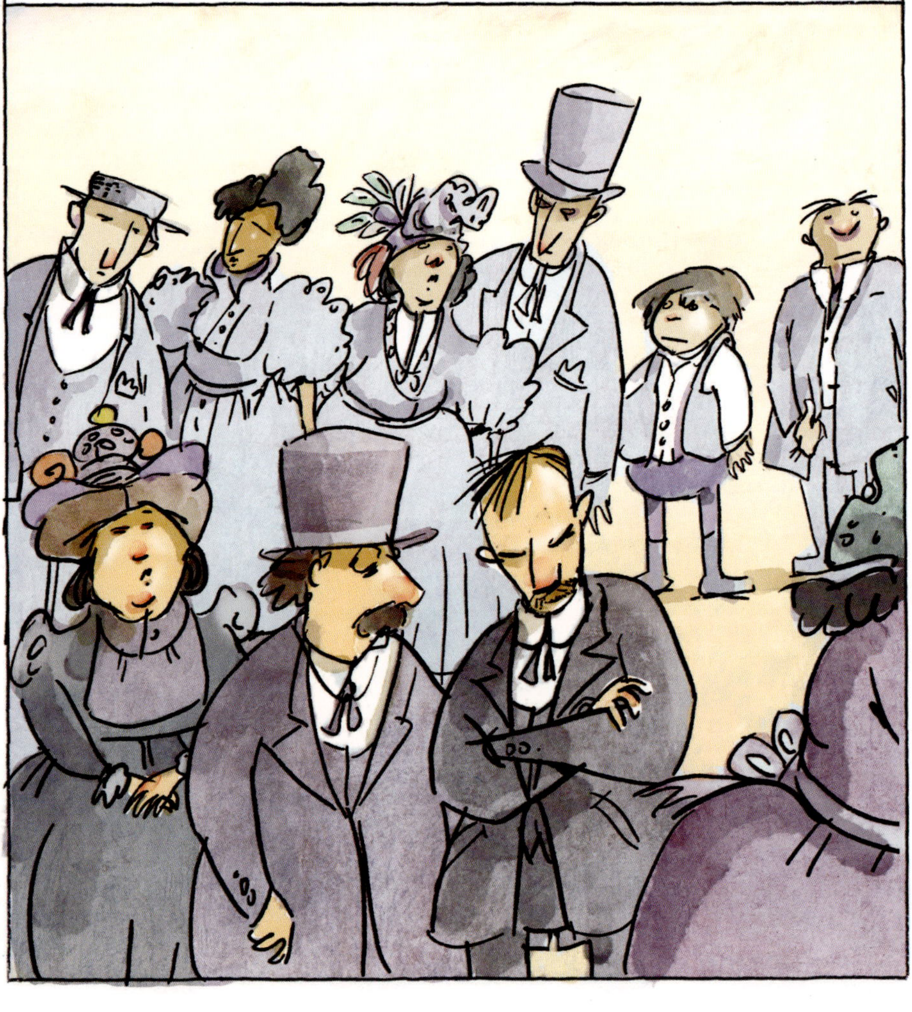

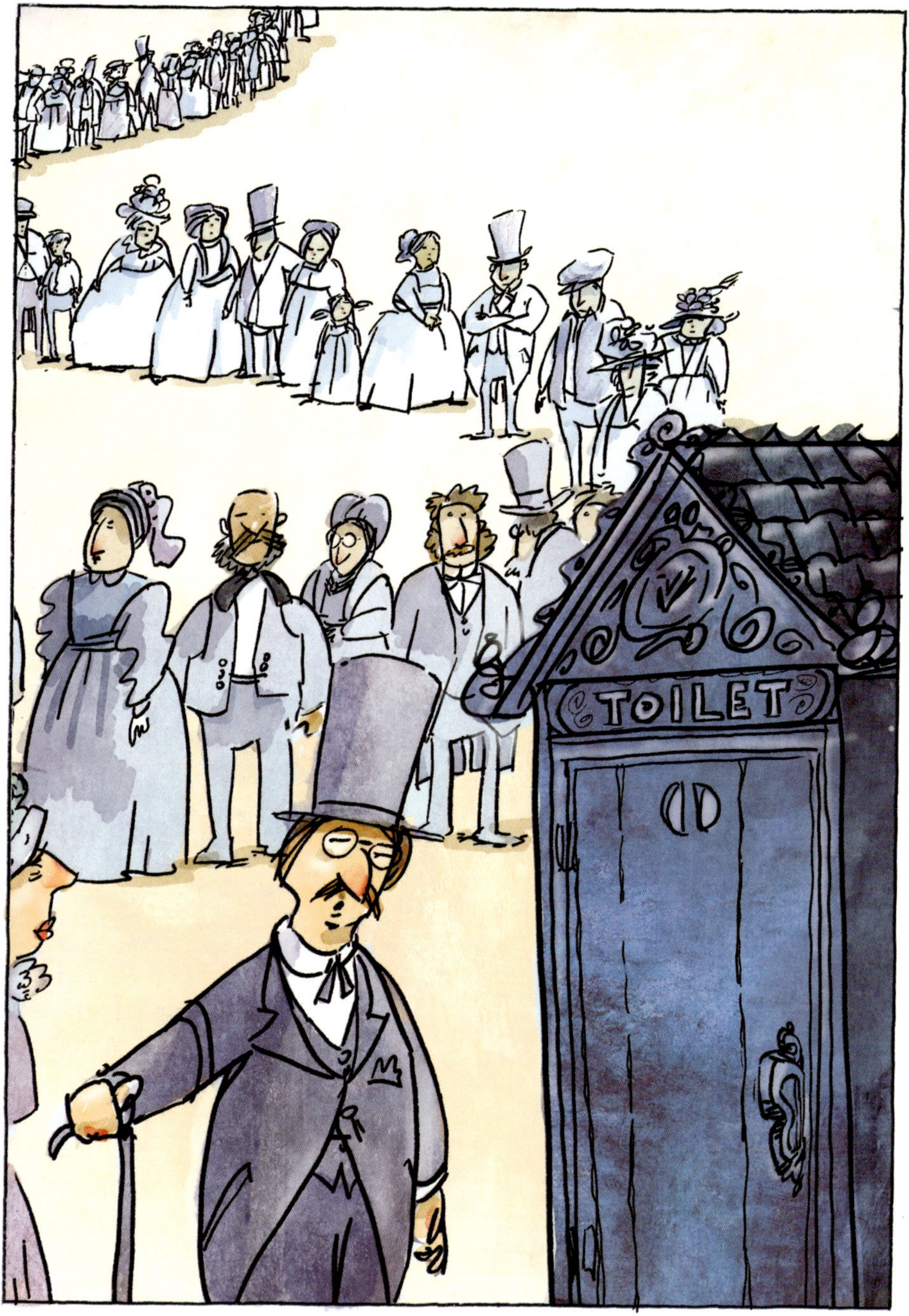
TOILET

Afterward, ordinary people began installing toilets in their homes.

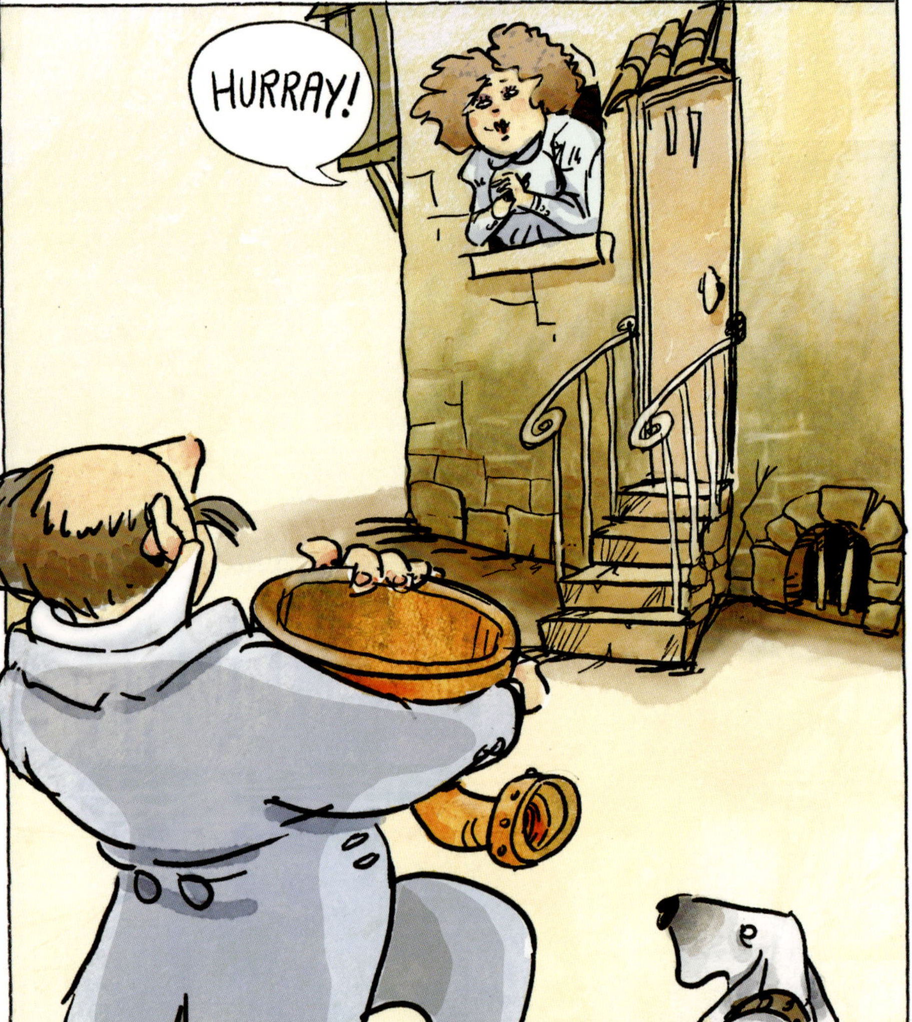
HURRAY!

Then, Thomas Crapper became plumber to the British royal family. His reputation soared, and when he manufactured a flush toilet, it became widely popular. Soon, people associated any toilet with a Crapper toilet until *toilet* and *Crapper* became interchangeable.

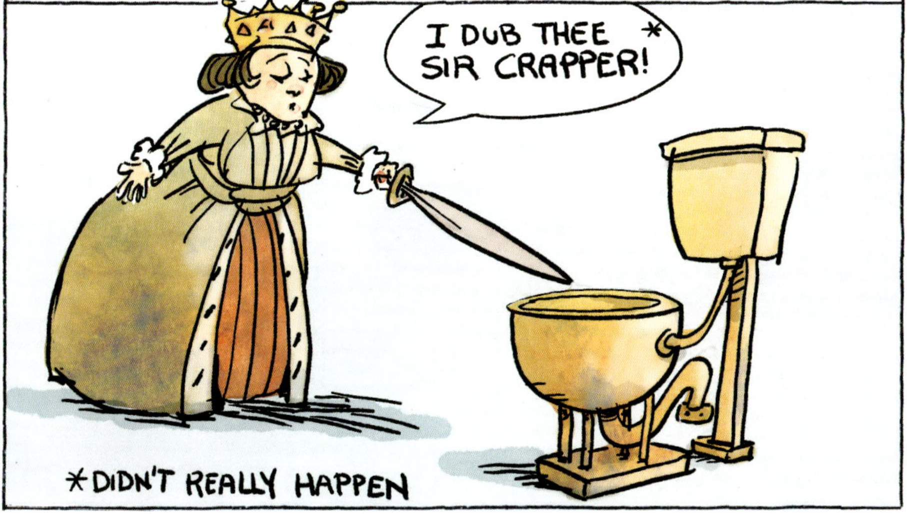
I DUB THEE SIR CRAPPER! *
*DIDN'T REALLY HAPPEN

In 1880, Crapper replaced the *S*-shaped pipe with a *U*-shaped pipe, an idea that has been adopted in modern toilets. So, we can say the modern toilet is really a combination of the Big Ideas of Harington, Cumming, and Crapper.

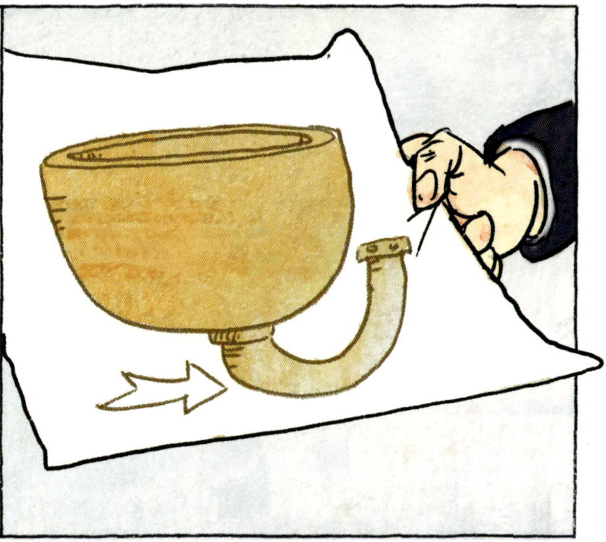

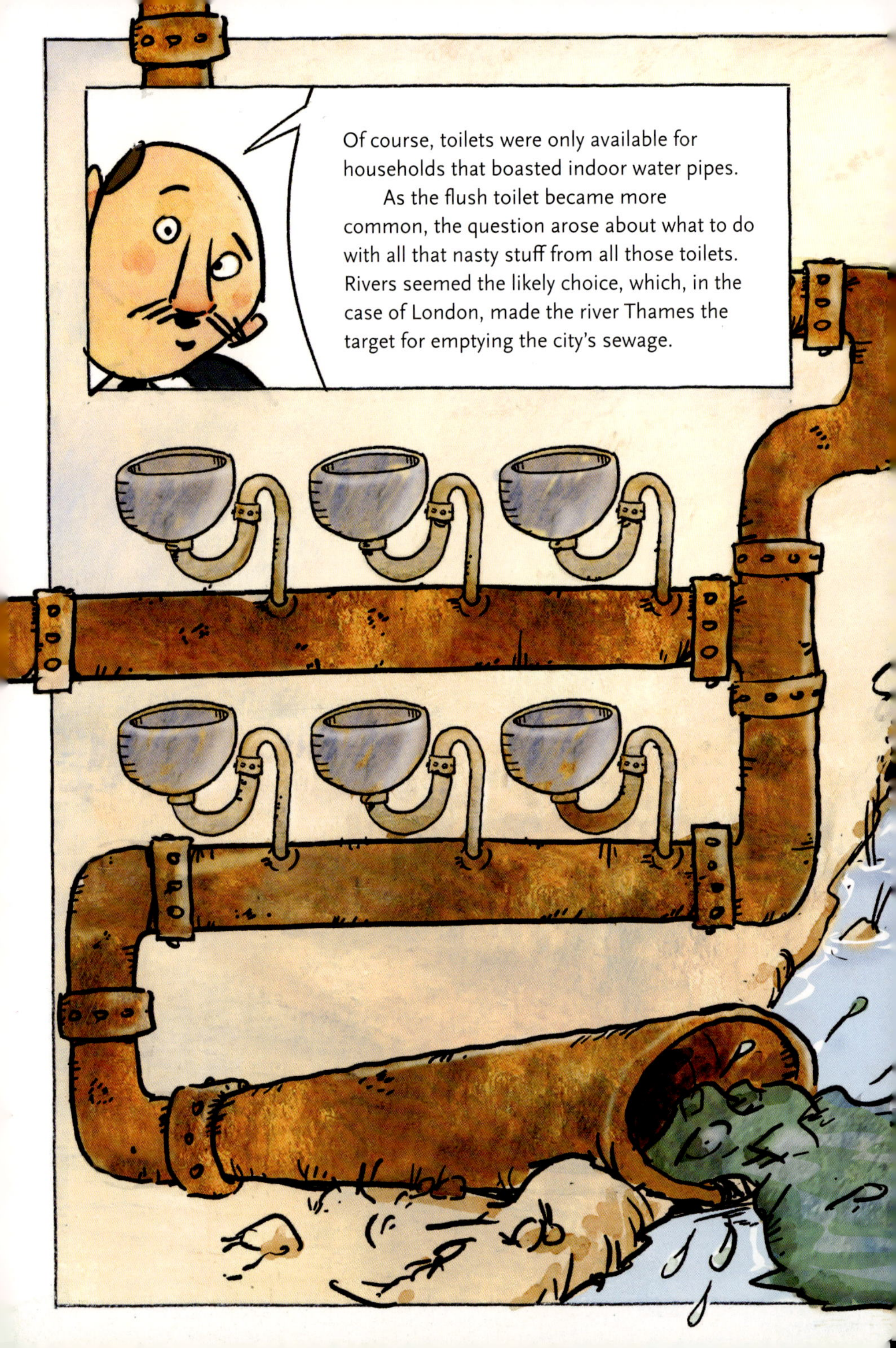
Of course, toilets were only available for households that boasted indoor water pipes.
As the flush toilet became more common, the question arose about what to do with all that nasty stuff from all those toilets. Rivers seemed the likely choice, which, in the case of London, made the river Thames the target for emptying the city's sewage.

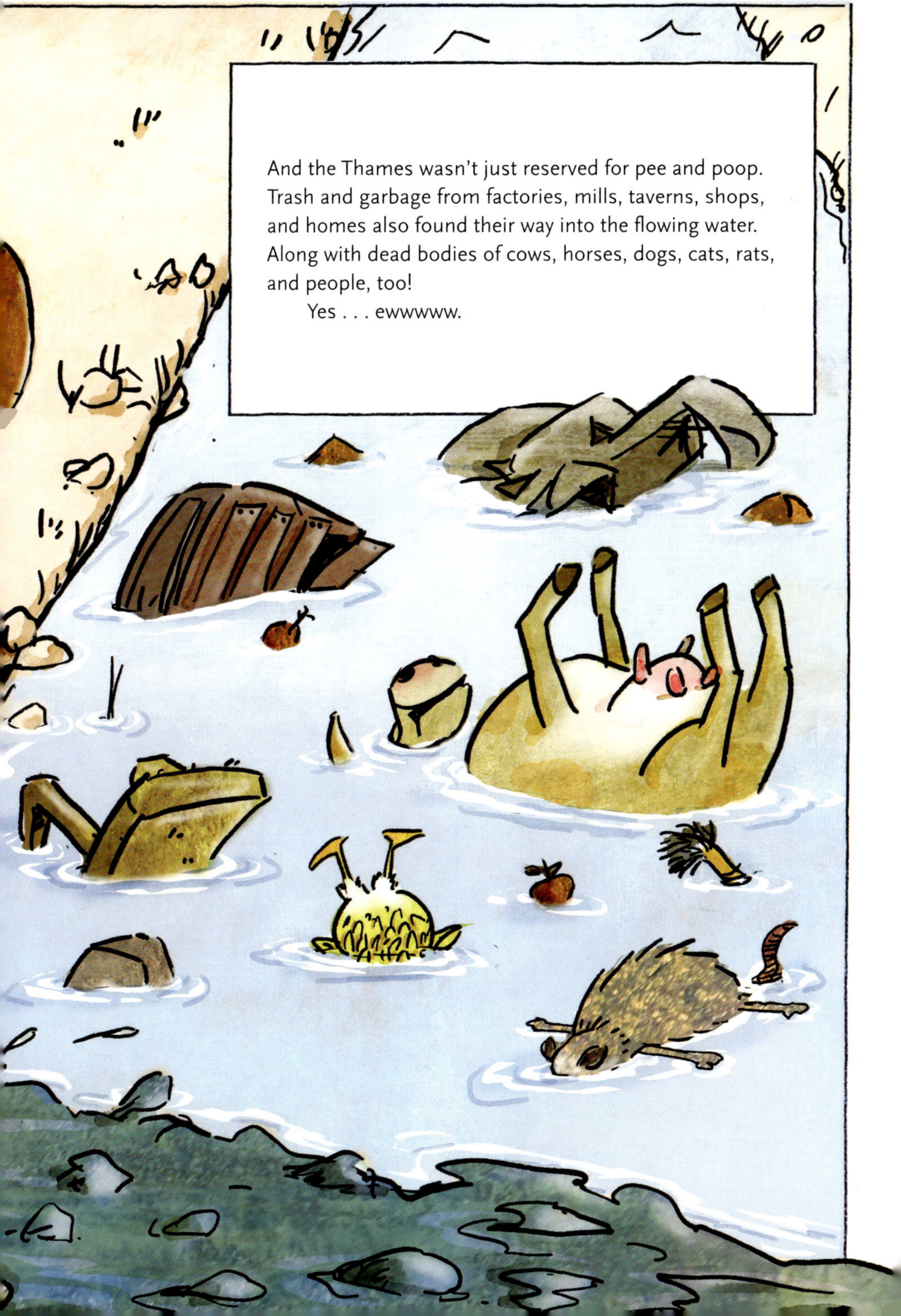

And the Thames wasn't just reserved for pee and poop. Trash and garbage from factories, mills, taverns, shops, and homes also found their way into the flowing water. Along with dead bodies of cows, horses, dogs, cats, rats, and people, too!

Yes . . . ewwwww.

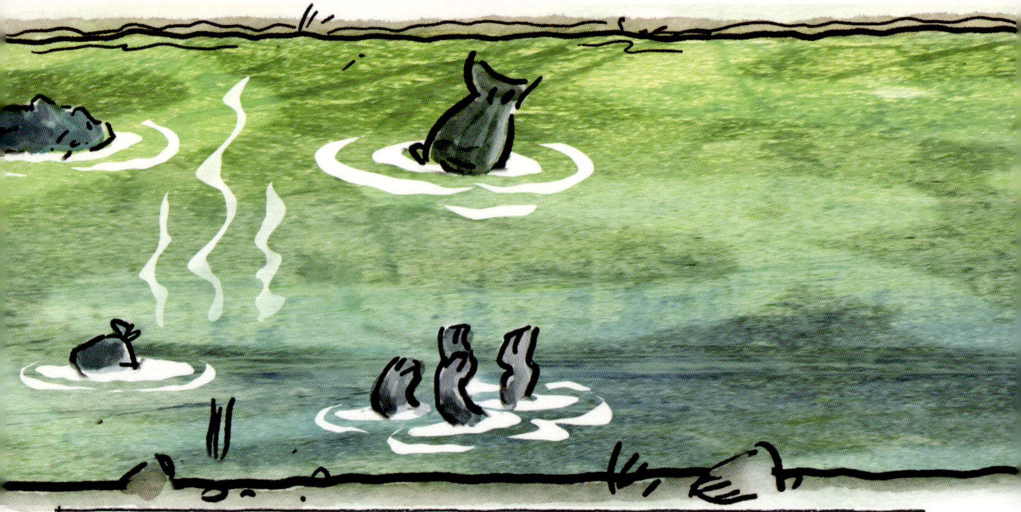

By 1858, the Thames was a “foul sewer, a river of pollution . . . festering and reeking with all abominable smells.”

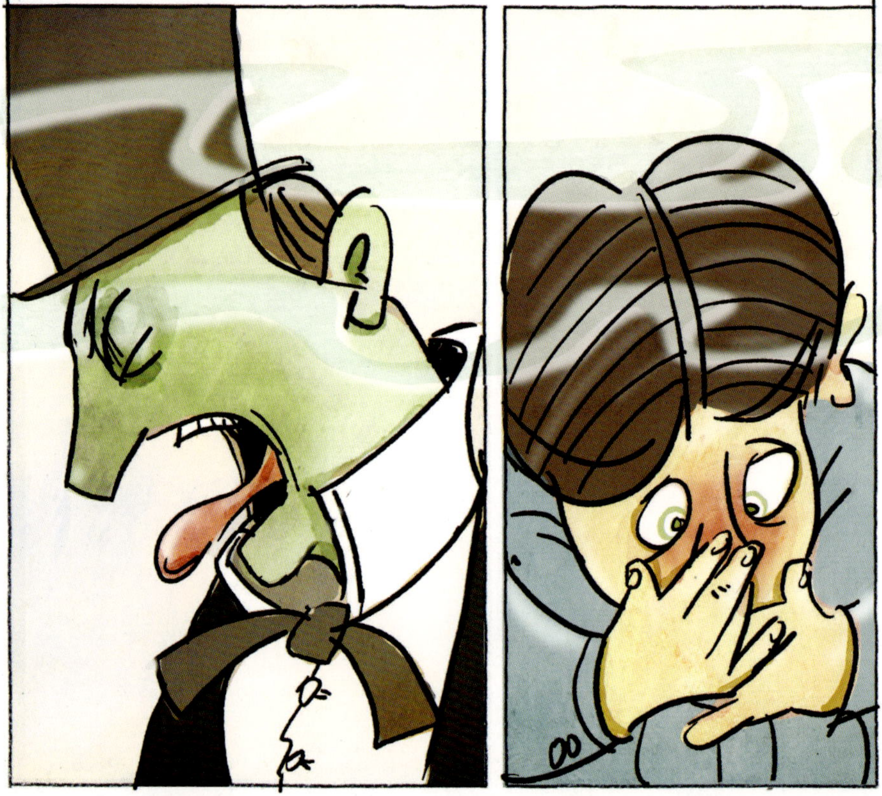

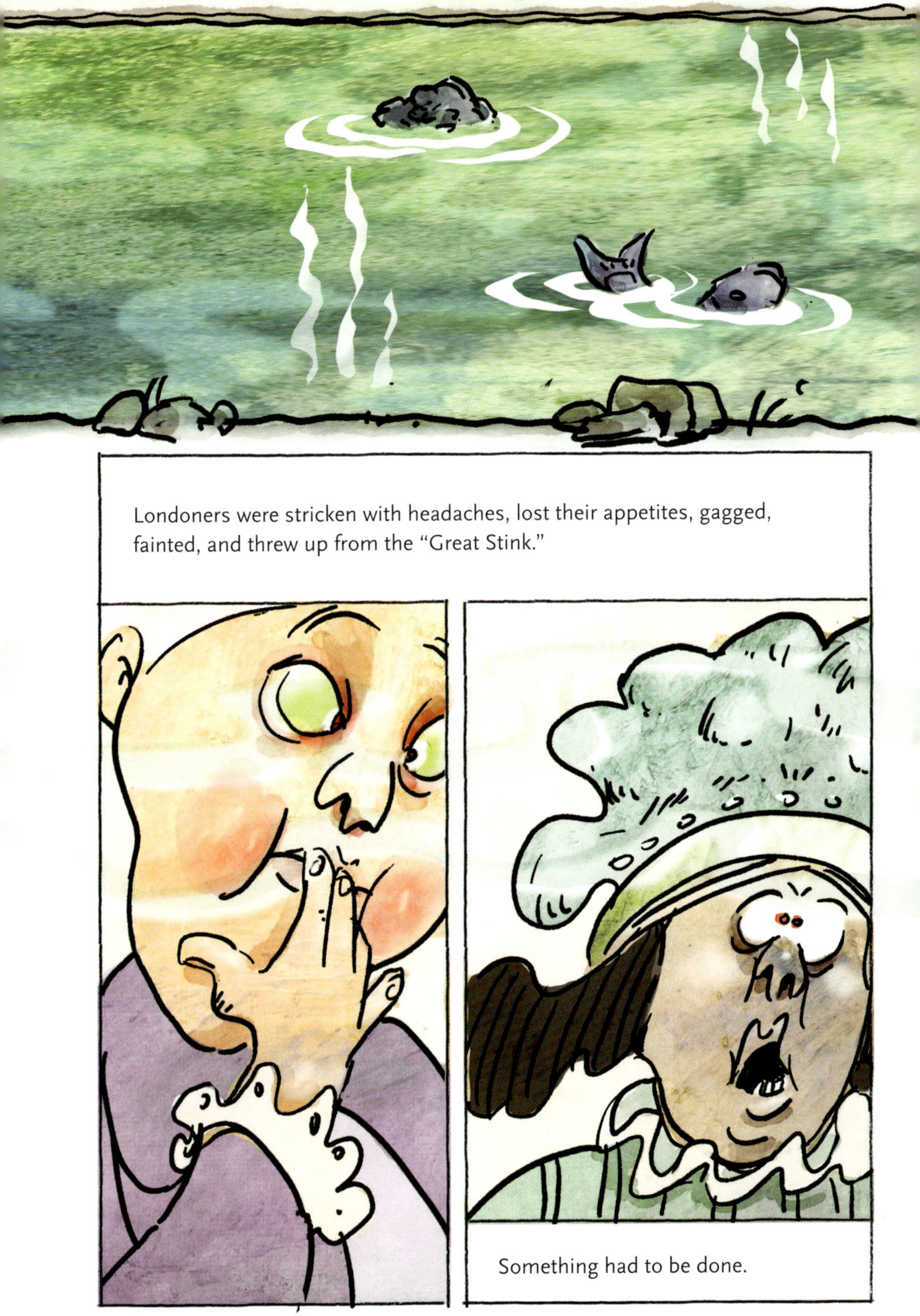
Londoners were stricken with headaches, lost their appetites, gagged, fainted, and threw up from the "Great Stink."
Something had to be done.

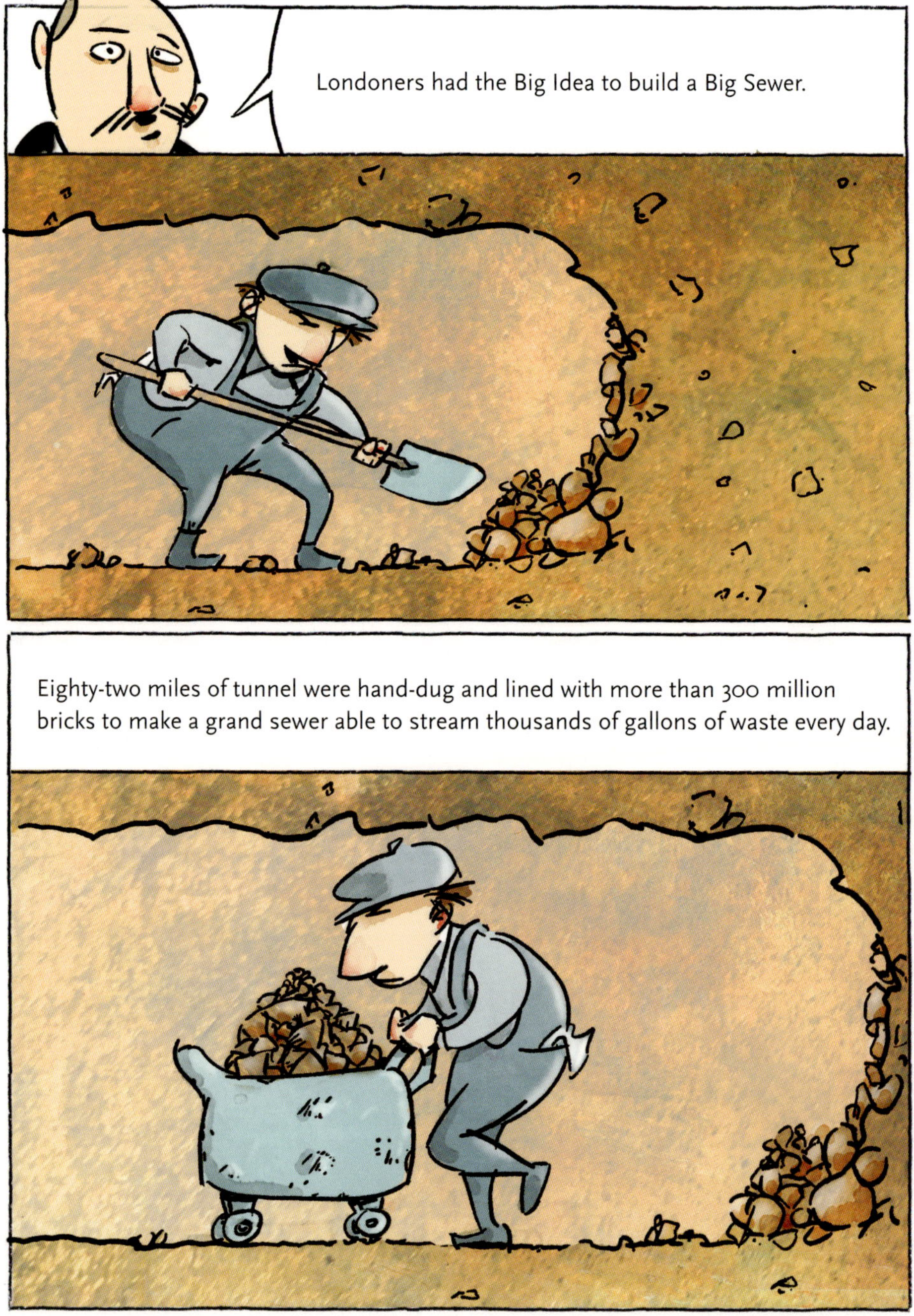
Londoners had the Big Idea to build a Big Sewer.
Eighty-two miles of tunnel were hand-dug and lined with more than 300 million bricks to make a grand sewer able to stream thousands of gallons of waste every day.

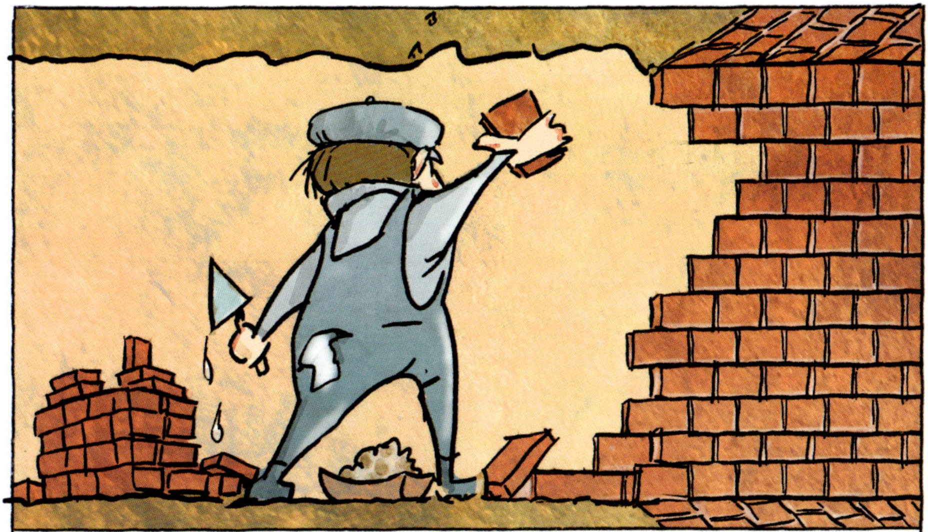

And where did all that disgusting, untreated sewage goop go?

It was dumped back in the Thames, eight miles downstream, becoming a black and poisonous mess.

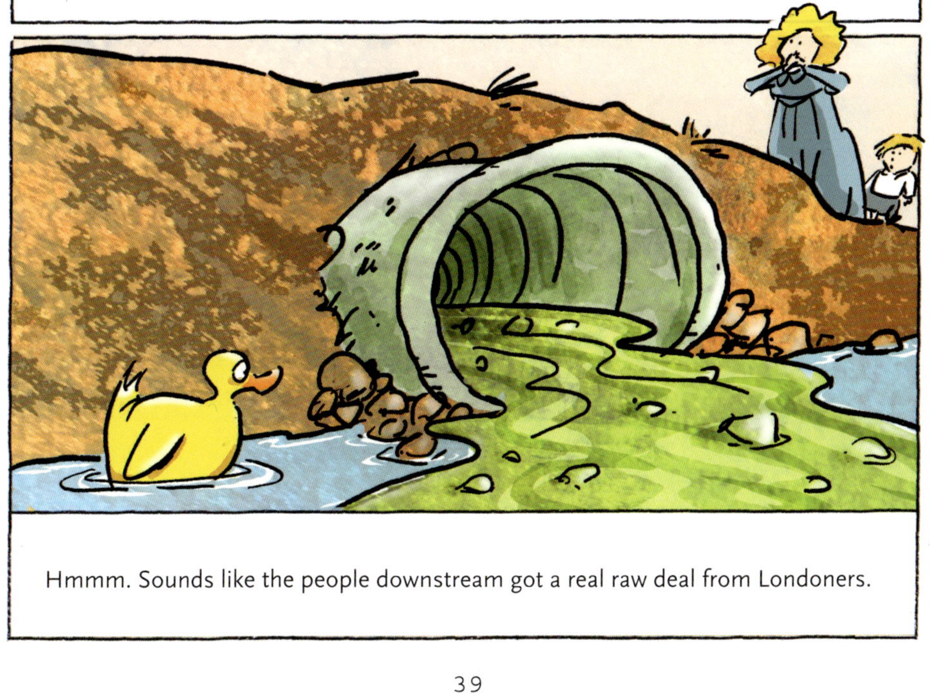

Hmmm. Sounds like the people downstream got a real raw deal from Londoners.

Of course, London wasn't alone when it came to the problem of filth.
At the end of the nineteenth century, New York City was a dirty mess, too.

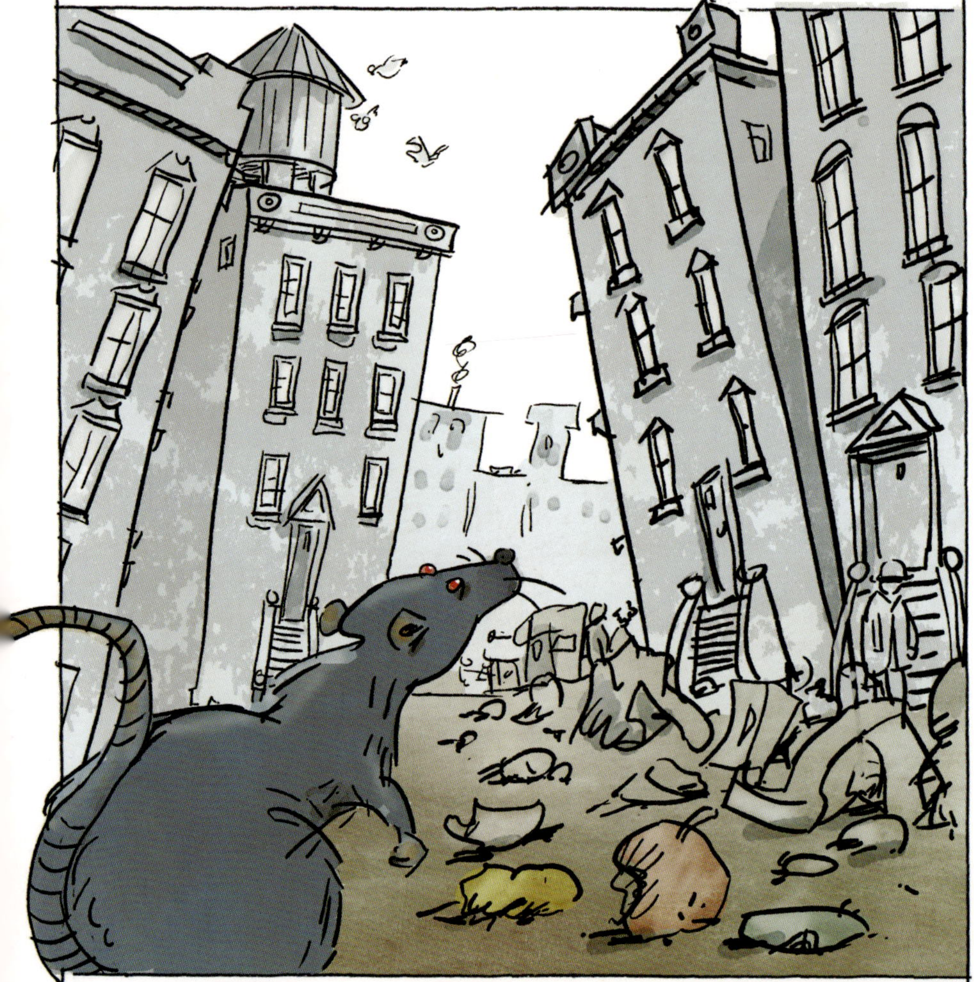

In the age of horsepower, the presence of horse poop and pee was a common experience everywhere.

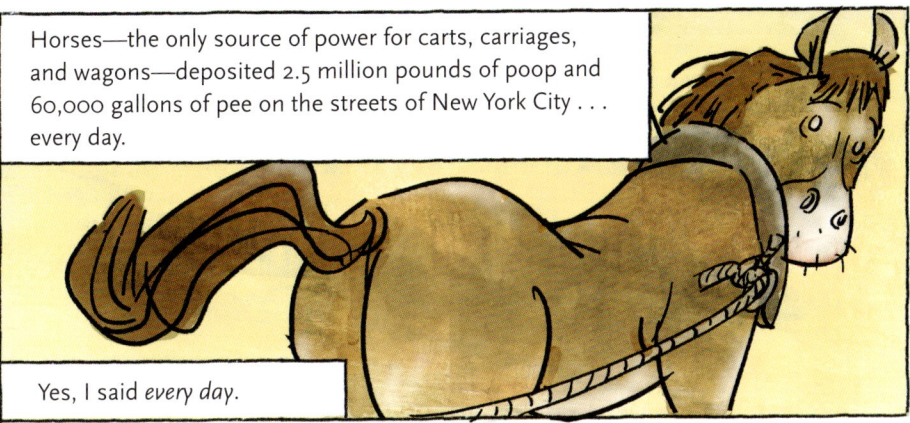

Horses—the only source of power for carts, carriages, and wagons—deposited 2.5 million pounds of poop and 60,000 gallons of pee on the streets of New York City . . . every day.

Yes, I said *every day*.

And the poor horses who were worked to death were left to rot on the street where they died.

Household trash, business garbage, rotting food, and poop thrown out of windows collected in the gutters in two-foot-high piles. Outdoor bathrooms, or outhouses, were everywhere.

"All the streets are one mass of reeking, disgusting filth . . . the dirt prevails all over . . . in the thoroughfares, in the by-streets, the alleyways, the lanes."

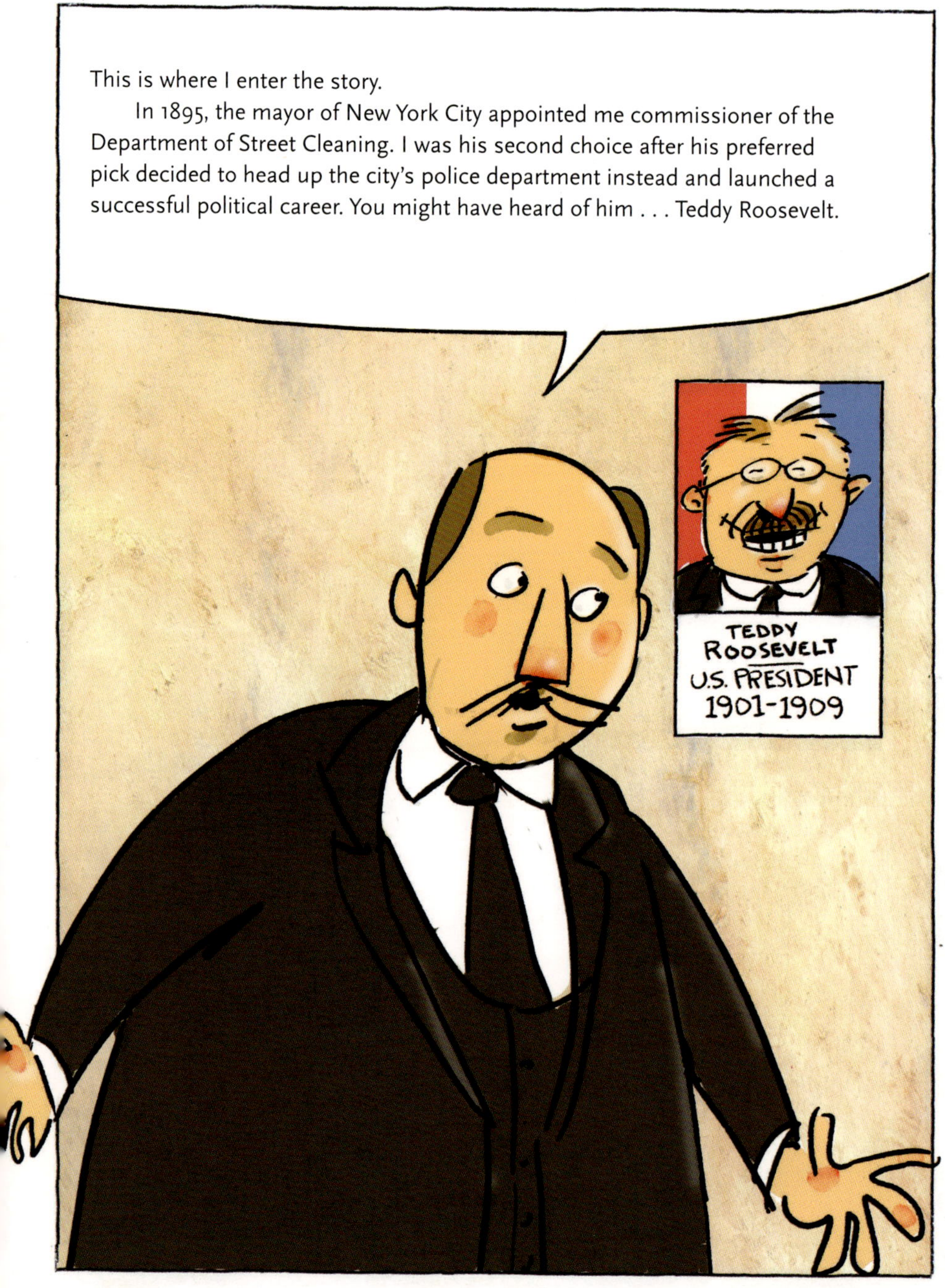
This is where I enter the story.
In 1895, the mayor of New York City appointed me commissioner of the Department of Street Cleaning. I was his second choice after his preferred pick decided to head up the city's police department instead and launched a successful political career. You might have heard of him . . . Teddy Roosevelt.
TEDDY ROOSEVELT U.S. PRESIDENT 1901-1909

In any case, as an engineer, I was probably better trained to be the head of sanitation.

I created an army of street cleaners, dressed in all-white.

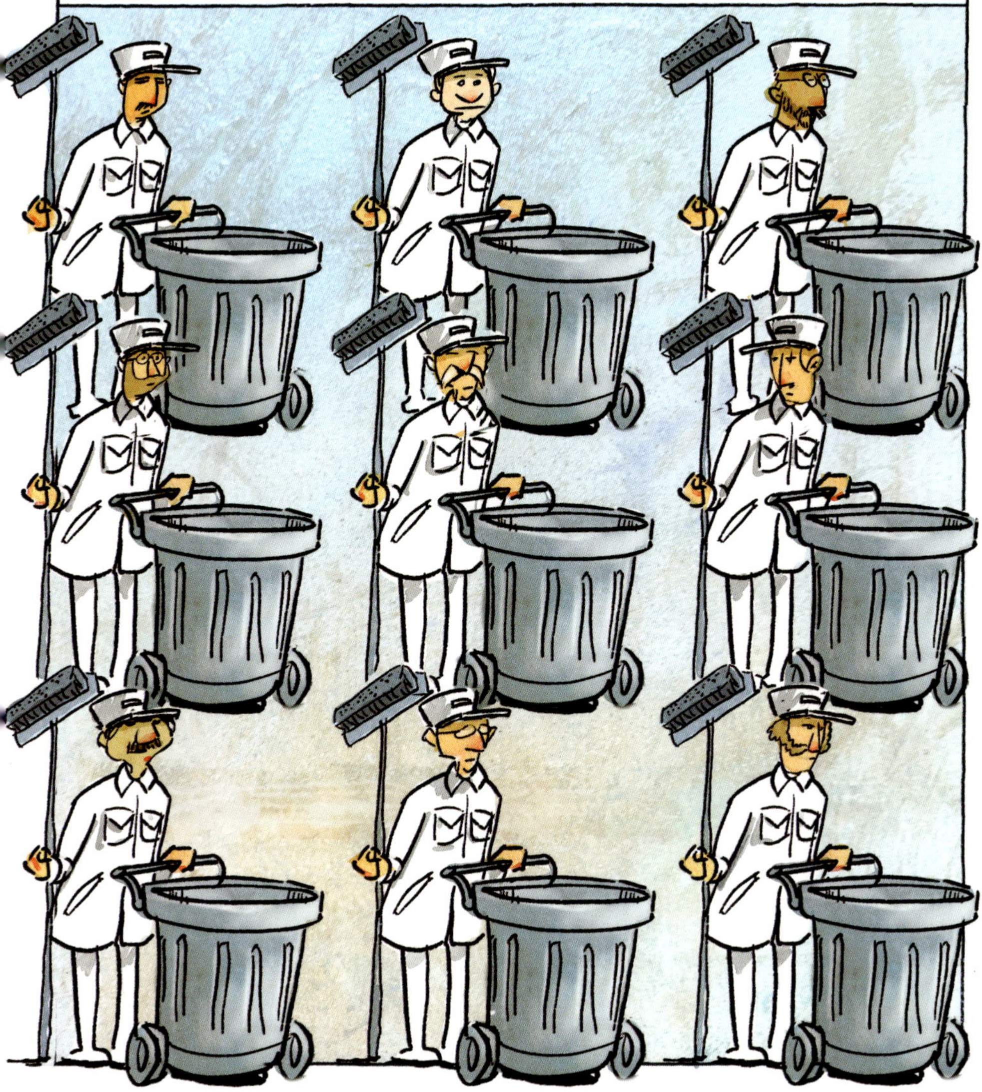

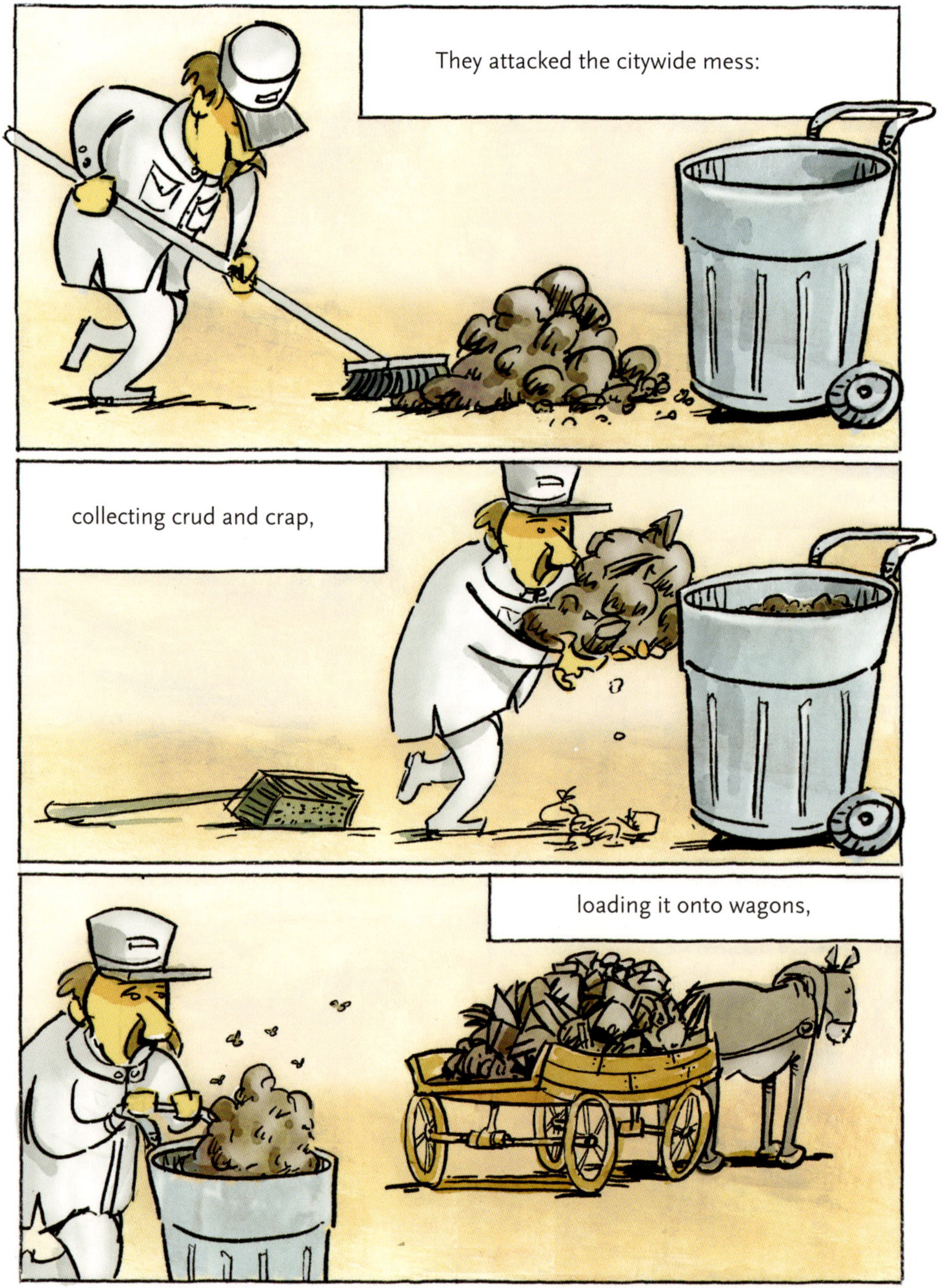
They attacked the citywide mess:
collecting crud and crap,
loading it onto wagons,

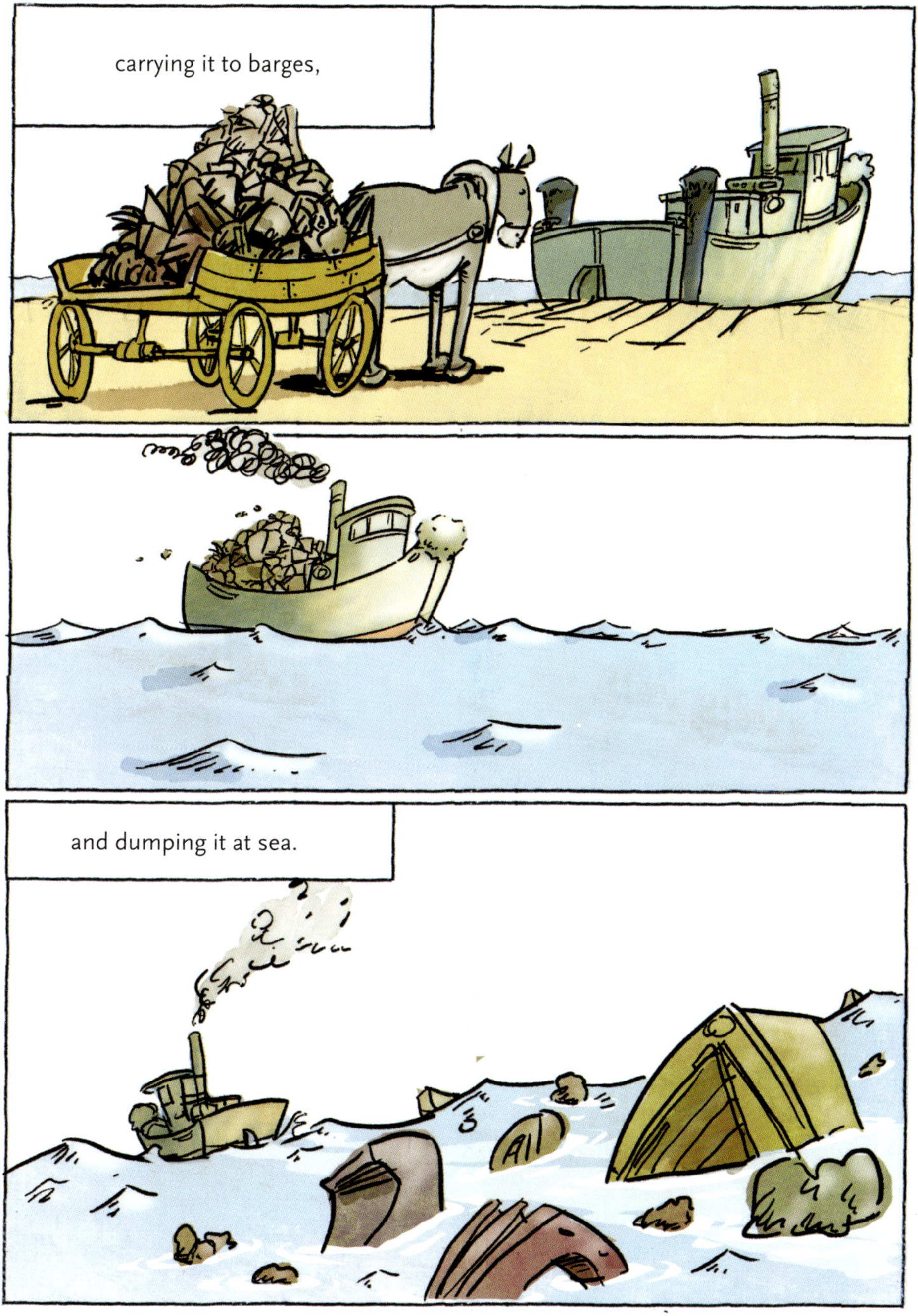
carrying it to barges,
and dumping it at sea.

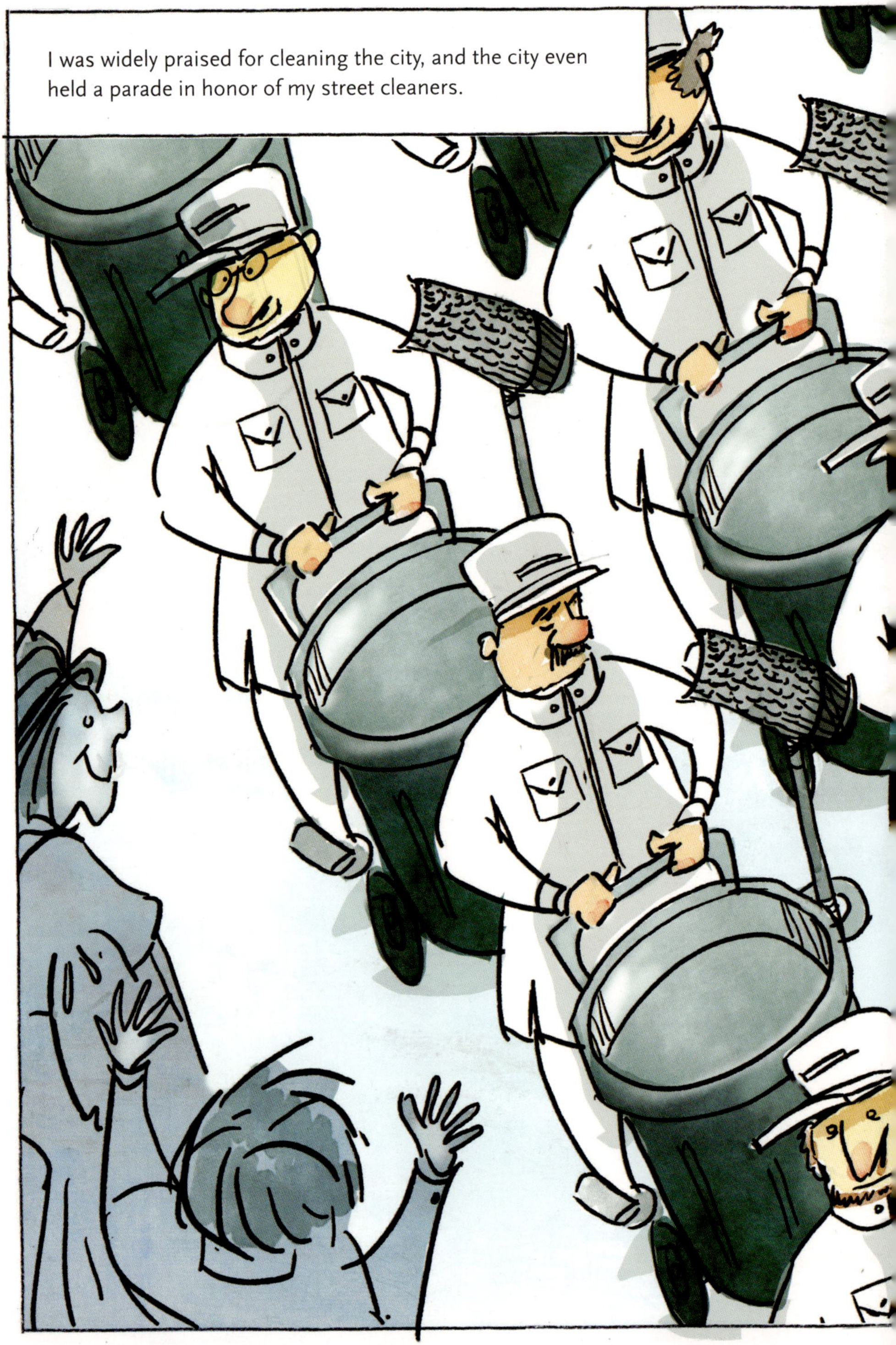
I was widely praised for cleaning the city, and the city even held a parade in honor of my street cleaners.

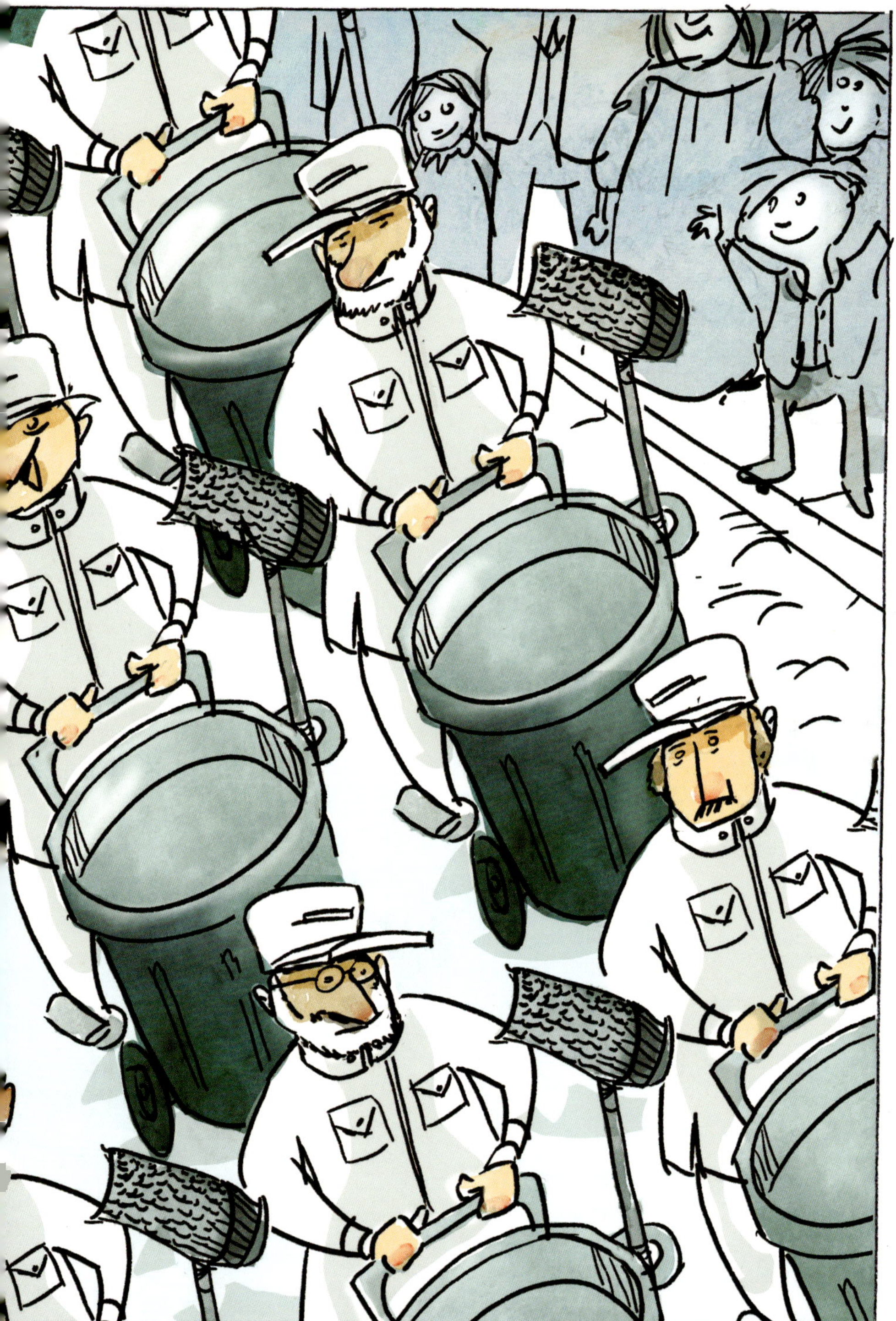

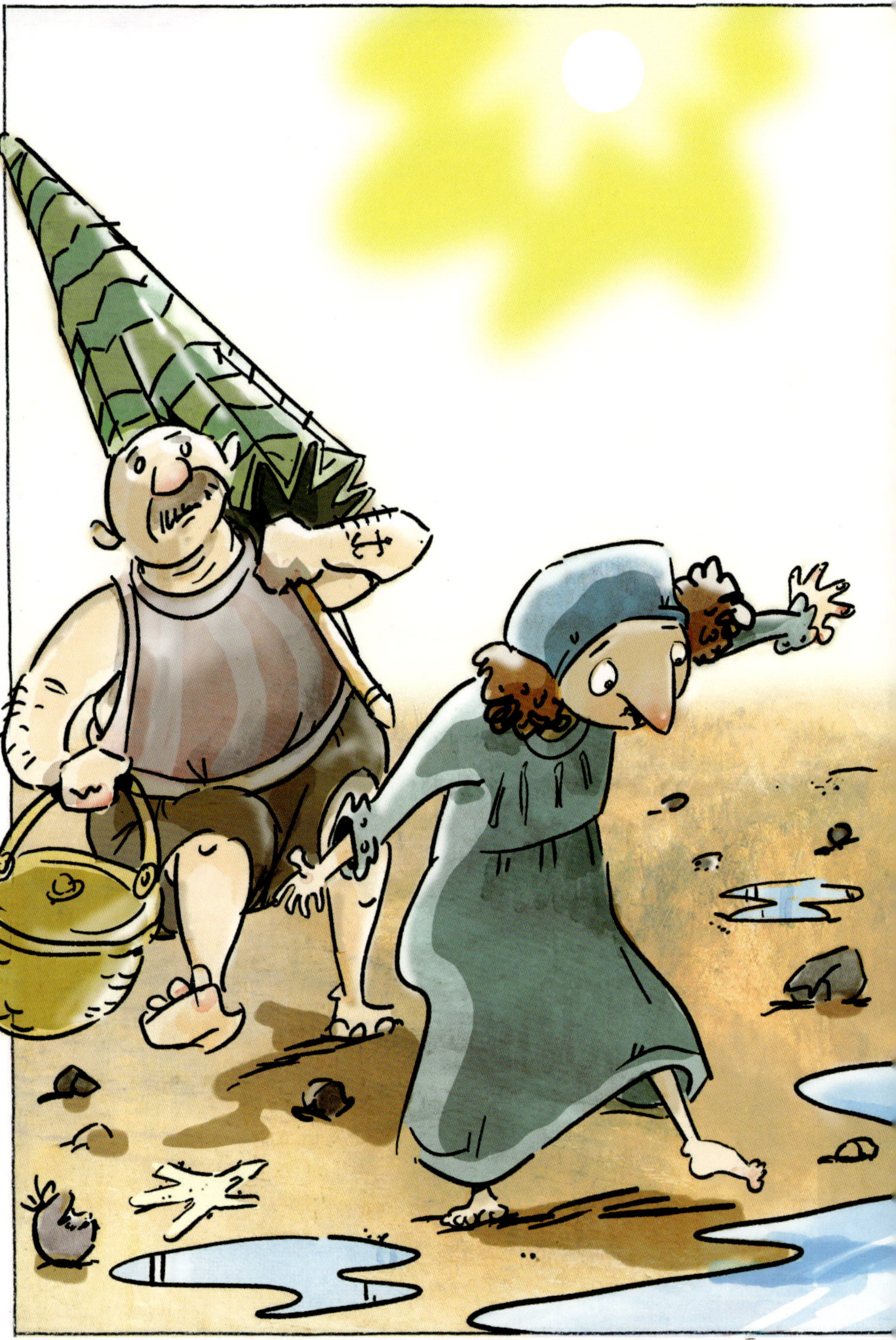

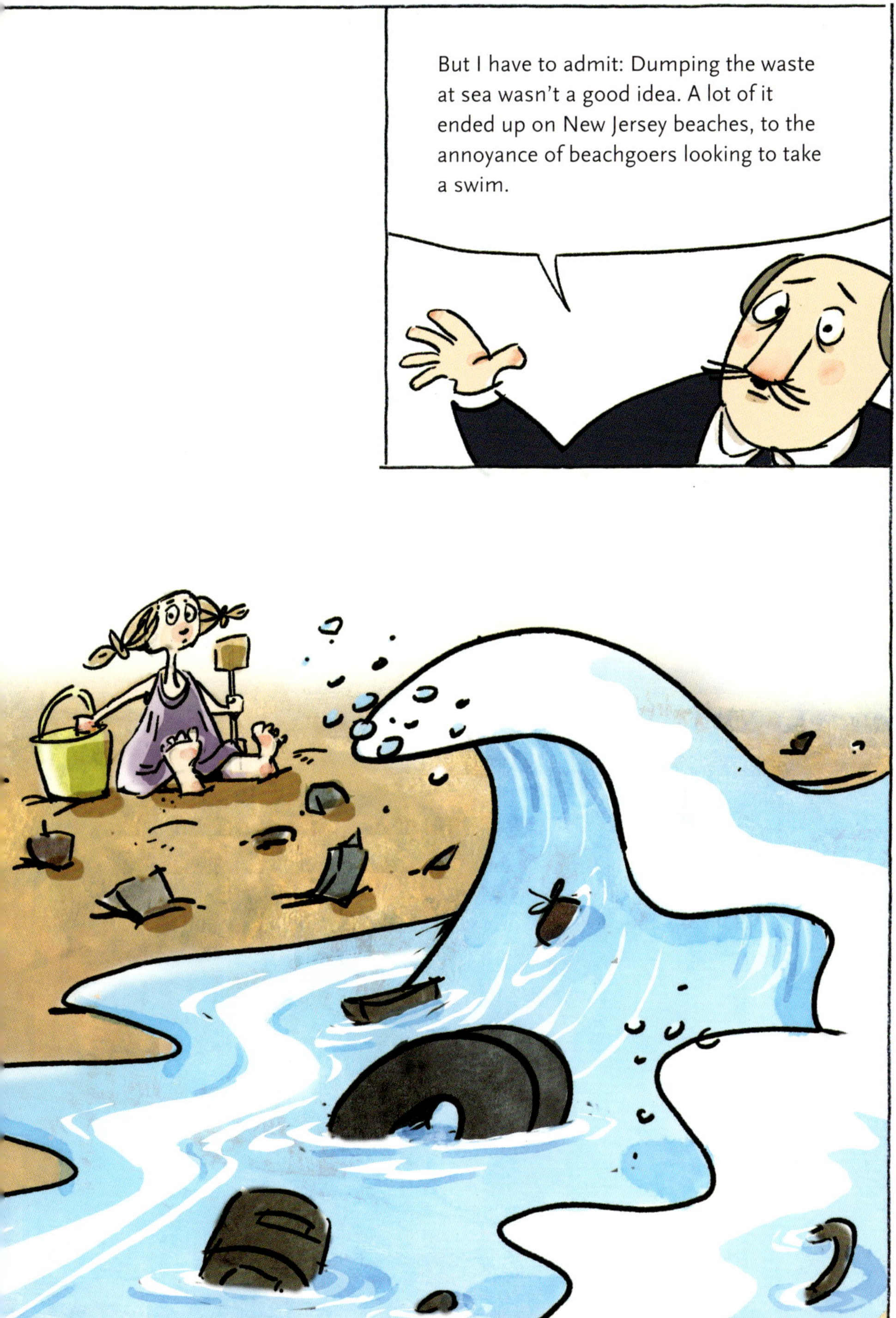
But I have to admit: Dumping the waste at sea wasn't a good idea. A lot of it ended up on New Jersey beaches, to the annoyance of beachgoers looking to take a swim.

While my men were shoveling poop in the gutters, the city was busy building sewers. *Lots* of sewers. By the beginning of the twenty-first century, the city had about 7,500 miles of them!

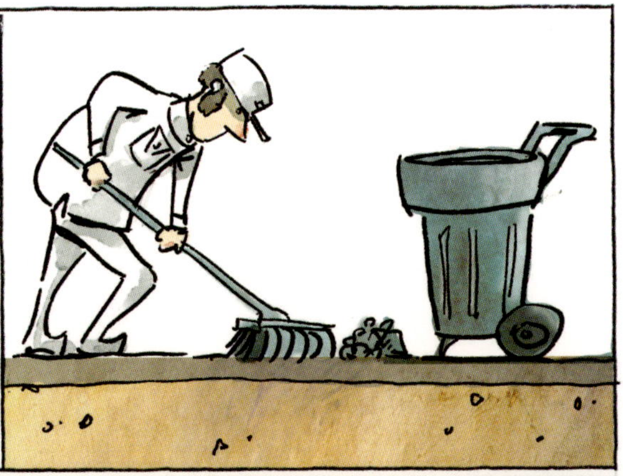

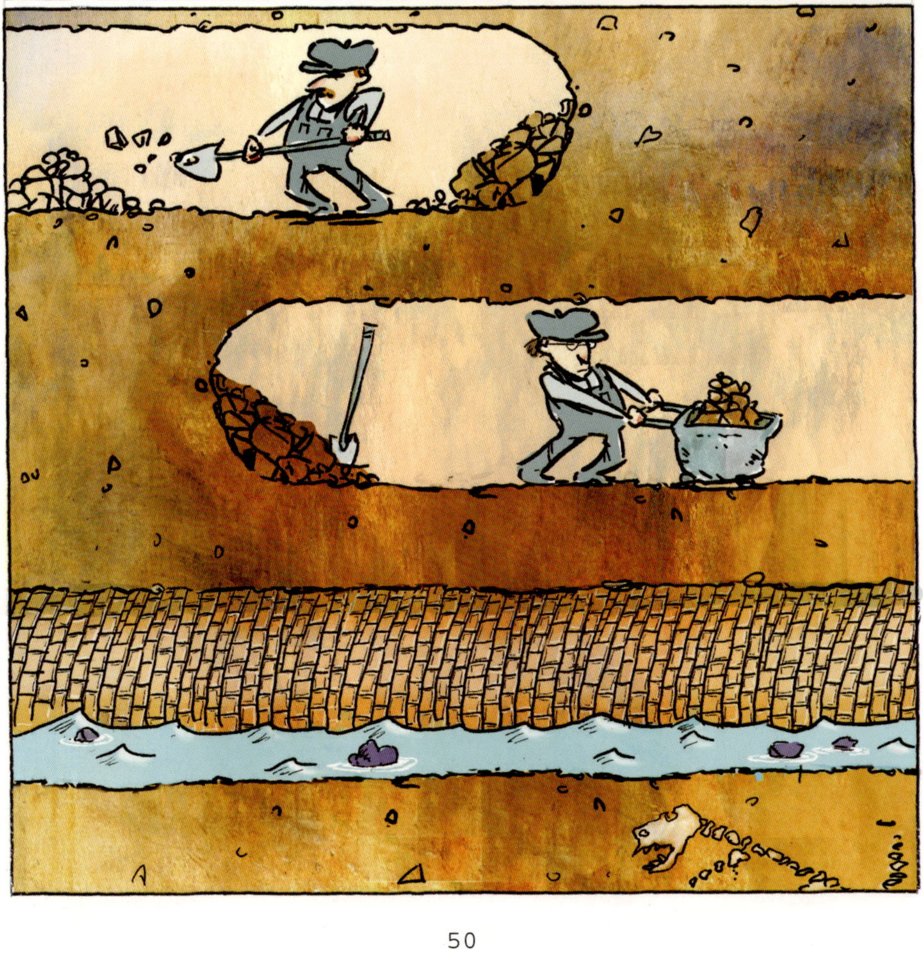

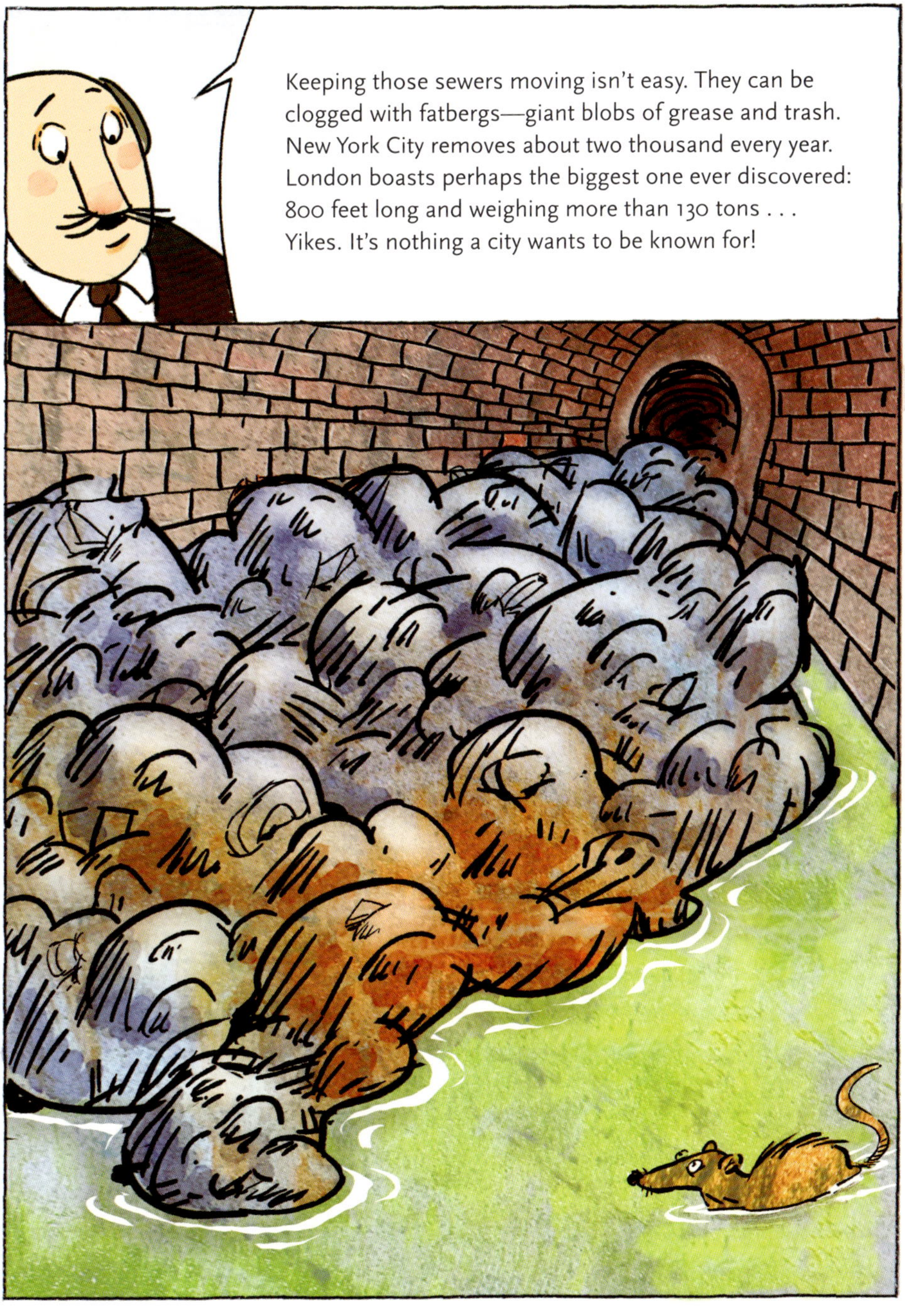
Keeping those sewers moving isn't easy. They can be clogged with fatbergs—giant blobs of grease and trash. New York City removes about two thousand every year. London boasts perhaps the biggest one ever discovered: 800 feet long and weighing more than 130 tons . . . Yikes. It's nothing a city wants to be known for!

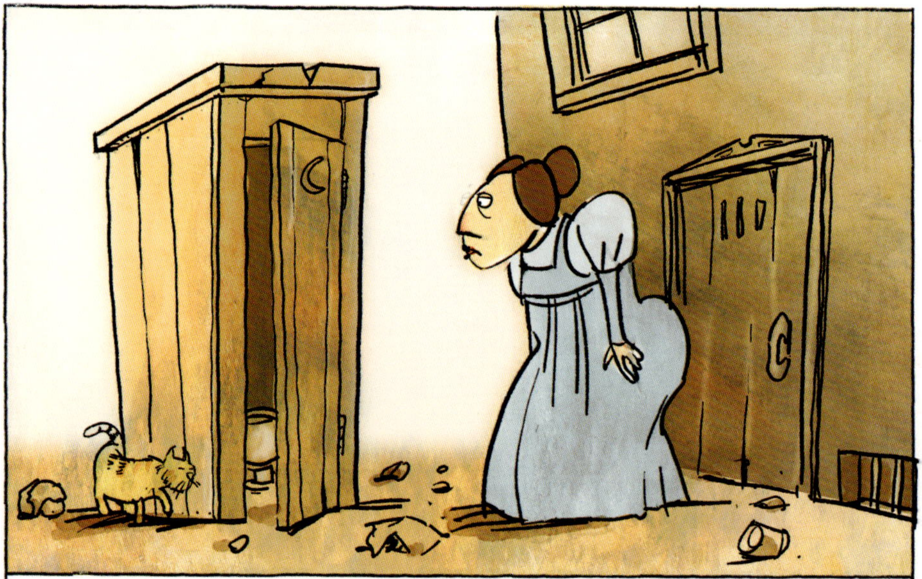

In New York City, new laws arrived requiring spaces or closets for indoor toilets within new buildings; outhouses and backyard cesspools—outdoor poop pits—began to disappear from the city . . .

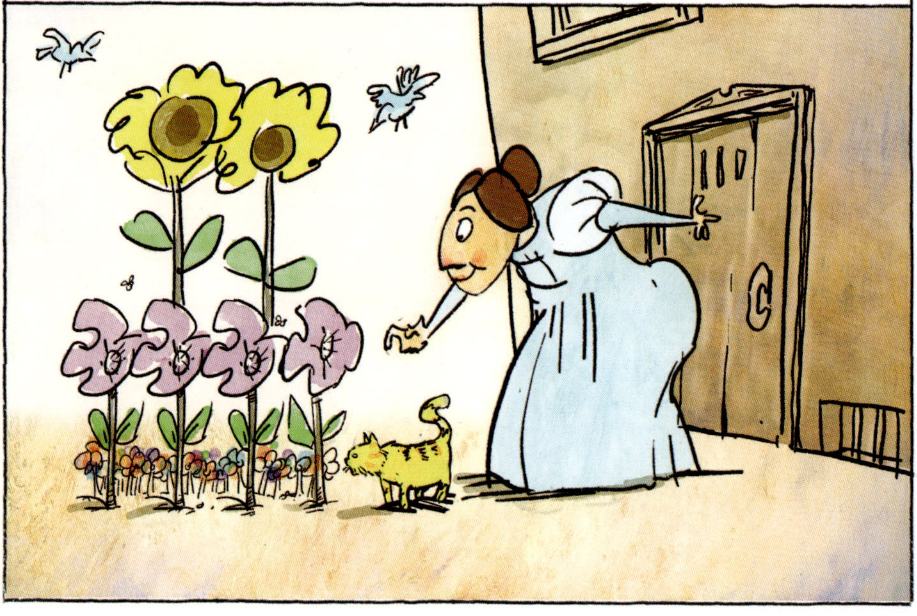

And they would disappear across the country, too . . .

But slowly . . .

In 1950, a quarter of American households didn't have toilets. In 2014, about a million and half Americans still used outhouses.

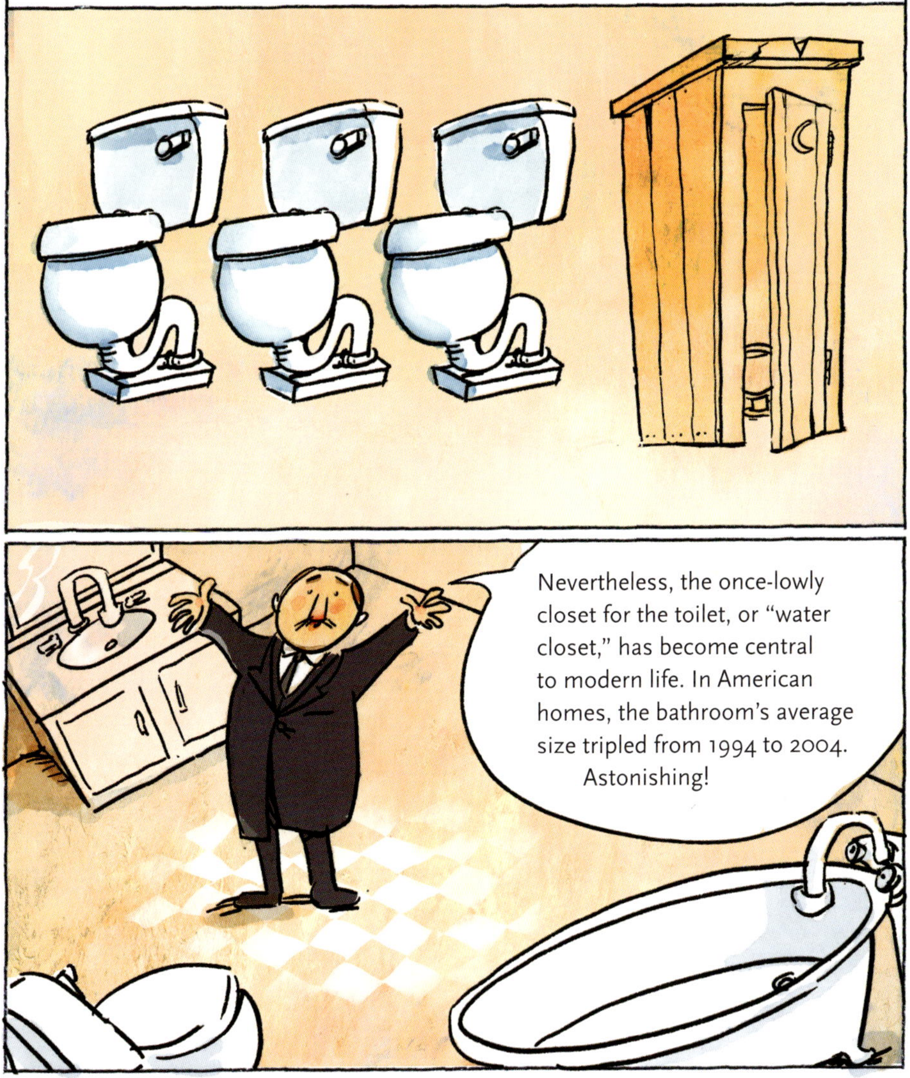
Nevertheless, the once-lowly closet for the toilet, or "water closet," has become central to modern life. In American homes, the bathroom's average size tripled from 1994 to 2004.
Astonishing!

We're even sending toilets into outer space . . . a Big Idea when you consider the problems early astronauts faced when their spacecrafts had none.

On Apollo 10, *something* escaped and prompted an uncomfortable conversation between the three astronauts.

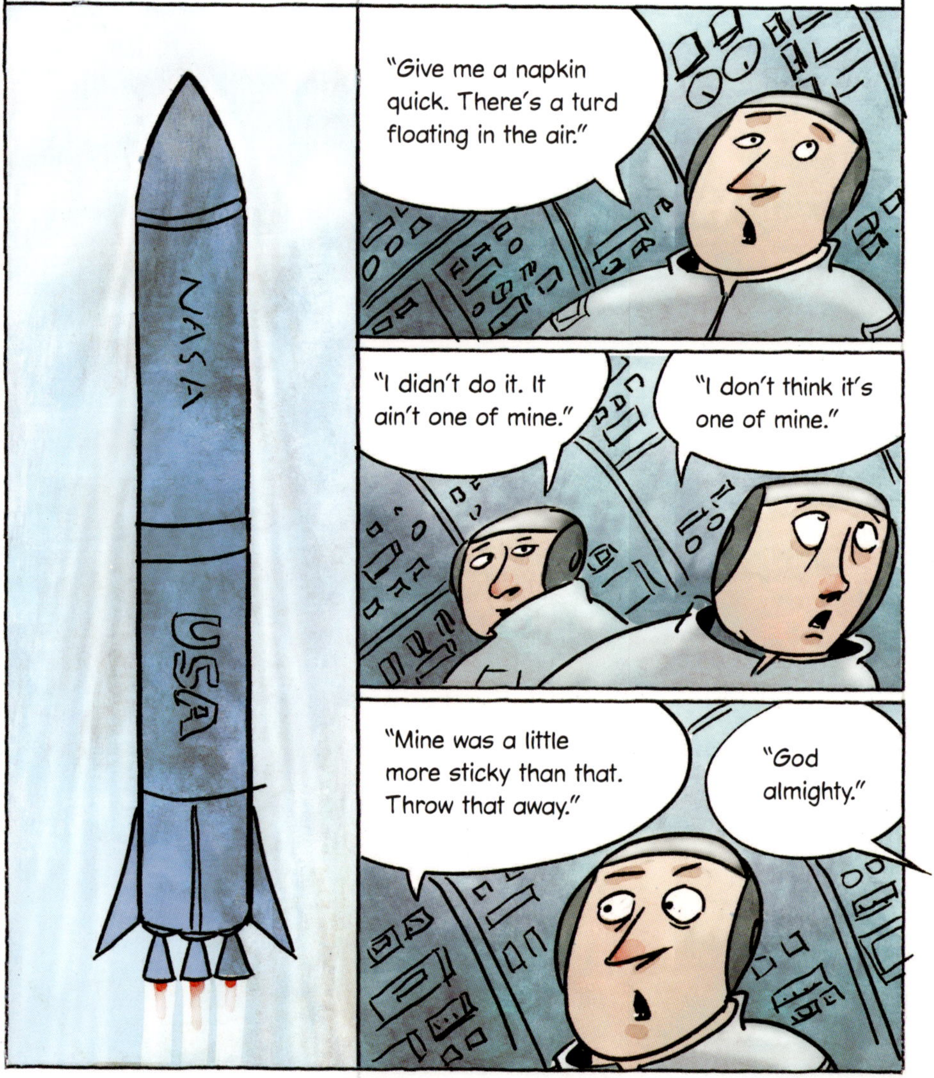
NASA
USA
"Give me a napkin quick. There's a turd floating in the air."
"I didn't do it. It ain't one of mine."
"I don't think it's one of mine."
"Mine was a little more sticky than that. Throw that away."
"God almighty."

Astronauts working in the International Space Station use a high-tech toilet, with funnels and specialty vacuums, and astronauts need to attend a training school before using it.

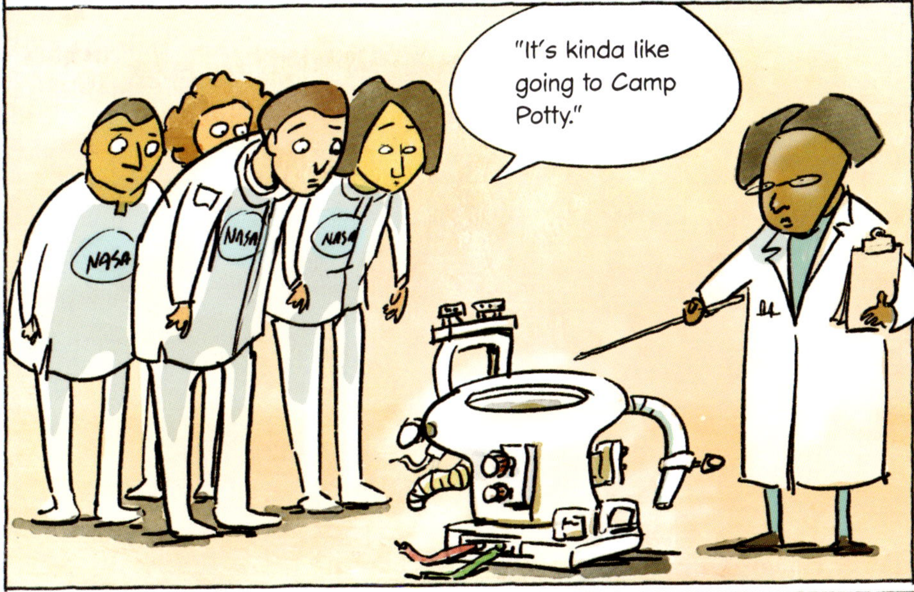

"It's kinda like going to Camp Potty."
NASA
NASA
NASA

There are foot straps and leg straps to keep the astronauts from floating away in zero gravity.

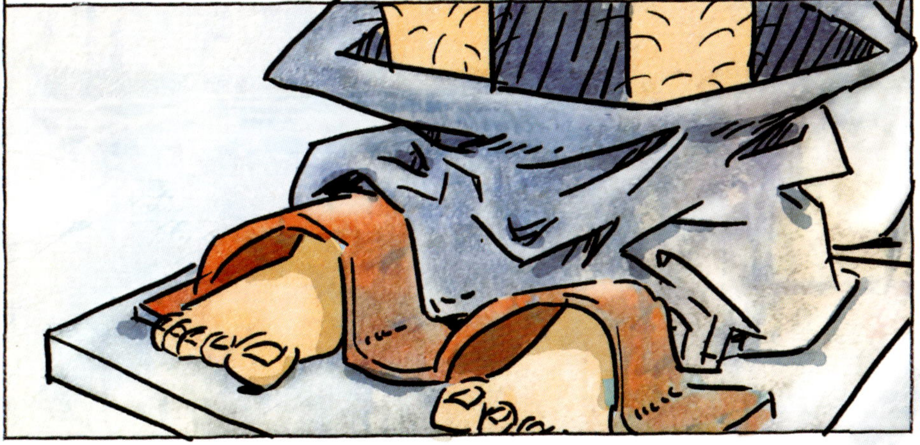

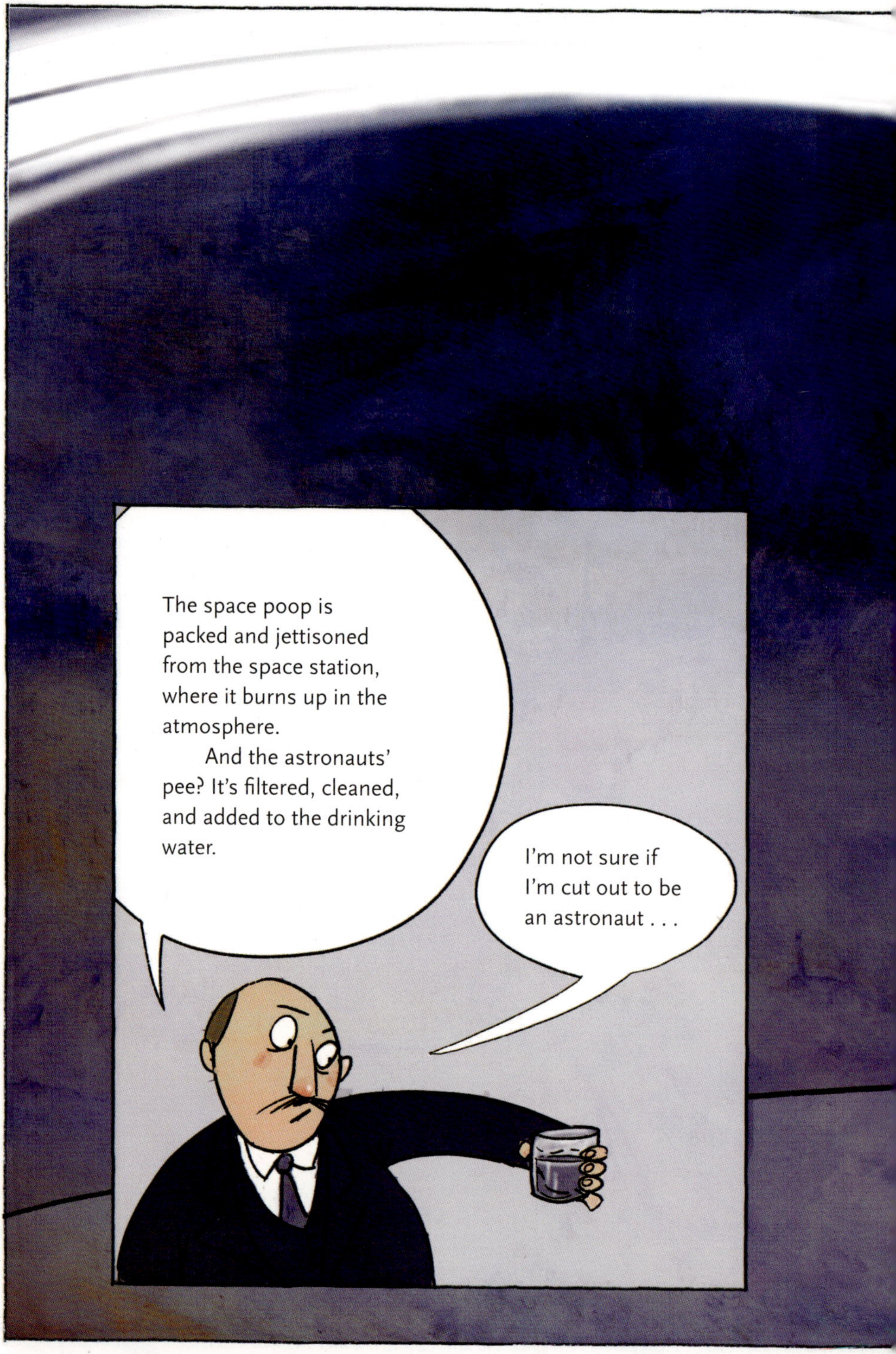
The space poop is packed and jettisoned from the space station, where it burns up in the atmosphere.
And the astronauts' pee? It's filtered, cleaned, and added to the drinking water.
I'm not sure if I'm cut out to be an astronaut . . .

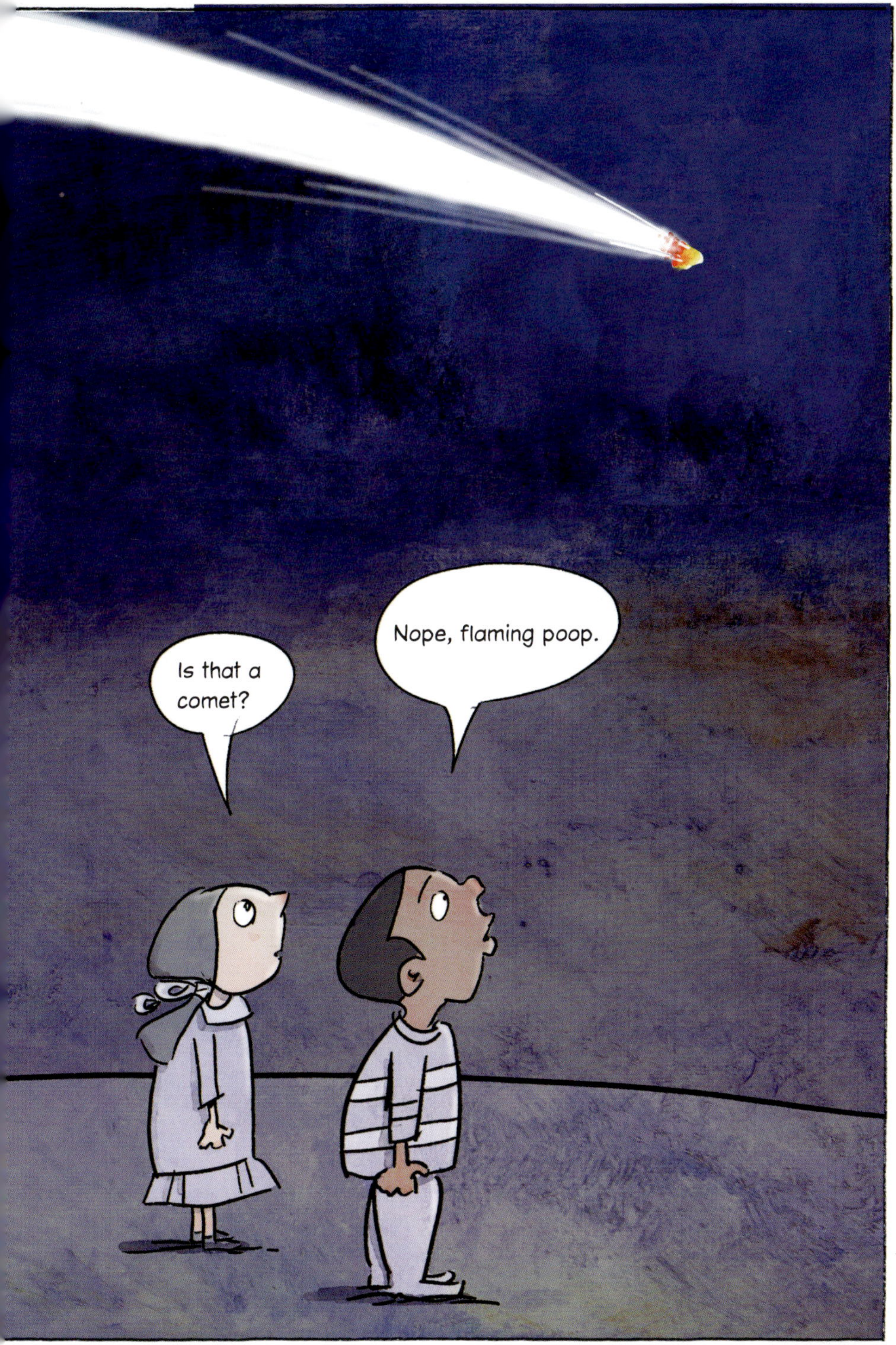
Is that a comet?
Nope, flaming poop.

On the moon, Apollo astronauts left behind unwanted stuff not needed for their return journey to Earth.

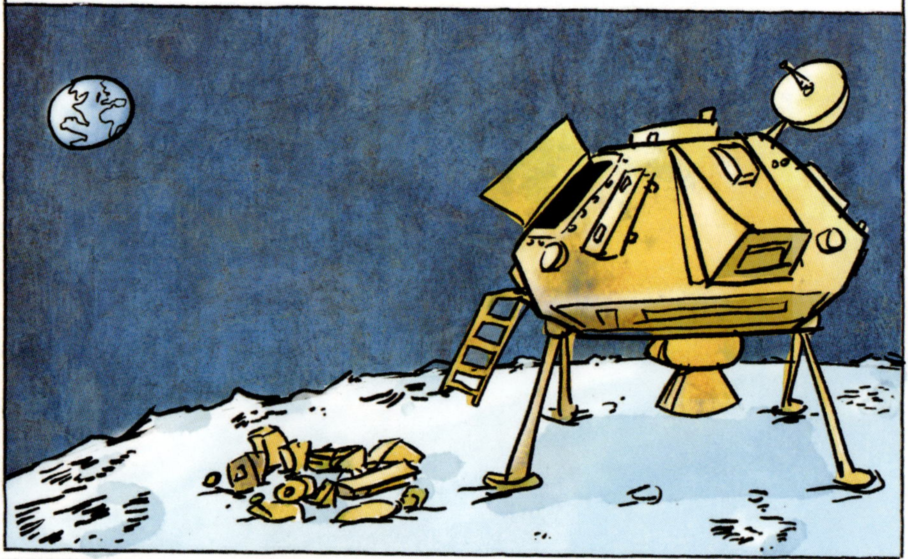

Among the stuff is spaceman poop.

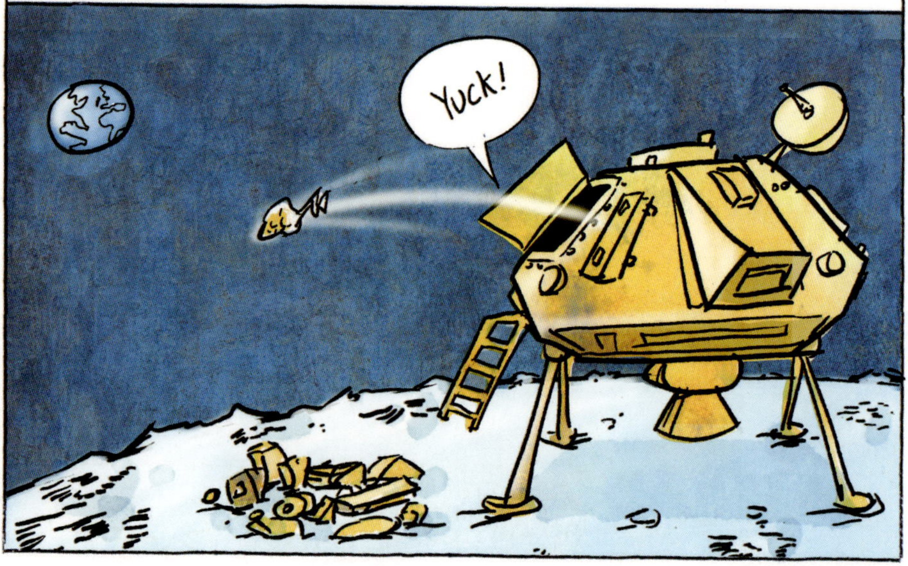
YUCK!

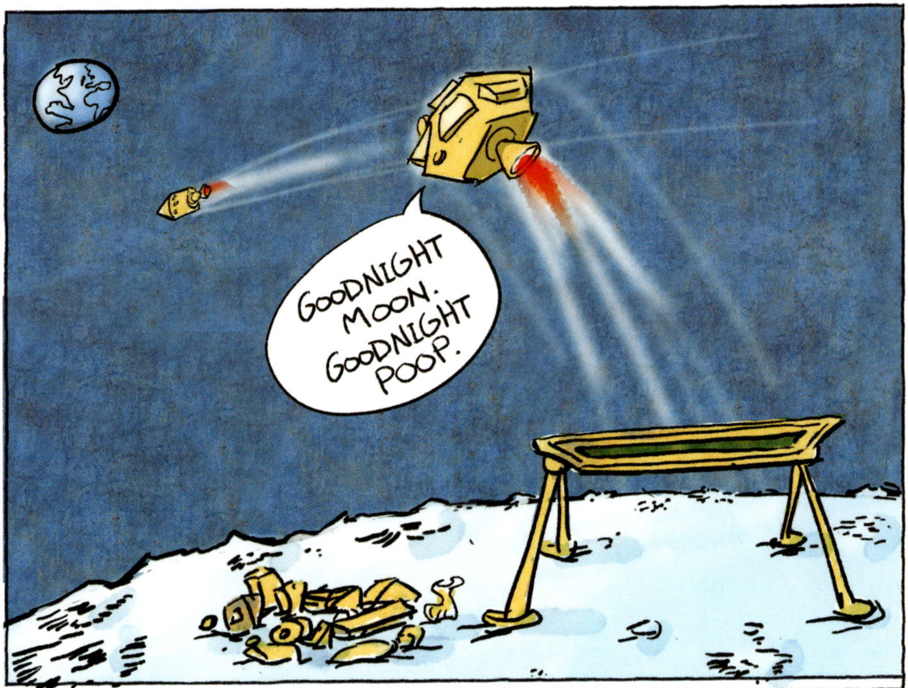
GOODNIGHT MOON. GOODNIGHT POOP.

Now scientists want to recover and examine the poop to see if the bacteria within it survived the harsh lunar landscape. I guess the first thing they will discover is if it still stinks.

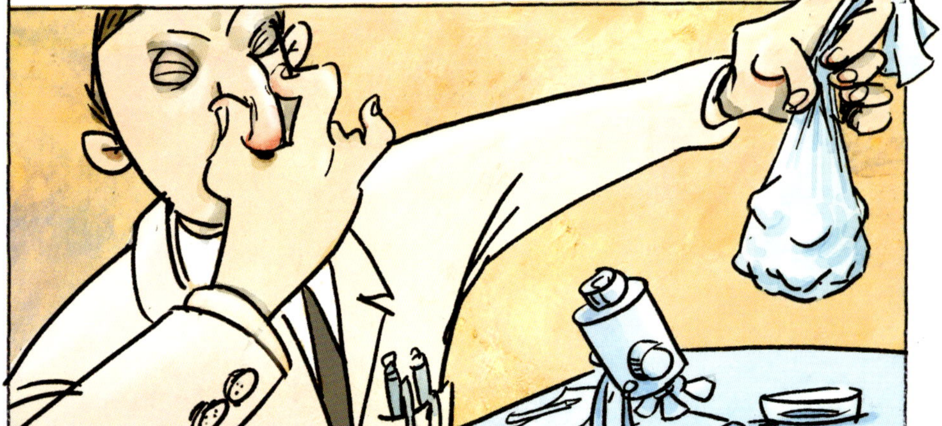

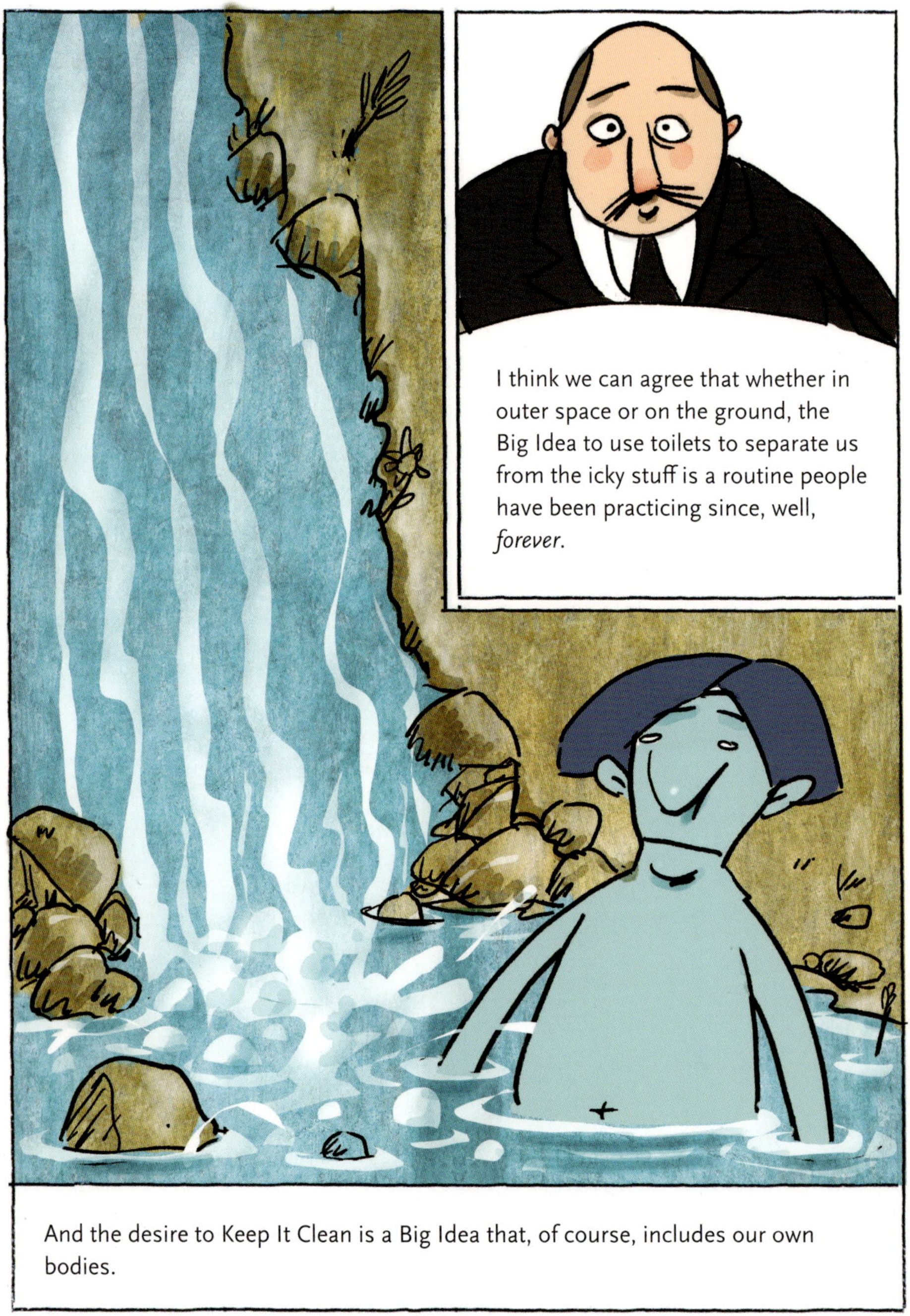
I think we can agree that whether in outer space or on the ground, the Big Idea to use toilets to separate us from the icky stuff is a routine people have been practicing since, well, *forever*.
And the desire to Keep It Clean is a Big Idea that, of course, includes our own bodies.

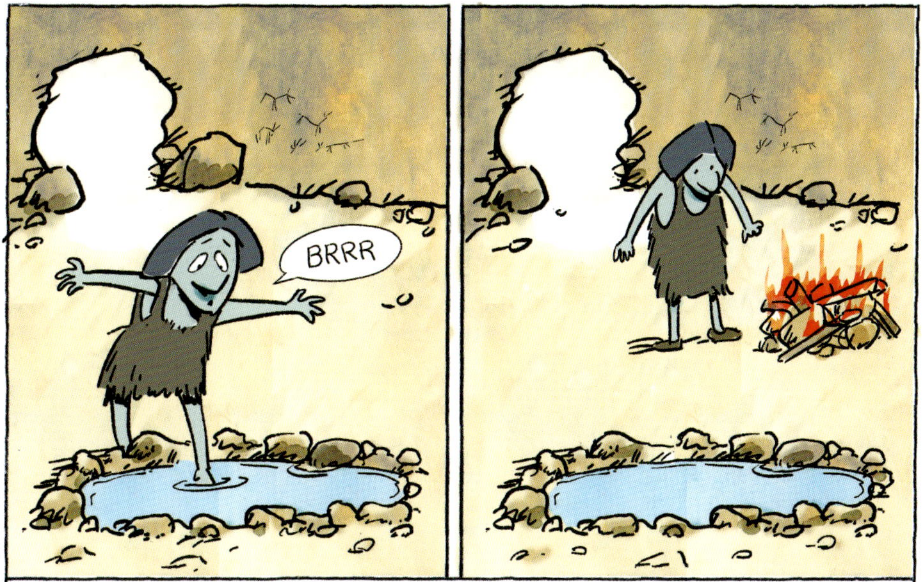
BRRR

Ancient peoples settled near natural springs that could be used for fresh water and bathing. And there's evidence that they used bowl-shaped pits in their caves as baths, even warming the water with heated stones.

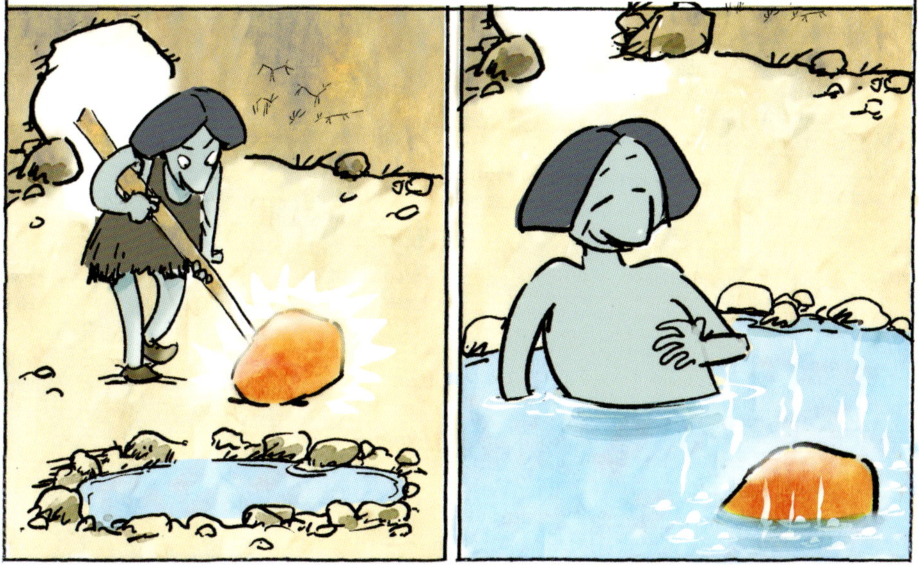

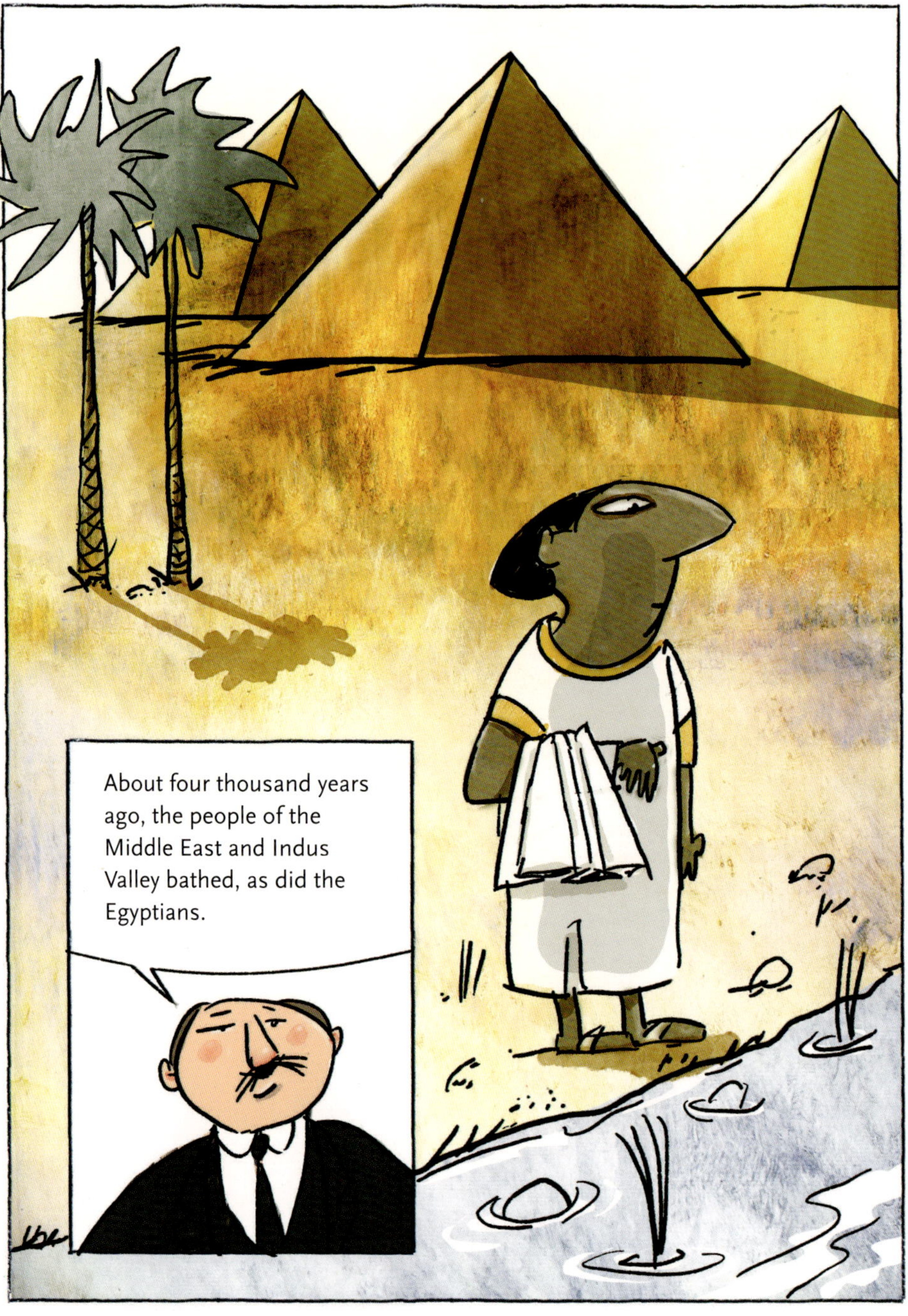
About four thousand years ago, the people of the Middle East and Indus Valley bathed, as did the Egyptians.

Despite bathing, Egyptians still worried about body odor. They would smear themselves with sweet-smelling pastes of cinnamon, lemongrass, myrrh, lily, and rose. Some pastes were thick and waxy and applied to the top of the head in the morning so that it would melt down the body as the day progressed.

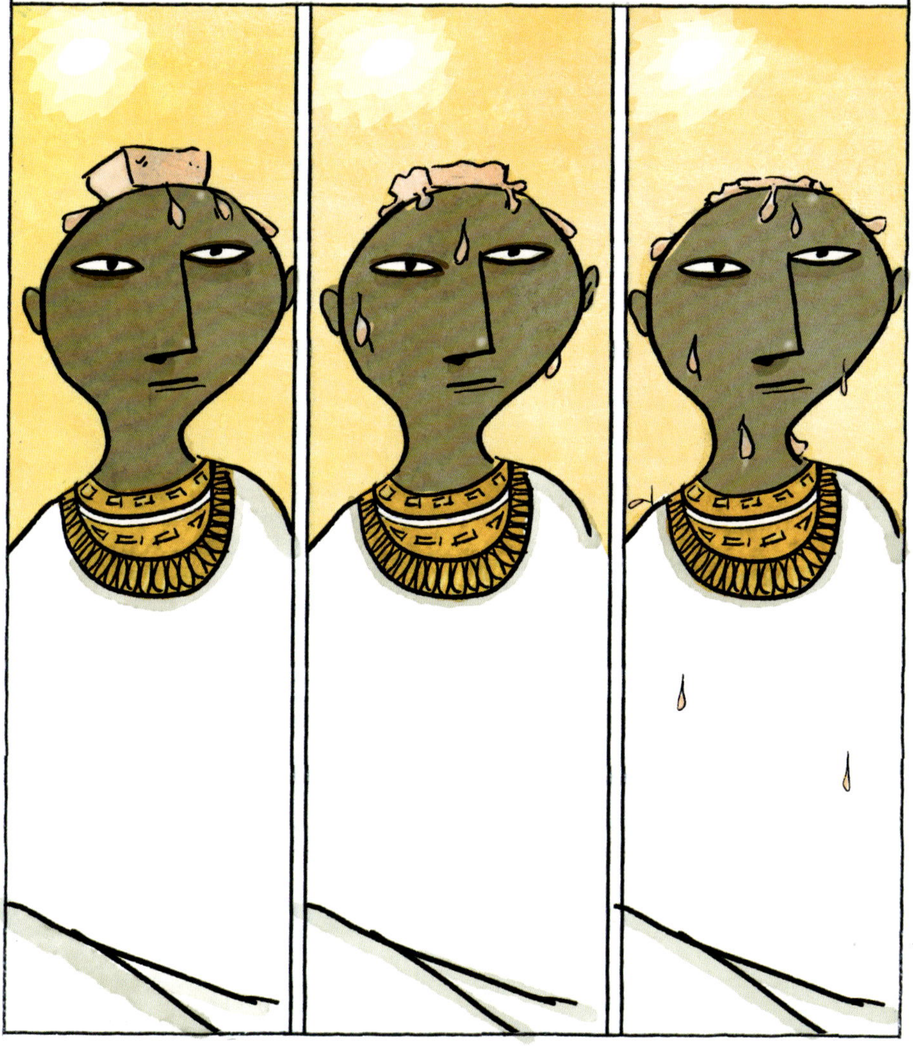

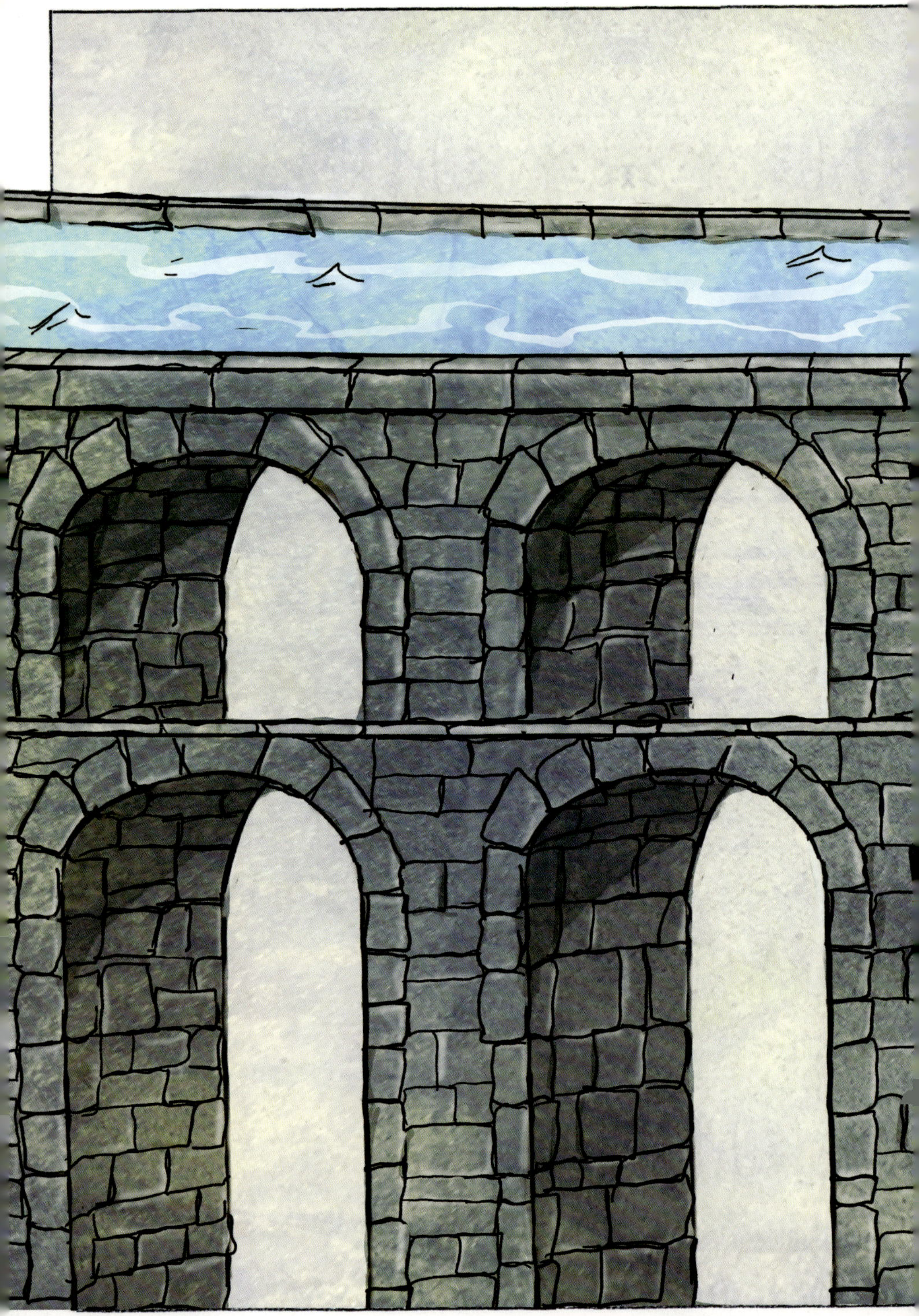

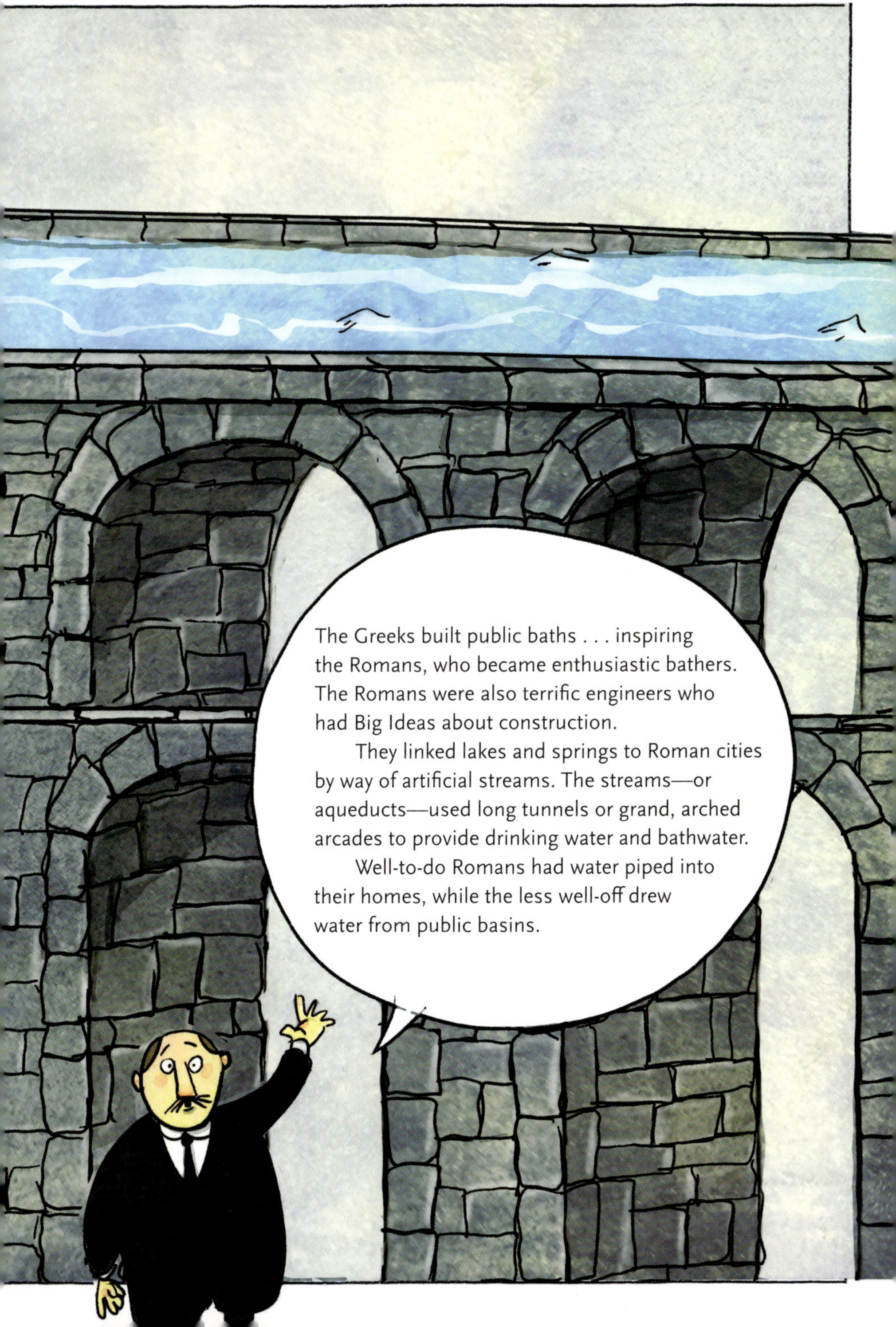
The Greeks built public baths . . . inspiring the Romans, who became enthusiastic bathers. The Romans were also terrific engineers who had Big Ideas about construction.
They linked lakes and springs to Roman cities by way of artificial streams. The streams—or aqueducts—used long tunnels or grand, arched arcades to provide drinking water and bathwater.
Well-to-do Romans had water piped into their homes, while the less well-off drew water from public basins.

Roman public baths were used for get-togethers as much as they were for cleaning.

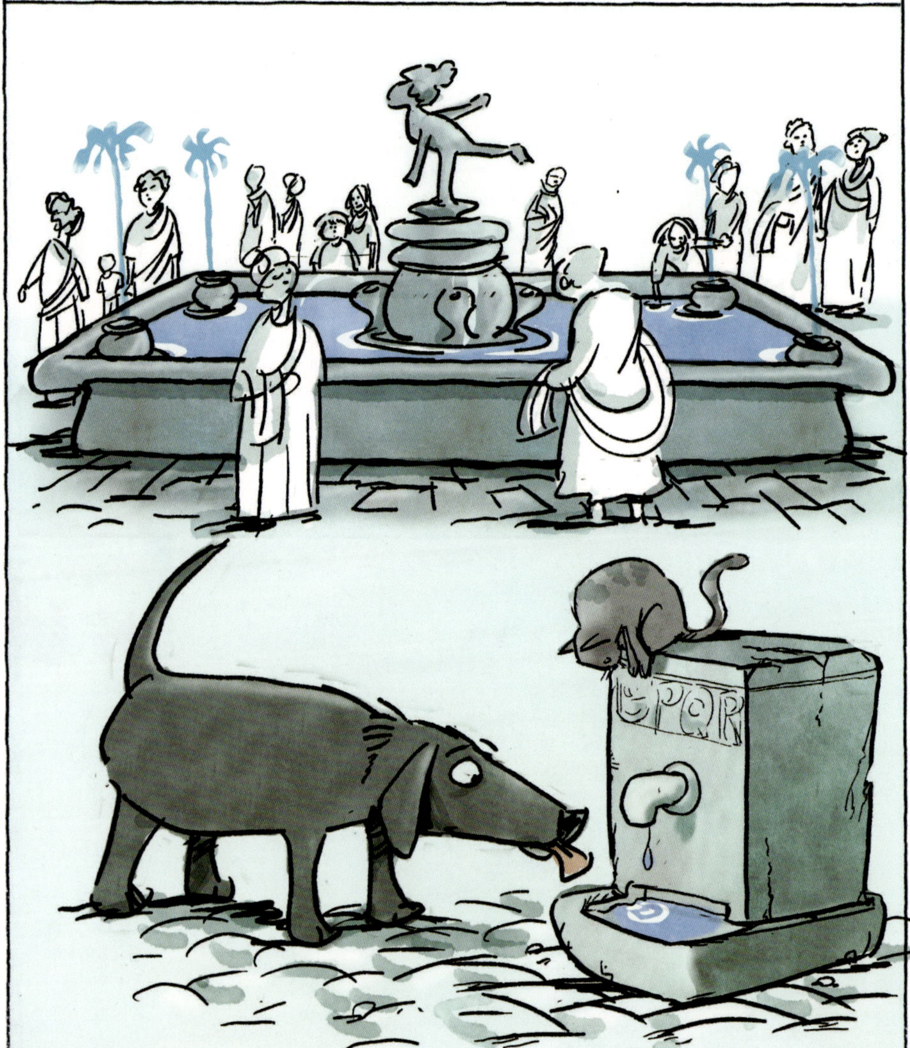
SPQR

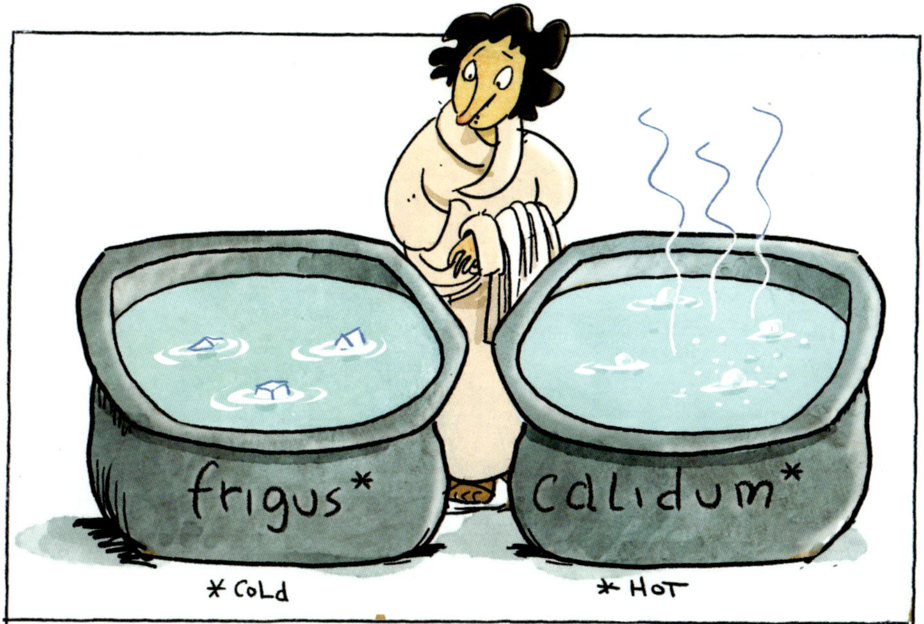
frigus*
calidum*
*COLD
*HOT

Bathers would alternate between cold water plunges and warm ones. Instead of soap, they used oil. Using a curved metal tool called a *strigil*, they scraped away the oil, along with dirt trapped in it.

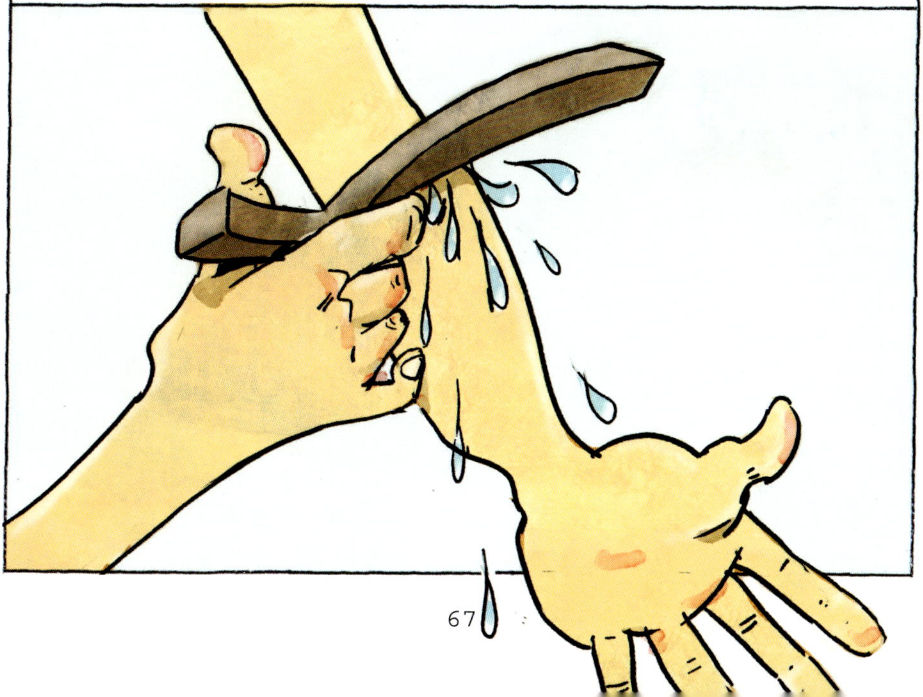

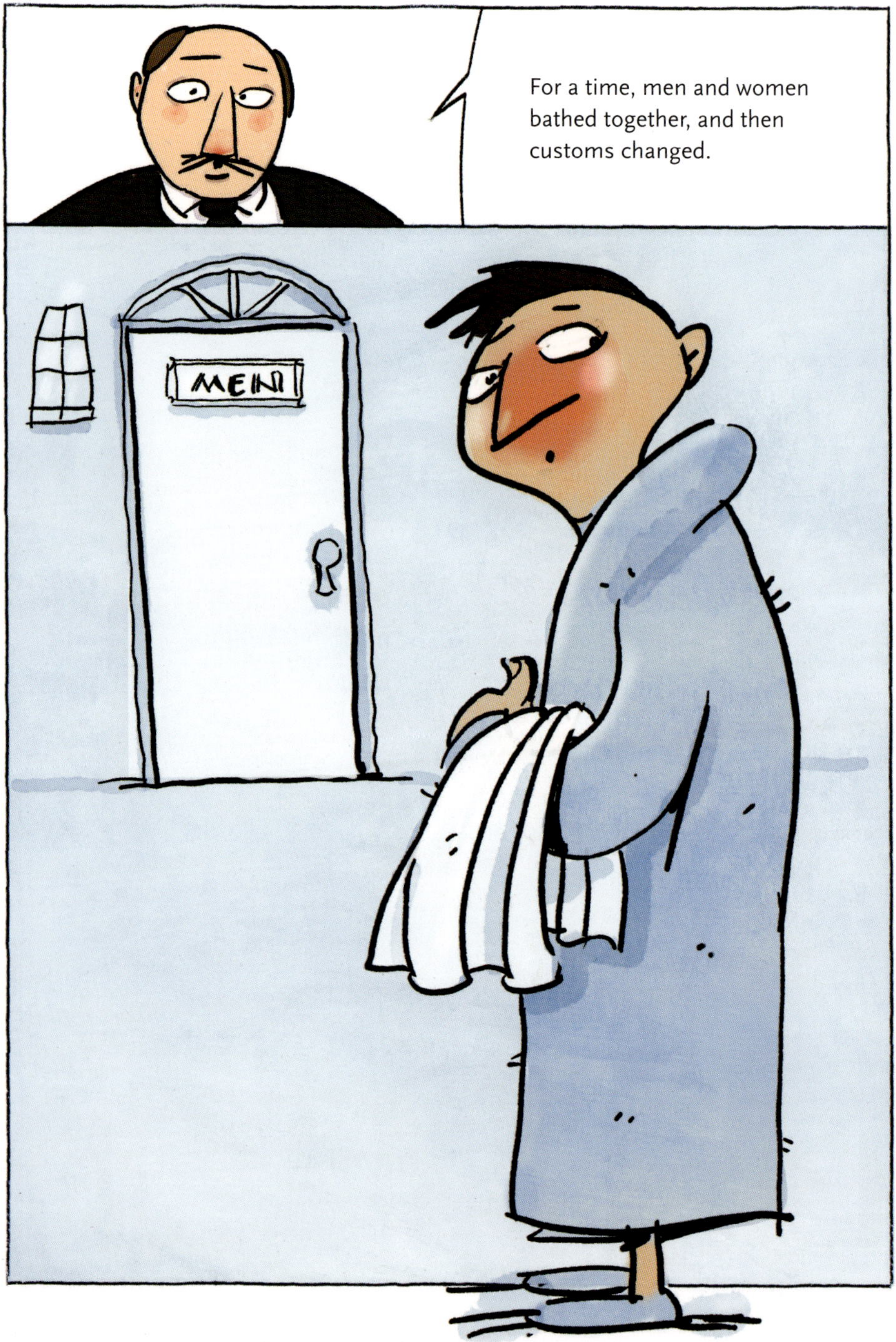
For a time, men and women bathed together, and then customs changed.
MEN

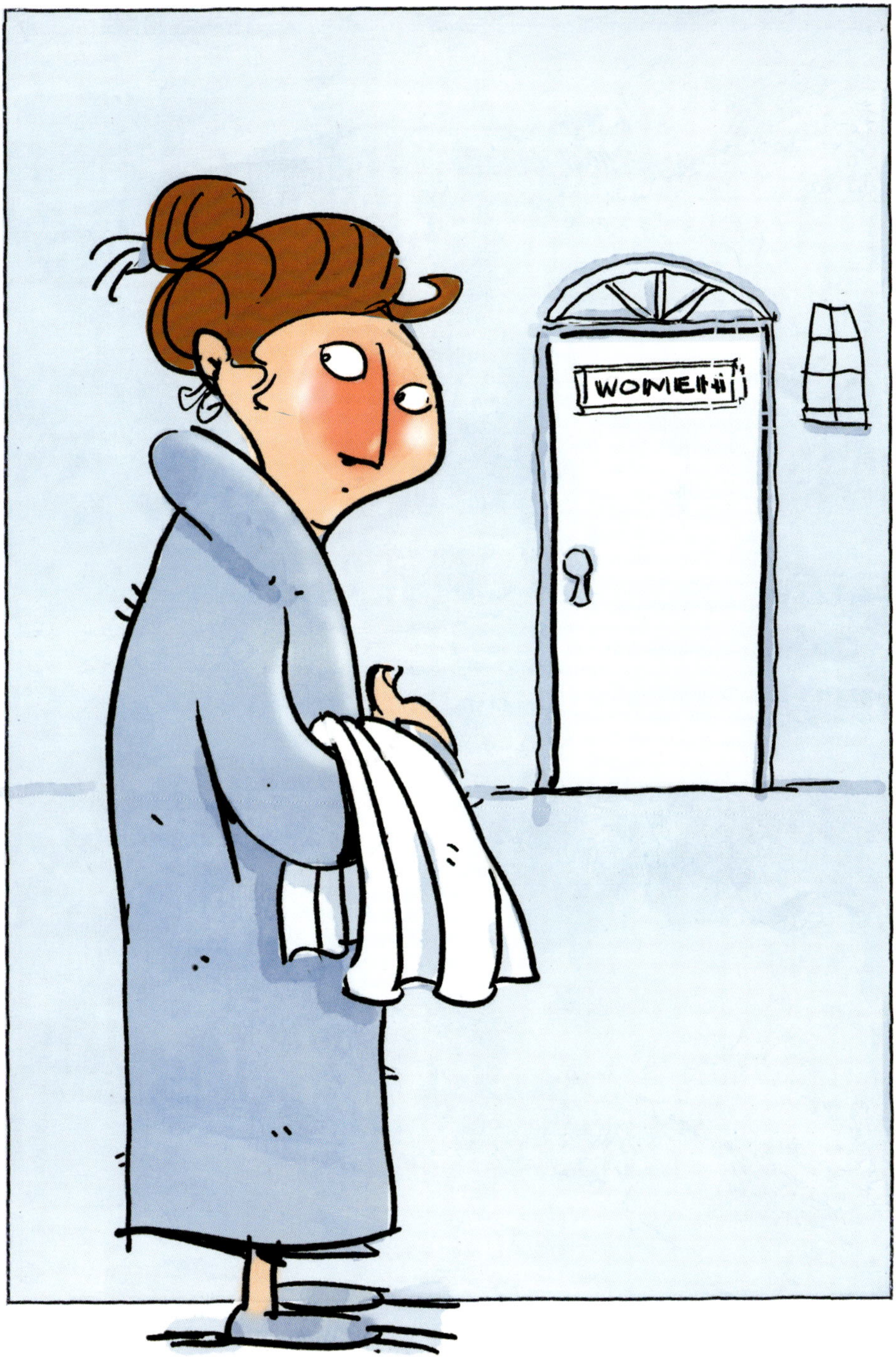
WOMEN

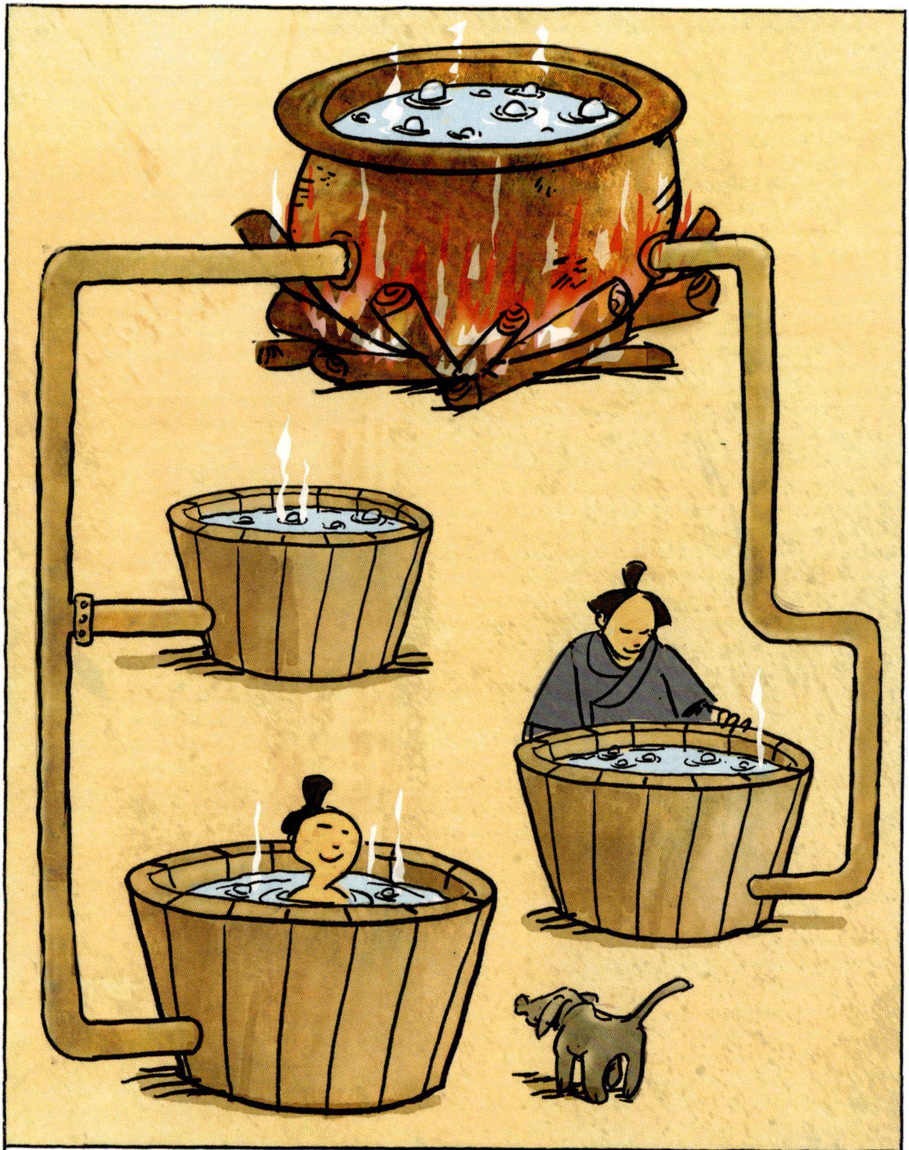

The Japanese matched the Romans' love of baths. By the mid-eighth century, they piped hot water from a fire-heated copper cauldron to nearby wooden bathtubs.

By the Middle Ages, Japanese towns and cities included public bathhouses. Bathing became a social activity that might include friends and family.

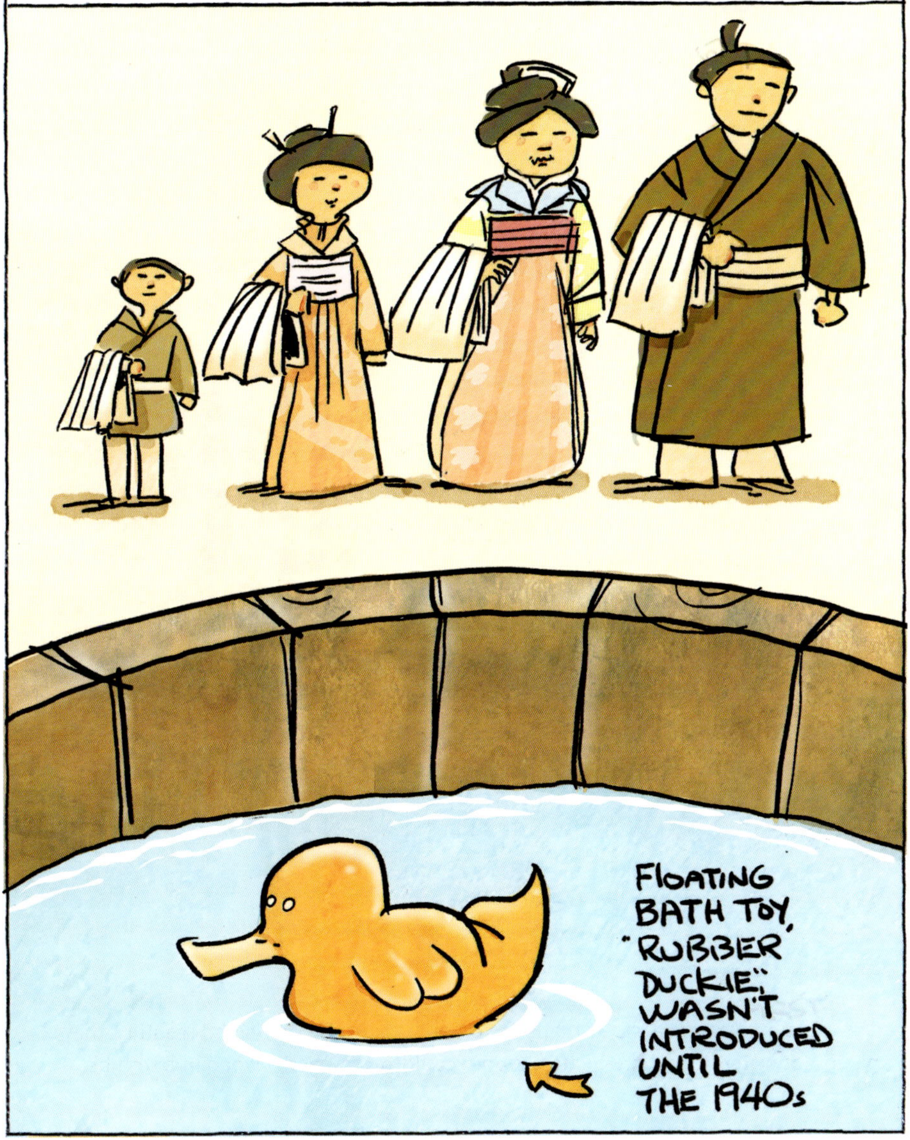
FLOATING BATH TOY, "RUBBER DUCKIE," WASN'T INTRODUCED UNTIL THE 1940s

Meanwhile in Europe, Roman rule ended, and public baths went in and out of fashion.

At times when they were popular, they were part community center and part banquet hall where men, women, and children ate, drank, gambled, danced, and listened to music. (And bathed.)

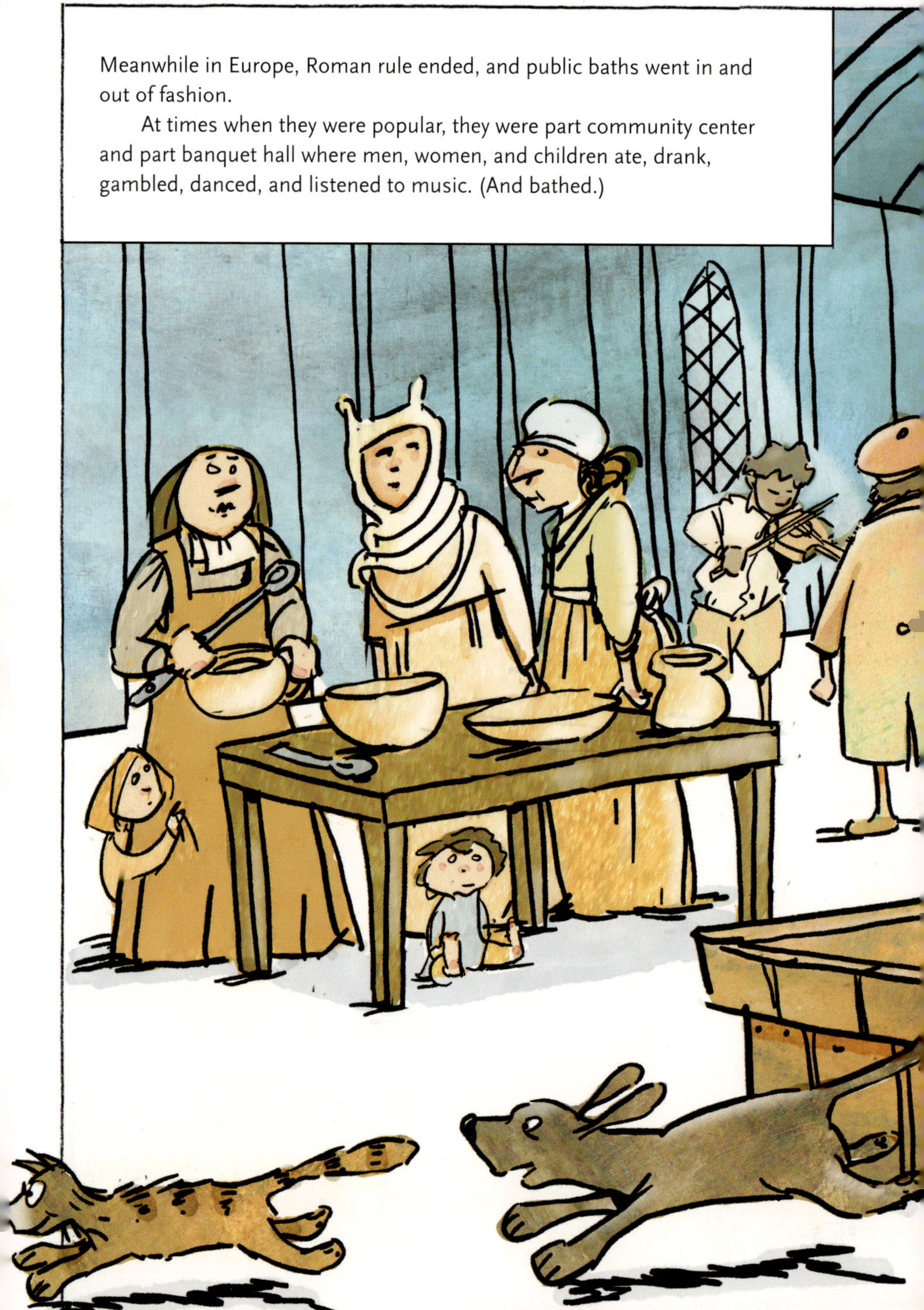

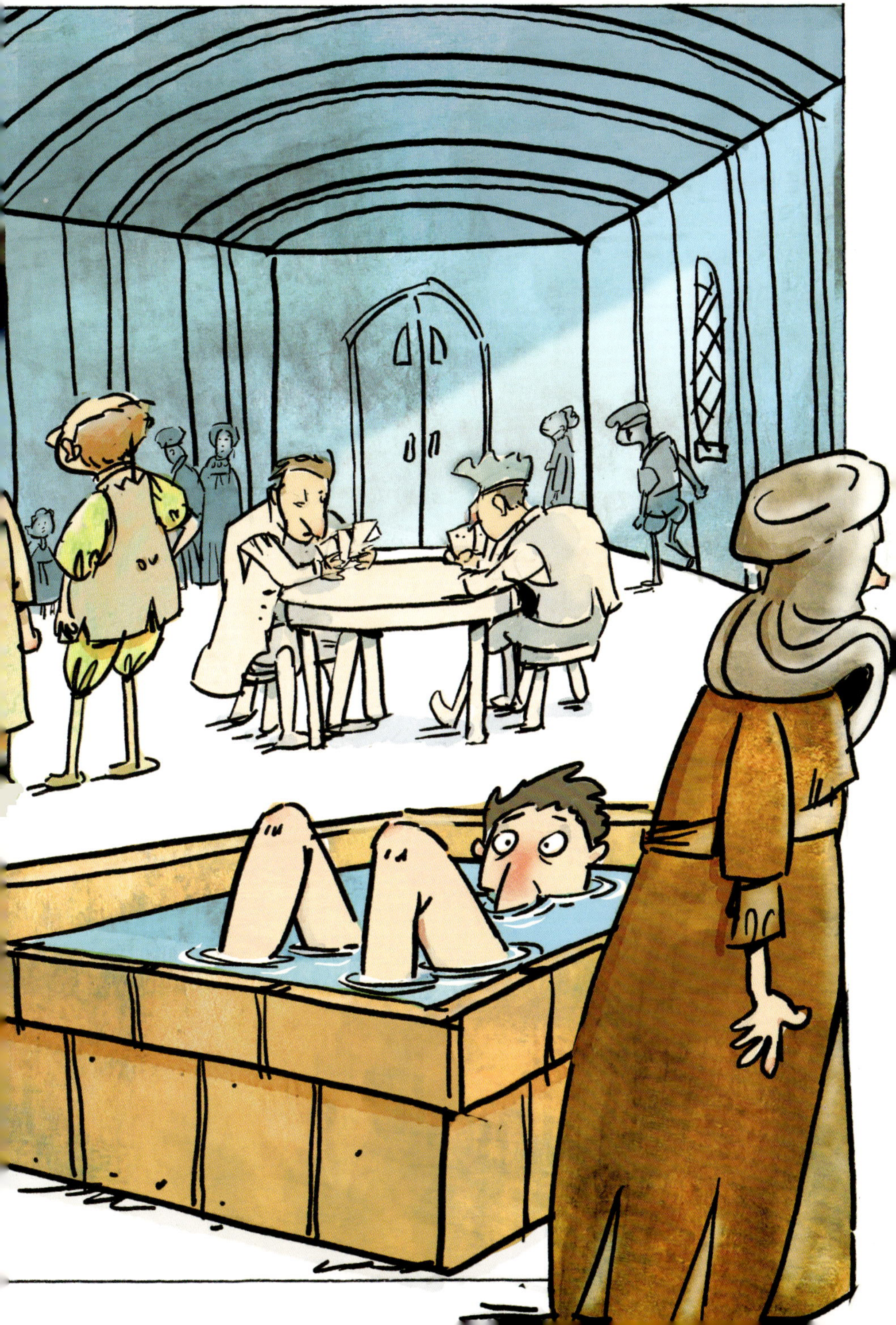

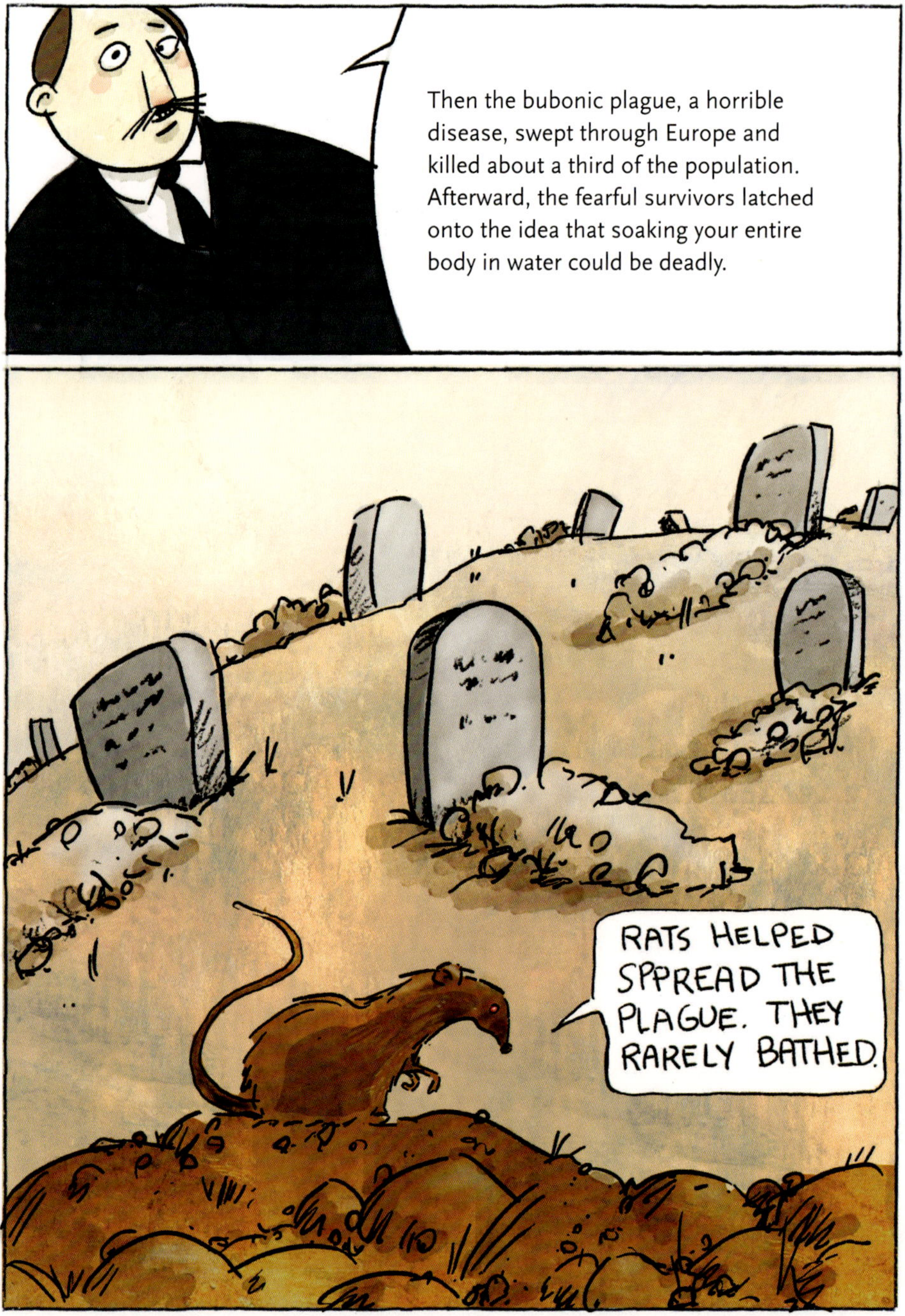
Then the bubonic plague, a horrible disease, swept through Europe and killed about a third of the population. Afterward, the fearful survivors latched onto the idea that soaking your entire body in water could be deadly.
RATS HELPED SPPREAD THE PLAGUE. THEY RARELY BATHED.

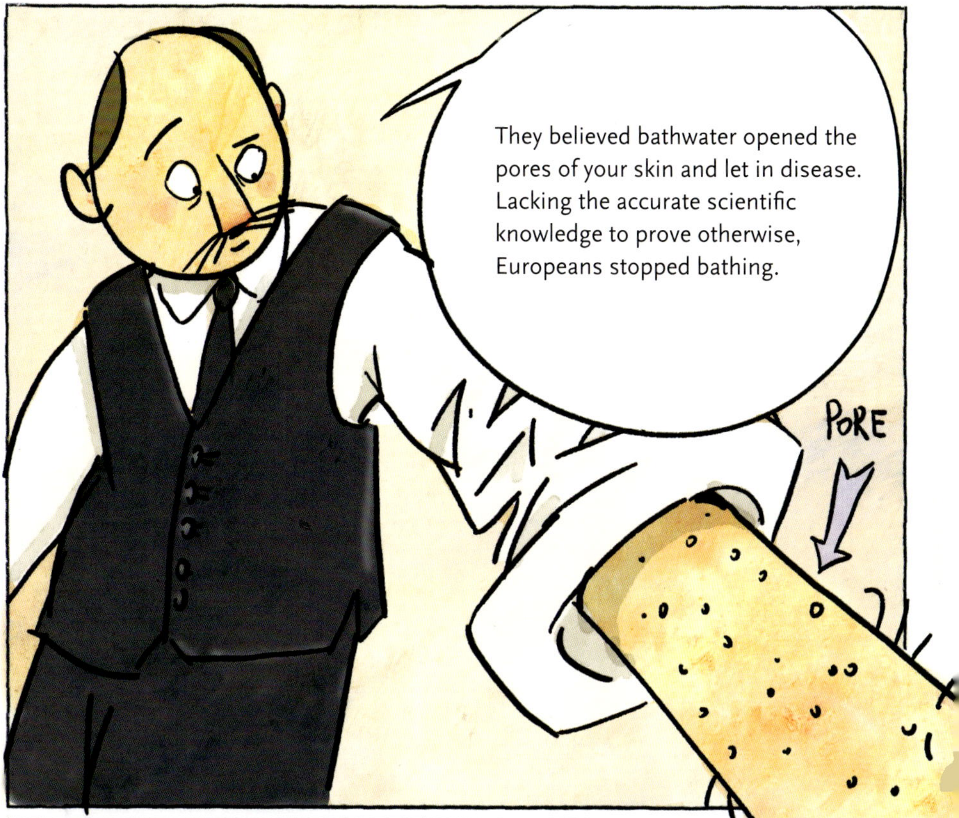
They believed bathwater opened the pores of your skin and let in disease. Lacking the accurate scientific knowledge to prove otherwise, Europeans stopped bathing.
PORE

The fear of water seemed restricted to warm, indoor baths. People still swam in rivers and lakes.

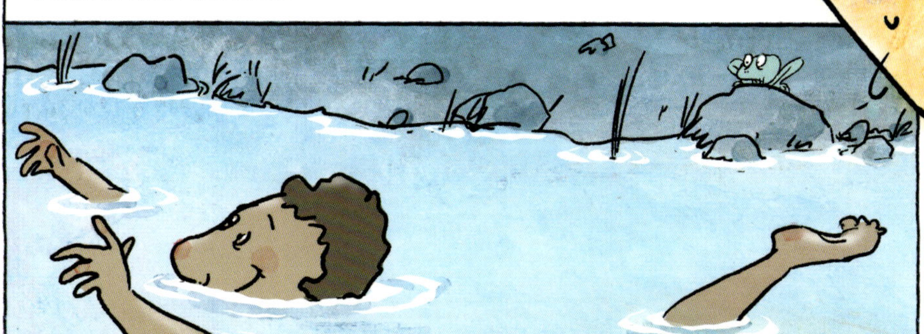

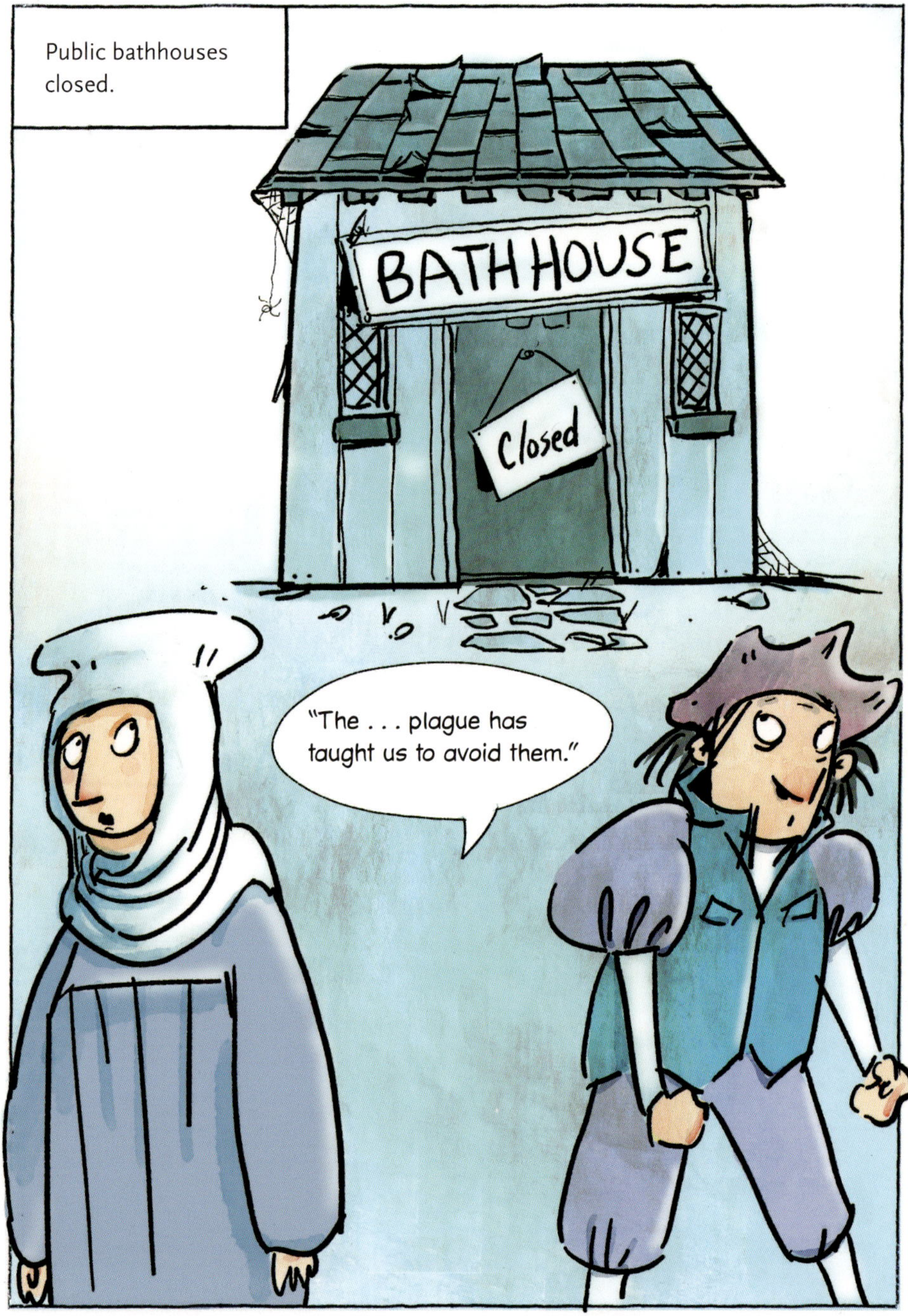
Public bathhouses closed.
BATHHOUSE
Closed
"The . . . plague has taught us to avoid them."

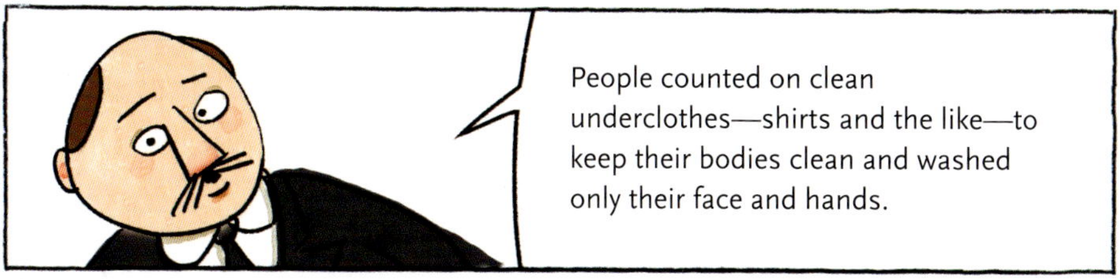
People counted on clean underclothes—shirts and the like—to keep their bodies clean and washed only their face and hands.

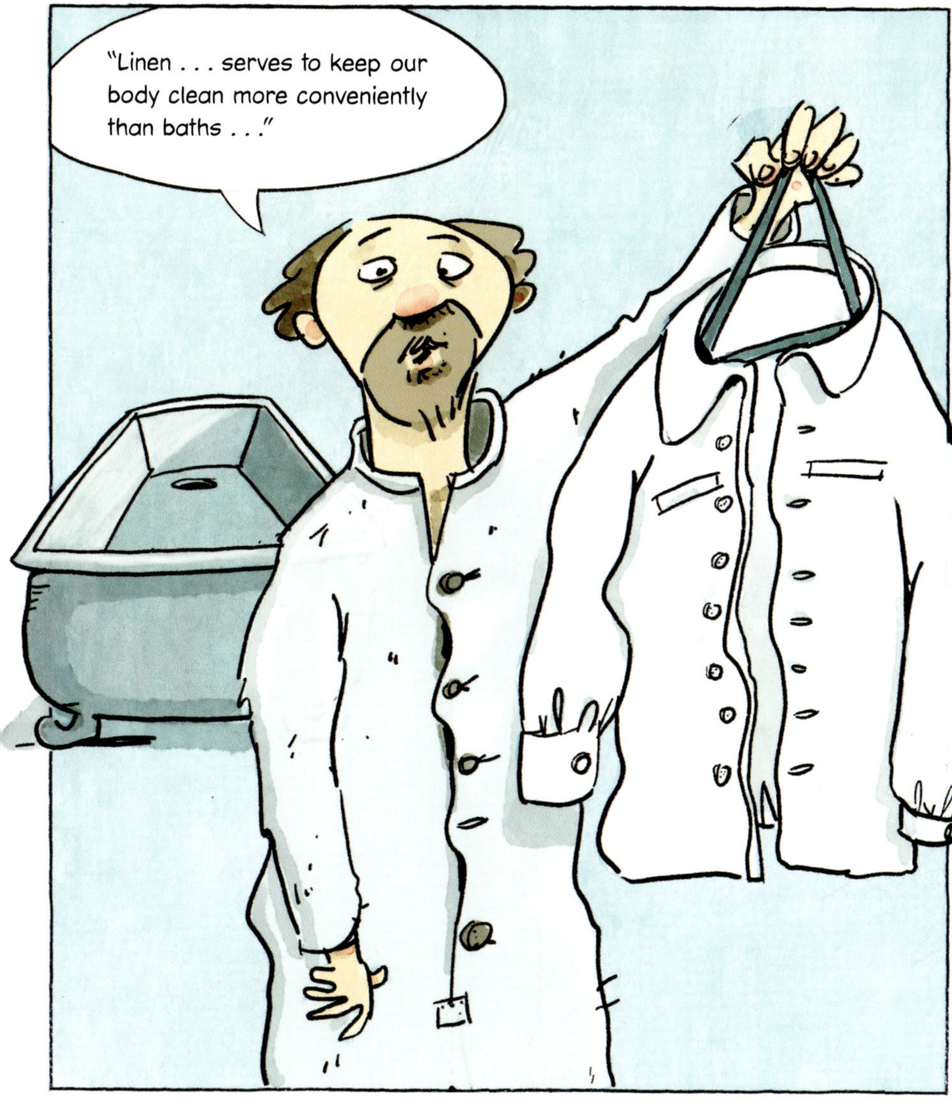
"Linen . . . serves to keep our body clean more conveniently than baths . . ."

For the years that followed, a lot of European people, old and young, rich and poor, townspeople and country folk . . . stank.

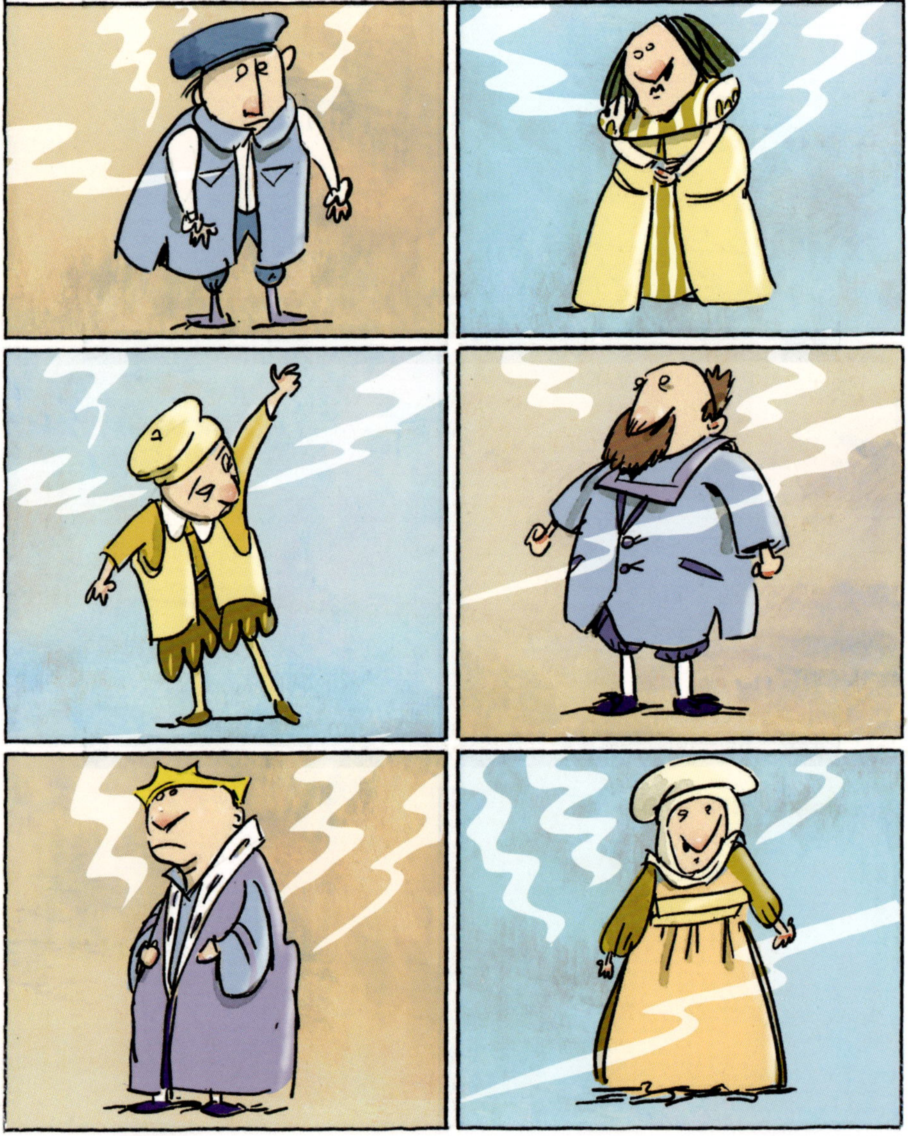

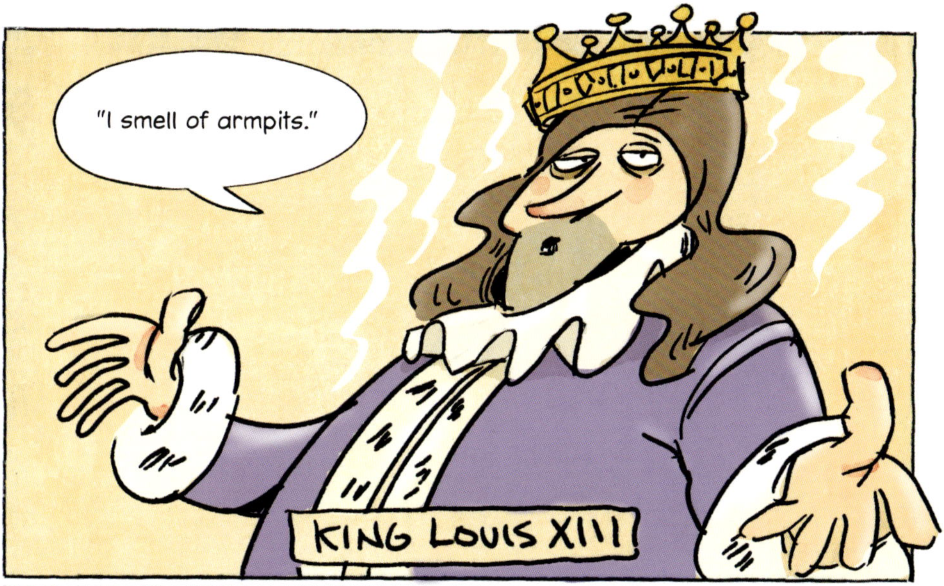
"I smell of armpits."
KING LOUIS XIII

People probably became used to the widespread stinky-ness and overlooked it. Or should I say, *over-smelled* it?

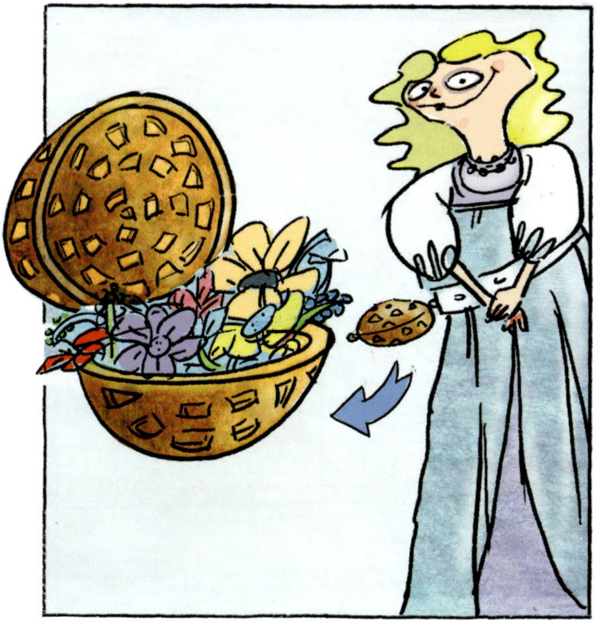

For those with delicate noses, bad odors were sweetened by scented lotions, perfumes, and the wearing of pomanders—globe-shaped jewelry filled with fragrant herbs or flower petals and hung from the waist.

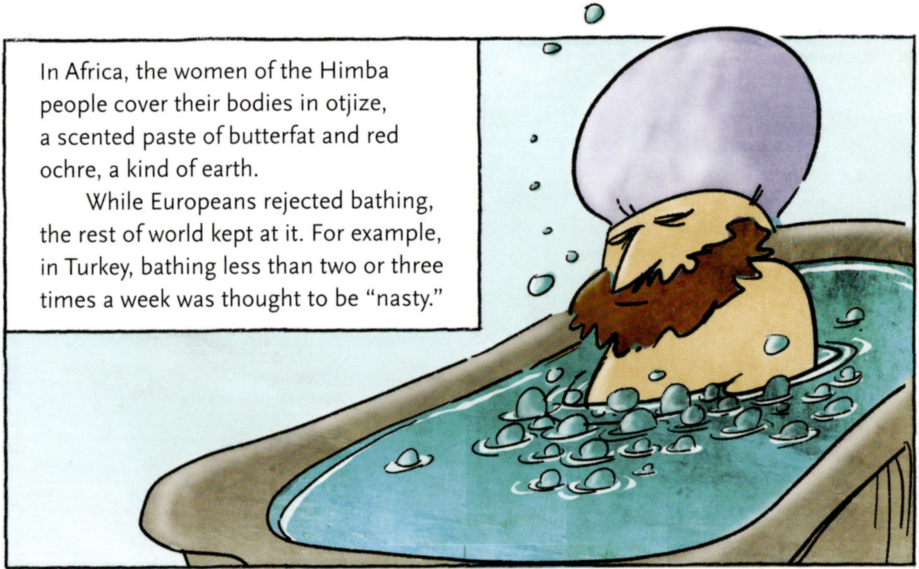
In Africa, the women of the Himba people cover their bodies in otjize, a scented paste of butterfat and red ochre, a kind of earth.
While Europeans rejected bathing, the rest of world kept at it. For example, in Turkey, bathing less than two or three times a week was thought to be "nasty."

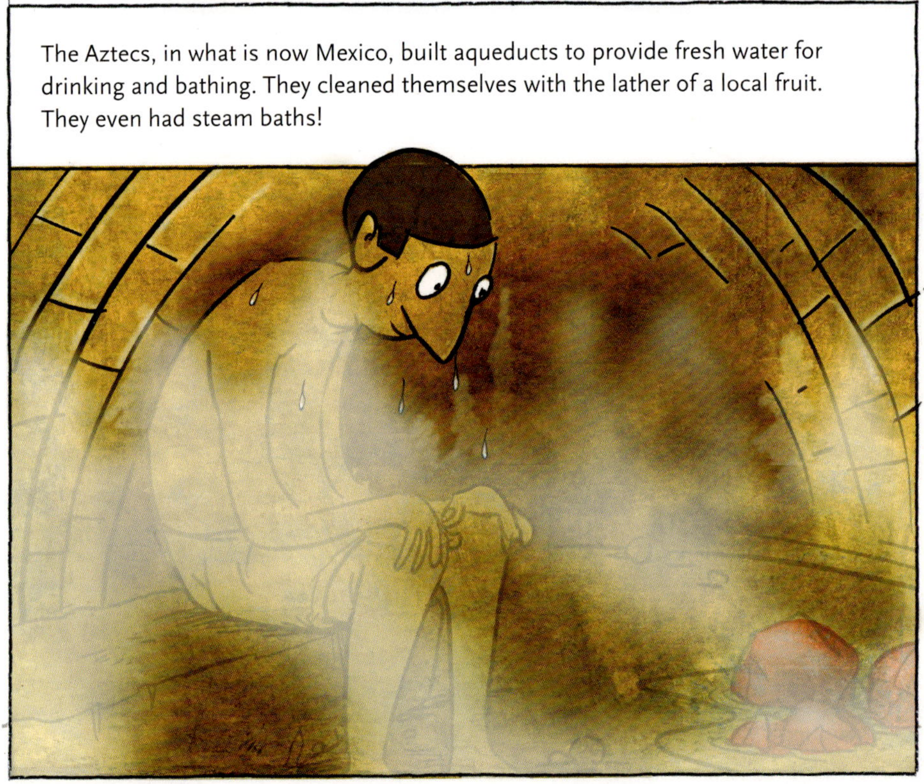
The Aztecs, in what is now Mexico, built aqueducts to provide fresh water for drinking and bathing. They cleaned themselves with the lather of a local fruit. They even had steam baths!

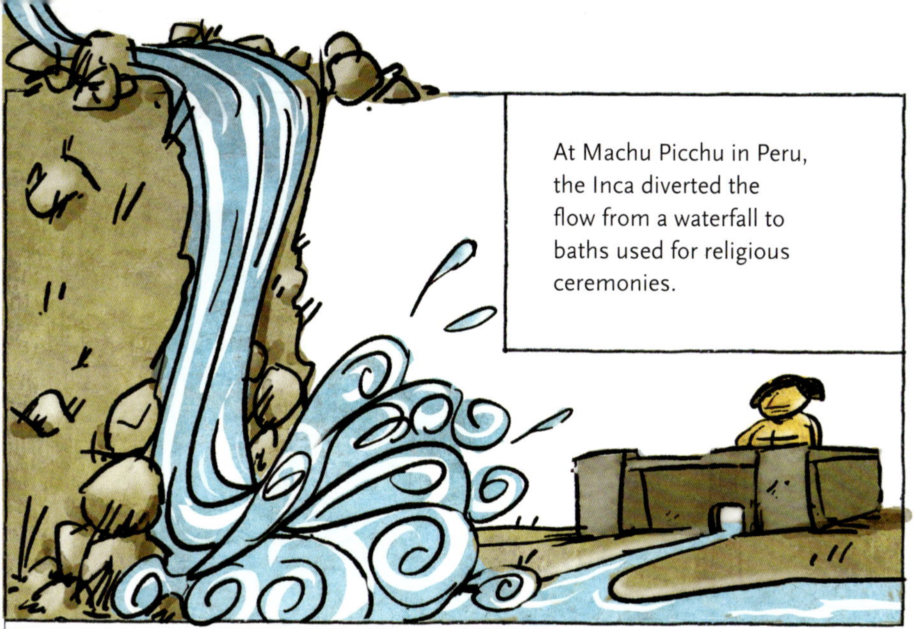
At Machu Picchu in Peru, the Inca diverted the flow from a waterfall to baths used for religious ceremonies.

In North America, indigenous peoples bathed in rivers and streams. When they met arriving Europeans, they found them barbaric and smelly.

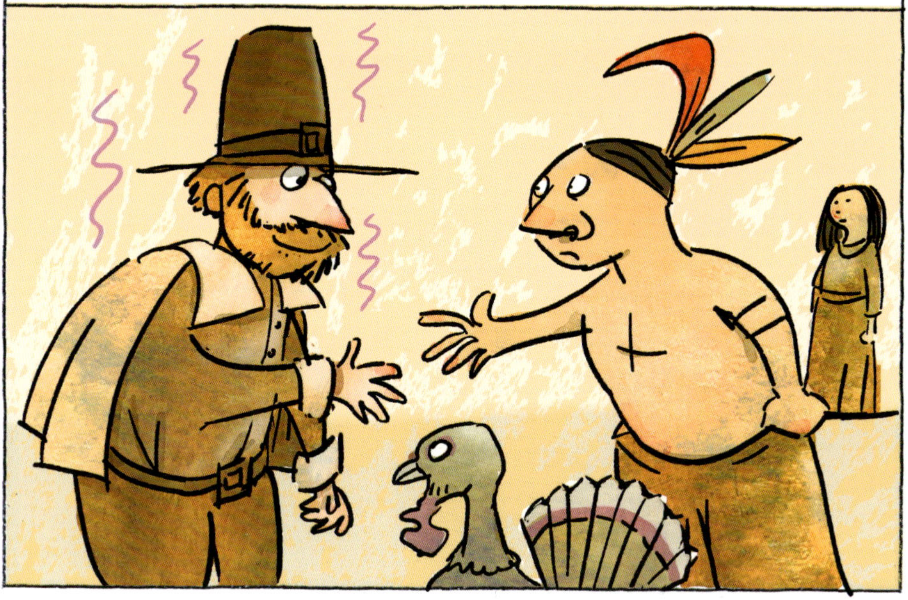

But by the time of the American Revolution, beliefs about bathing were changing, and most of the Founding Fathers probably didn't stink. George Washington "bathed" in rivers during warm weather . . .

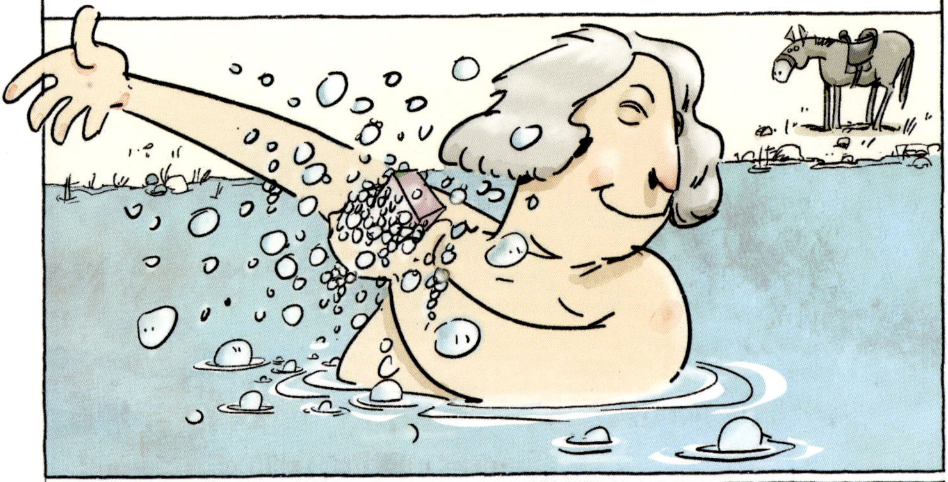

. . . and cleaned himself at a washbasin during the cold.

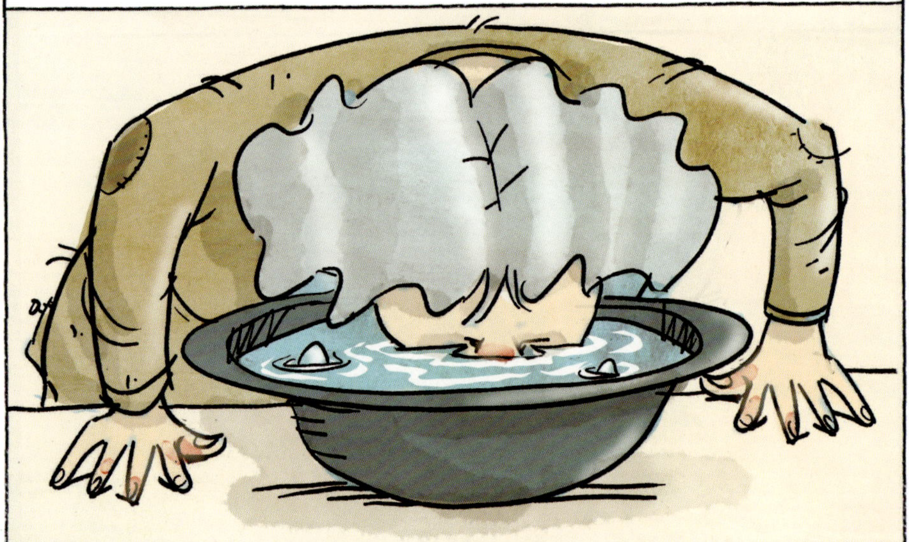

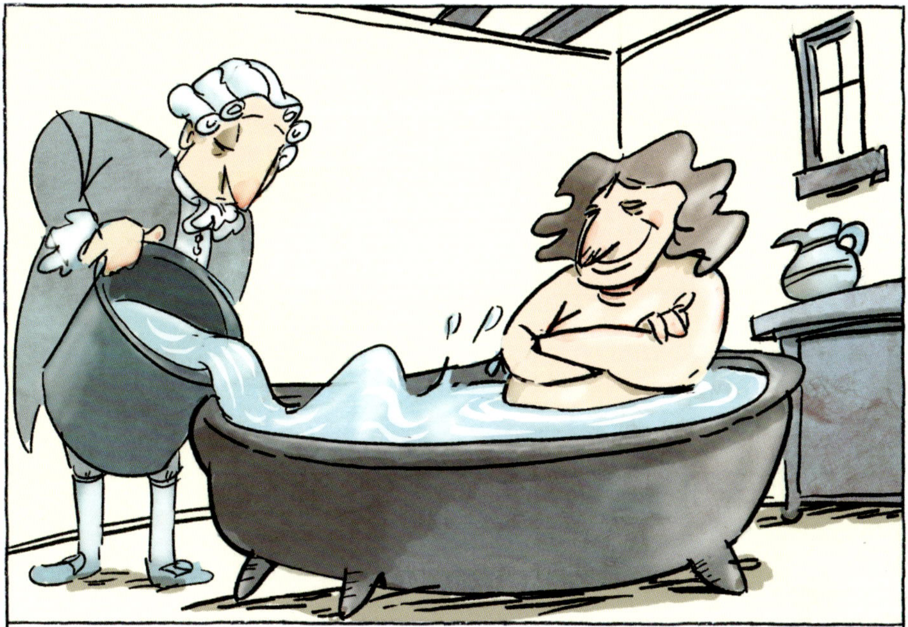

John Hancock used his tub daily, since he was wealthy enough to afford servants to haul the buckets of water to fill it. No tub for Thomas Jefferson, who used cold water from a basin to wash his face, hands, and feet every day.

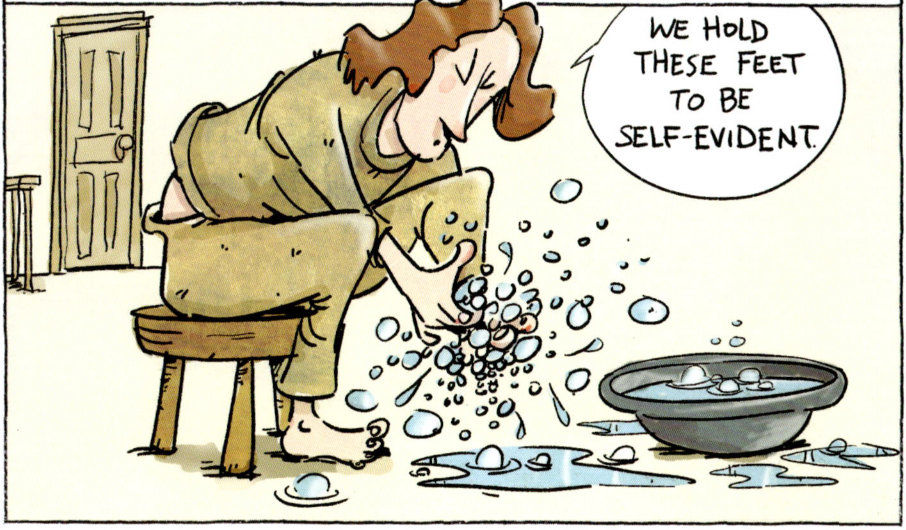
WE HOLD THESE FEET TO BE SELF-EVIDENT.

Ben Franklin used a tub—that is, when he wasn't skinny-dipping in streams and rivers, a practice he brought to London's river Thames while acting as a colonial representative to the English king.

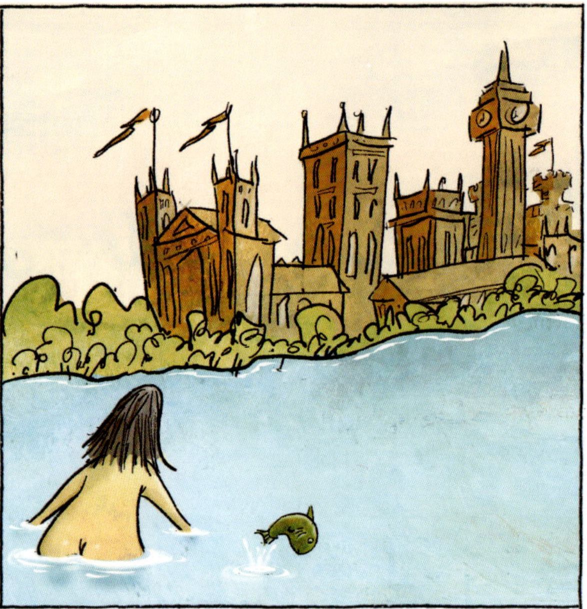

And it was in London where Franklin indulged in his "air baths." He'd sit at his open, first-floor window "without any clothes whatever, half an hour or an hour, according to the season."

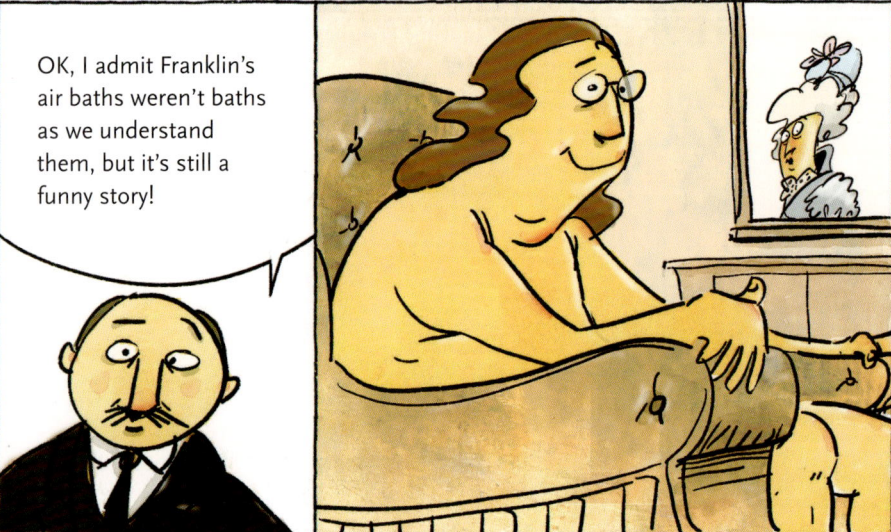

OK, I admit Franklin's air baths weren't baths as we understand them, but it's still a funny story!

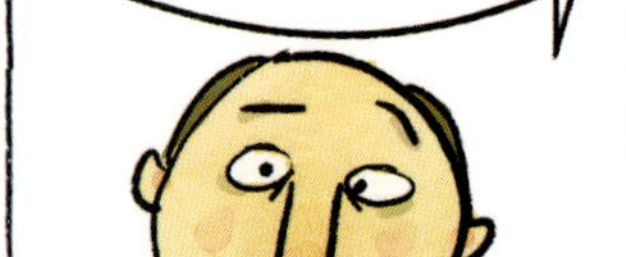

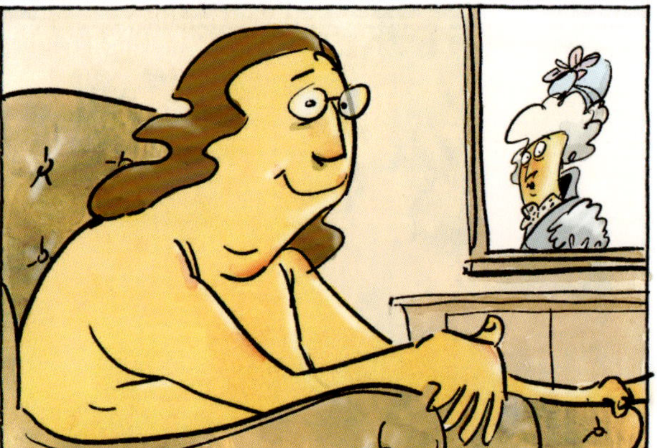

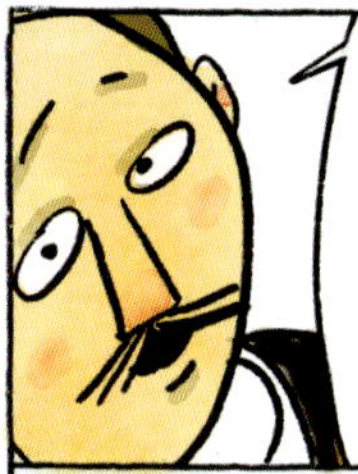

But what about showers, you ask?

Greeks and Romans used showers—water spilling out of pipes and onto your head and body—but the shower in the sense we're familiar with one wasn't invented until 1767 by William Feetham in England.

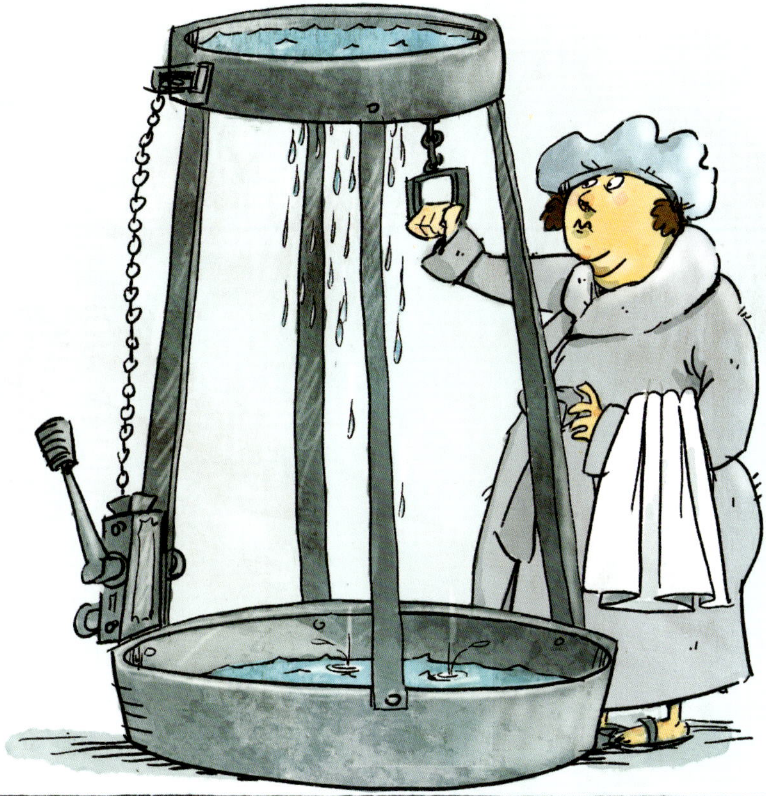

The bather used a hand pump to carry the water into an overhead basin. The water poured out by way of a chain pull.

Unfortunately, the water not only was cold but also modest in supply, meaning that the user would have to reuse dirty water.

It's not surprising Feetham's invention wasn't a success.

The world would have to wait for modern plumbing to enjoy a hot shower.

Bathing—and bathtubs in the home—increased in popularity in America and Europe throughout the nineteenth century. But we should remember it was mostly a feature of the people who could afford it: the middle and upper classes.

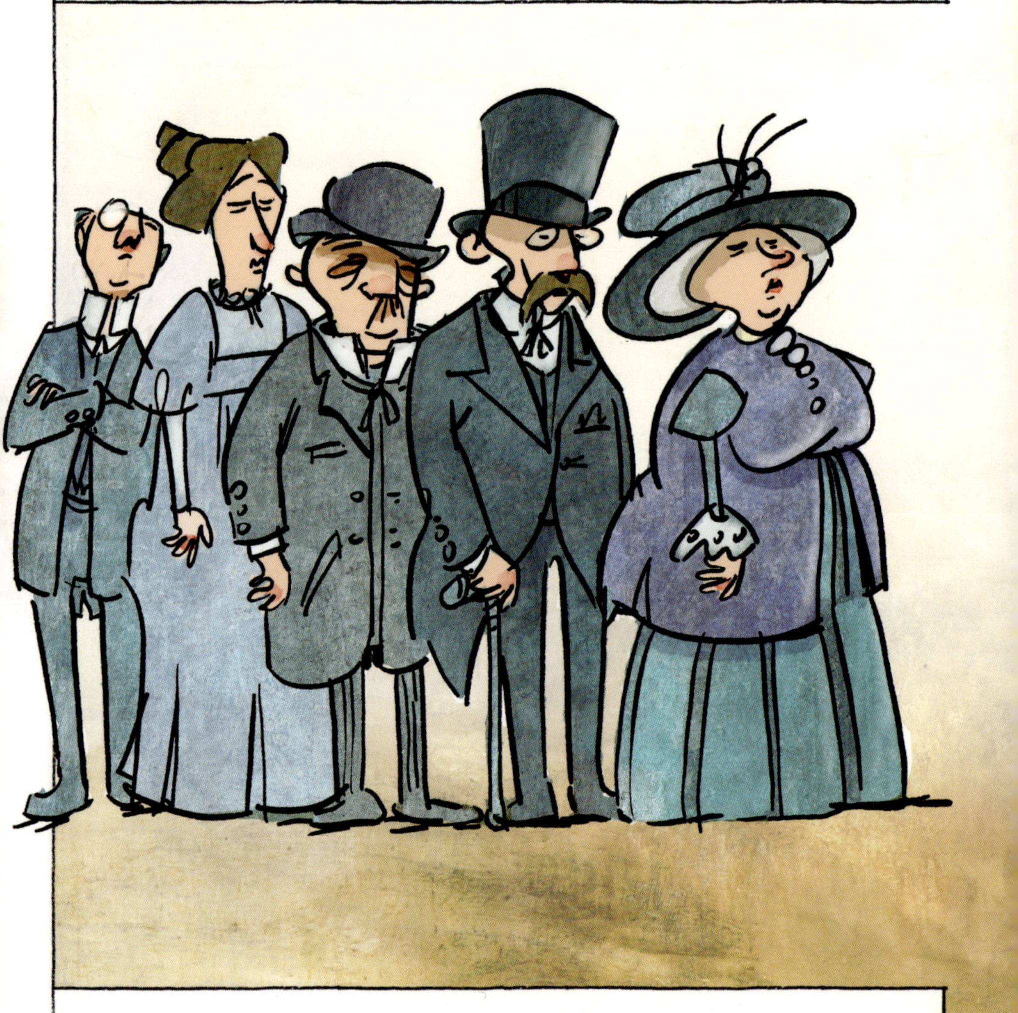

Poor people went without baths, giving us the expression "the great unwashed" as a way to describe the lower class.

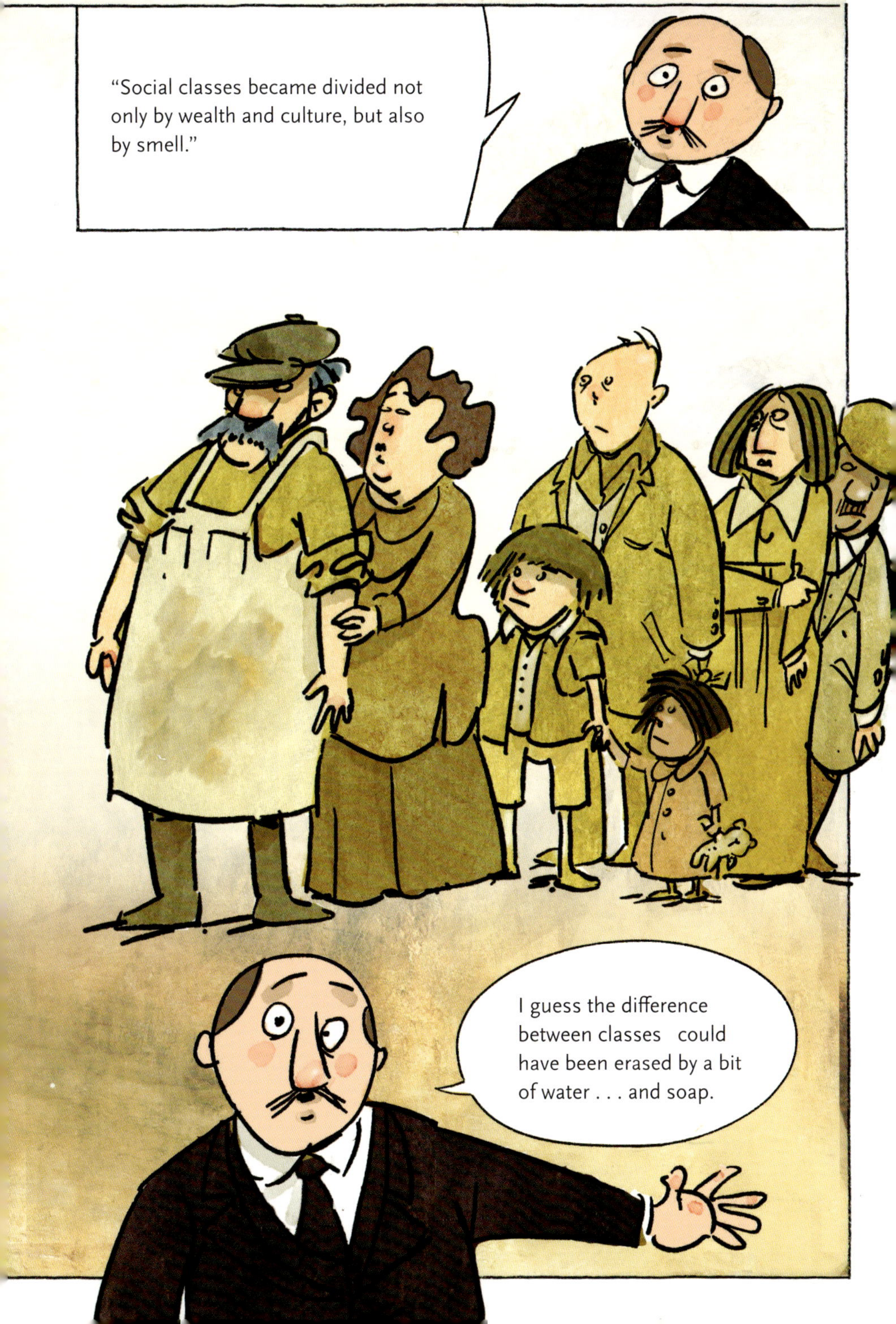
"Social classes became divided not only by wealth and culture, but also by smell."
I guess the difference between classes could have been erased by a bit of water . . . and soap.

Soap was the Big Idea of an unknown Middle Eastern person who mixed wood ashes, water, and animal fat or oil about five thousand years ago. The first soap was probably a bucket of ashy, greasy water and used to clean cloth.

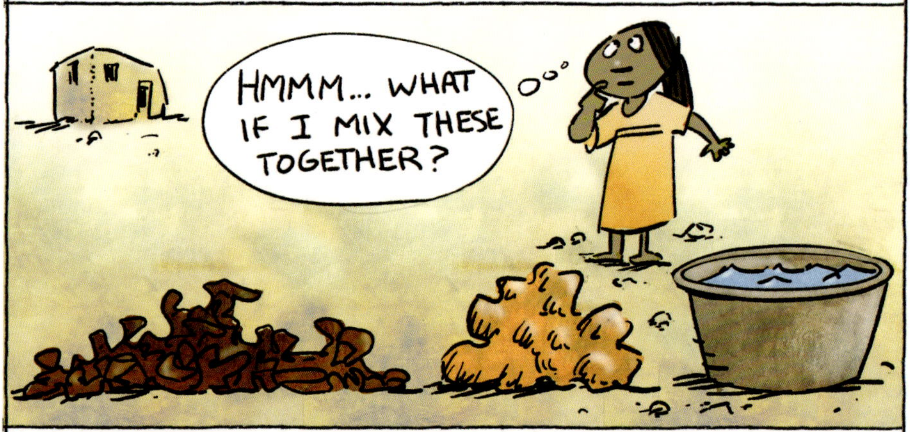
HMMM... WHAT IF I MIX THESE TOGETHER?

It took another thousand years before someone had the Big Idea to use soap to clean our bodies.

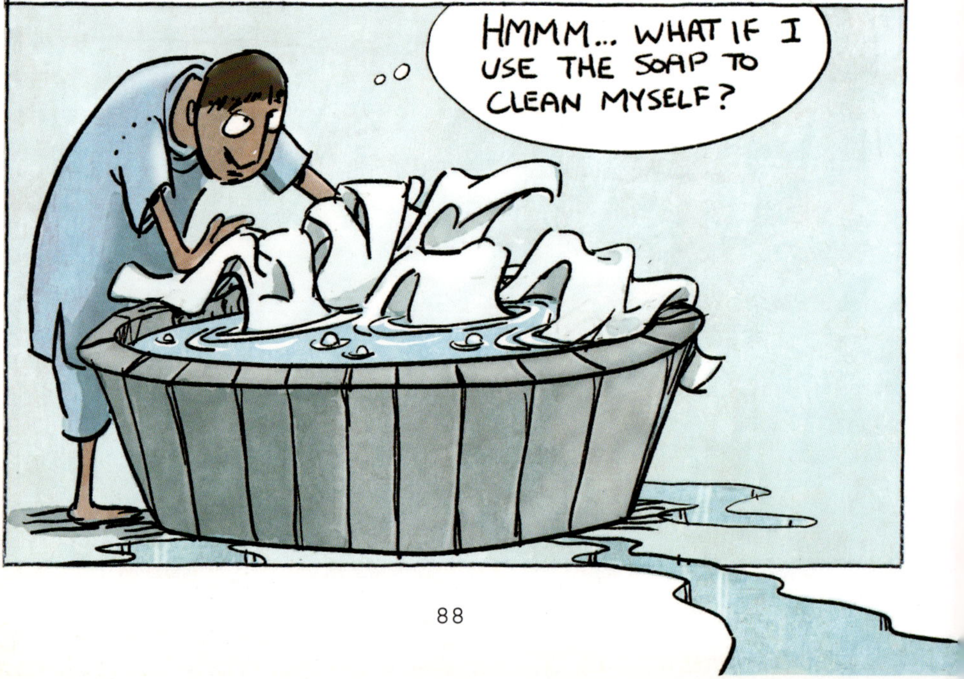
HMMM... WHAT IF I USE THE SOAP TO CLEAN MYSELF?

We have to forgive them for the long delay. Early soap was harsh on the skin. It could smell bad, too. Years and years passed before gentle, pleasant-smelling bars of soap arrived.

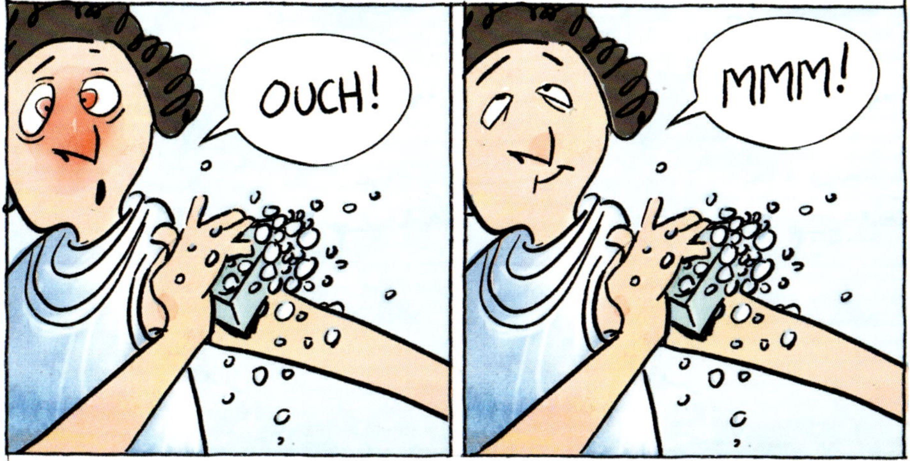
OUCH!
MMM!

Arab soap makers became popular throughout the Middle East and Europe in the eighth century.

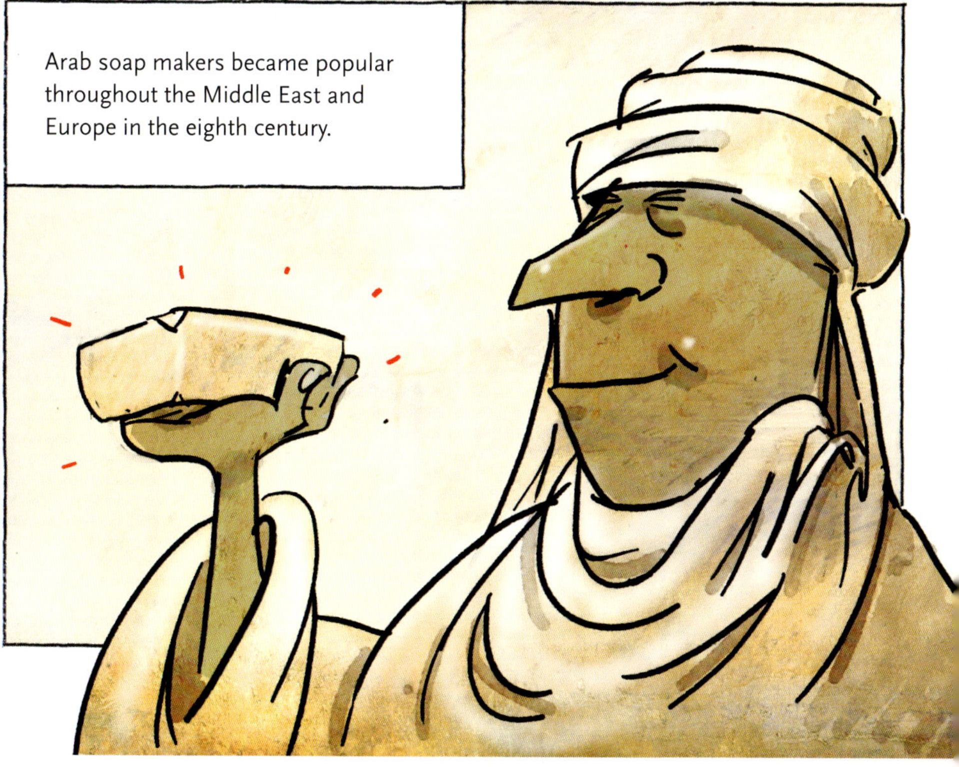

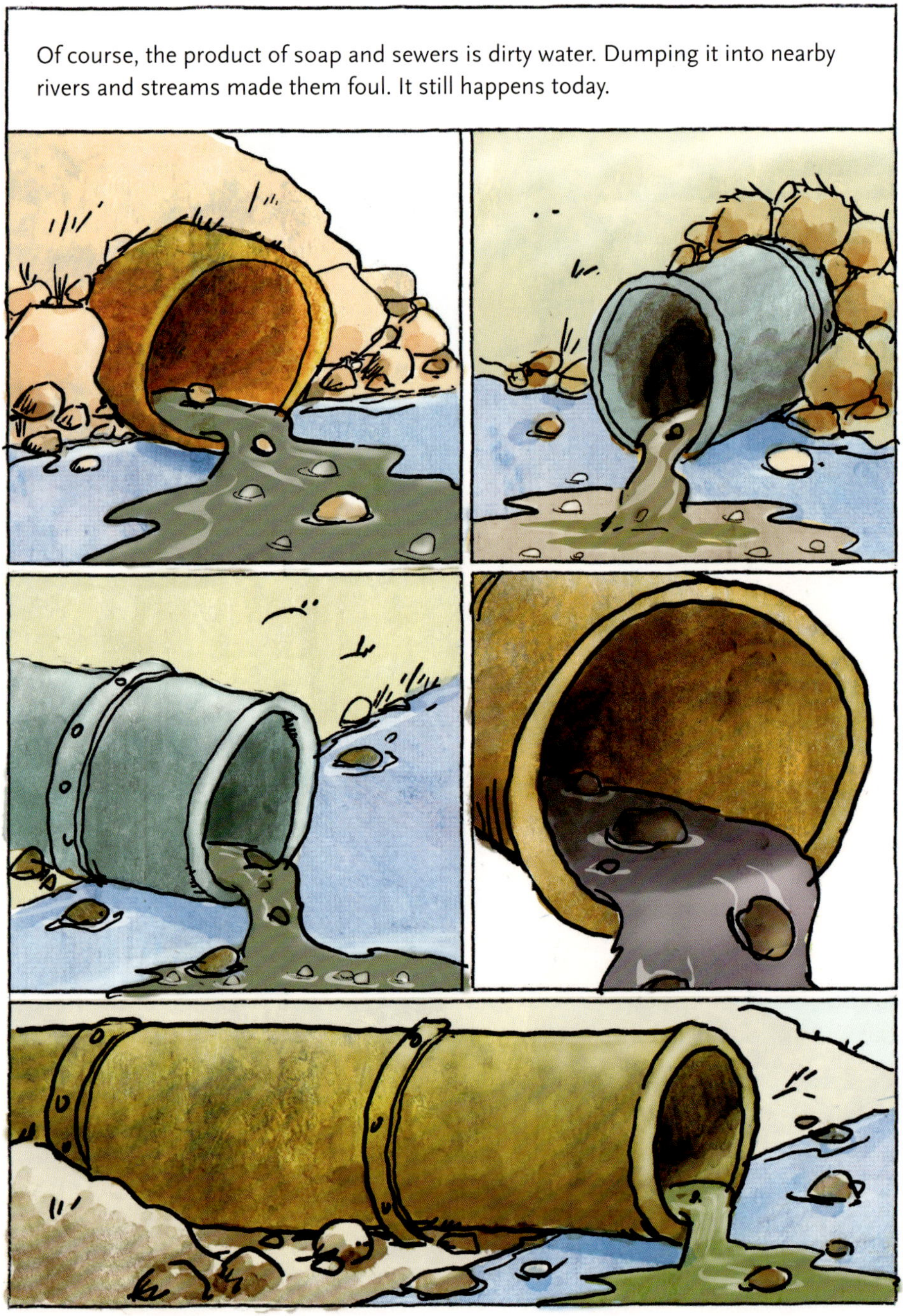
Of course, the product of soap and sewers is dirty water. Dumping it into nearby rivers and streams made them foul. It still happens today.

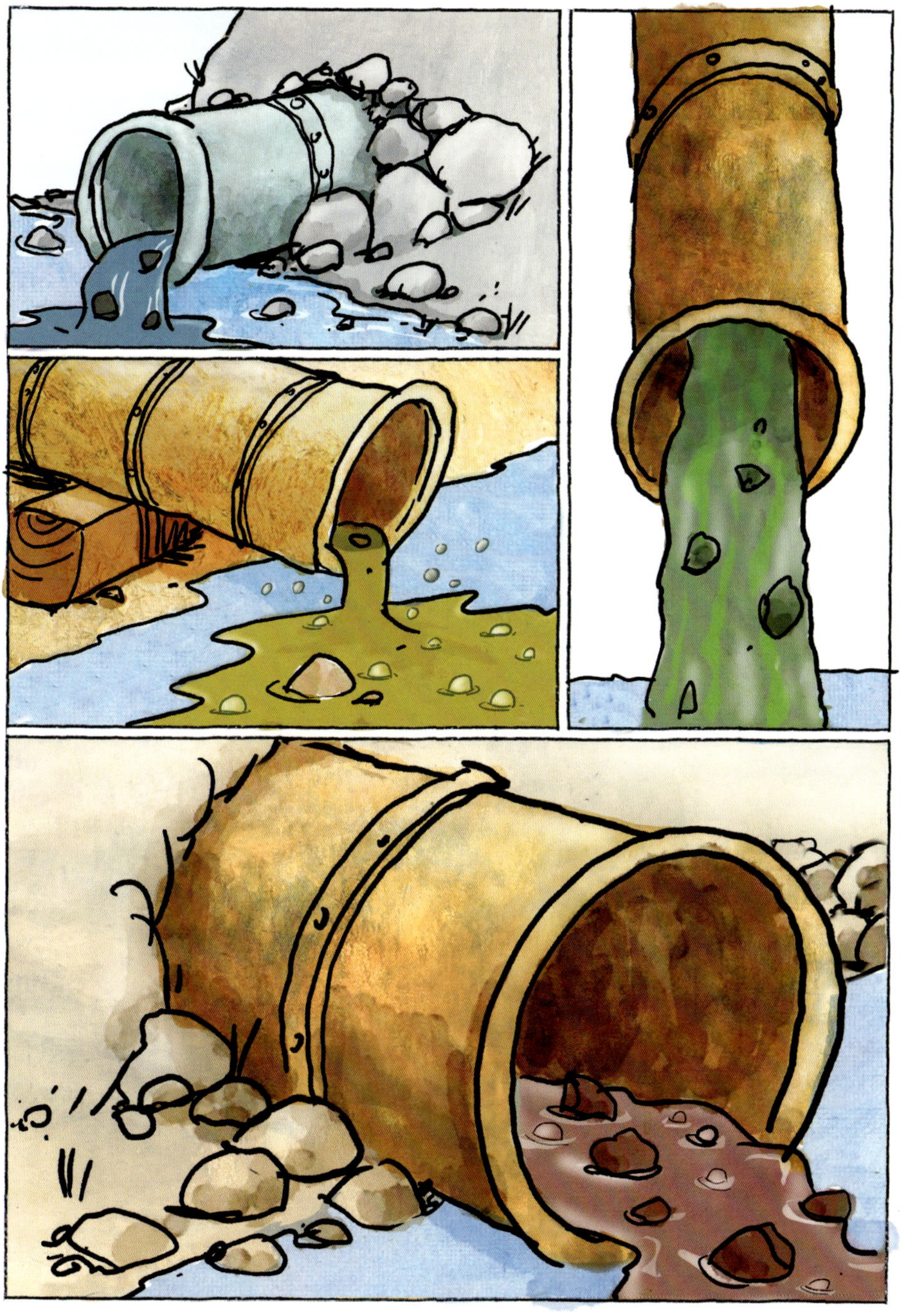

Whether made dirty from pollution or occurring naturally, most water must be made safe for washing and drinking. Ancient peoples of China, India, the Middle East, and Greece had the Big Idea to boil or filter it through cloth, sand, or charcoal.

About 2,500 years ago, both Indian and Chinese civilizations somehow discovered that the grindings of certain rocks added to a pool or jug of murky water attracted dirt, making icky clumps that settled on the bottom of the container, leaving clear, drinkable water on top.

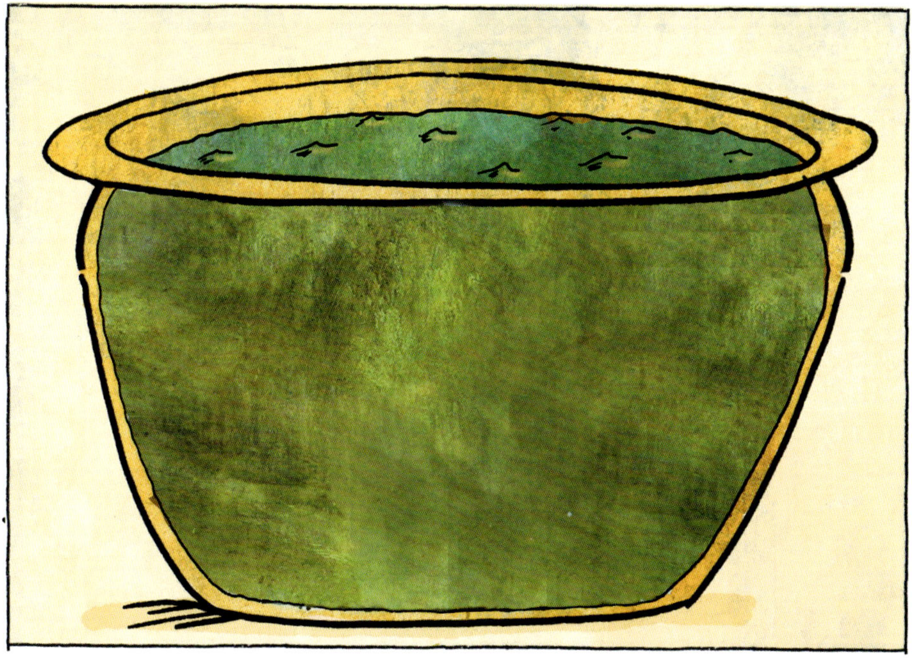

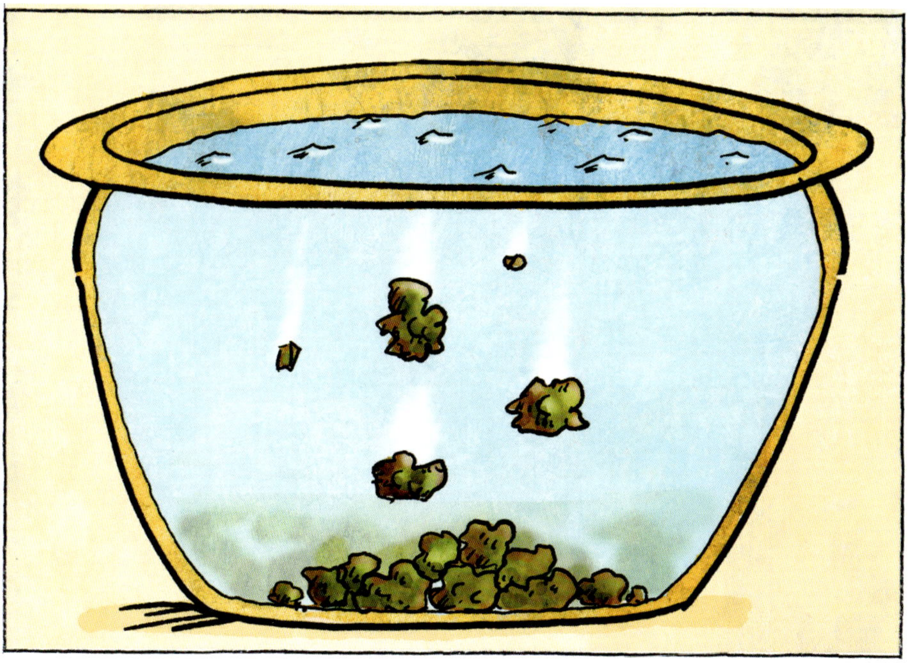

But for the longest time, people were only interested in the appearance, smell, and taste of the water. They didn't grasp the idea of truly "clean" water and that water that looked, smelled, and tasted good could still make you sick. Very sick. Even dangerously so.

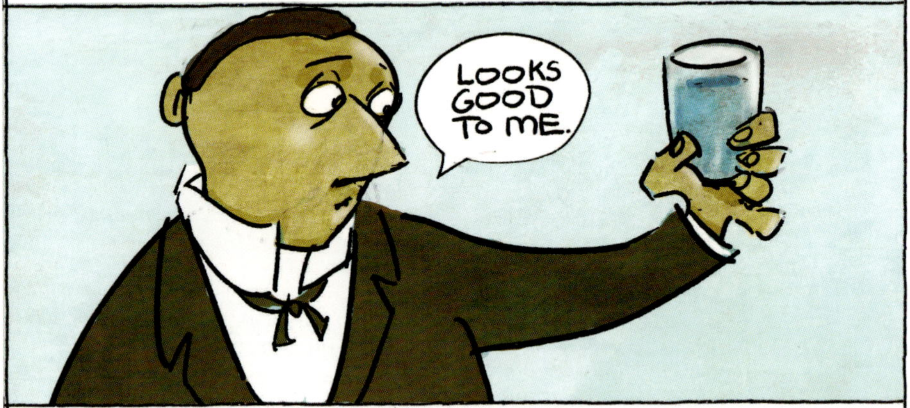
LOOKS GOOD TO ME.

Then, in the 1880s, scientists like Louis Pasteur and Robert Koch uncovered the link between microbes—germs—and disease. People began to understand that they needed to rid public water of disease-causing microbes.

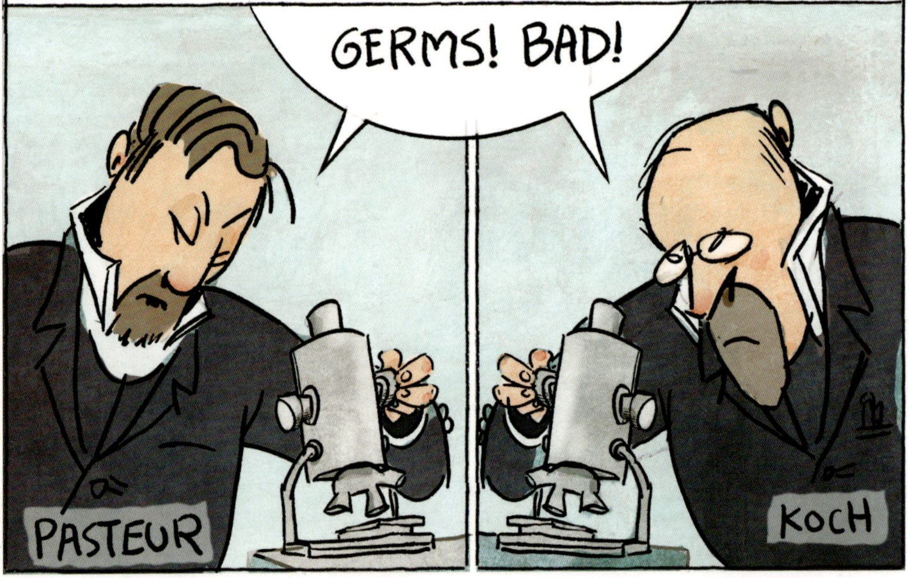
GERMS! BAD!
PASTEUR
KOCH

At the beginning of the twentieth century, New Jersey doctor John L. Leal promoted the idea of adding a tiny bit of chlorine—a safe chemical—to public water, knowing it would kill harmful germs.

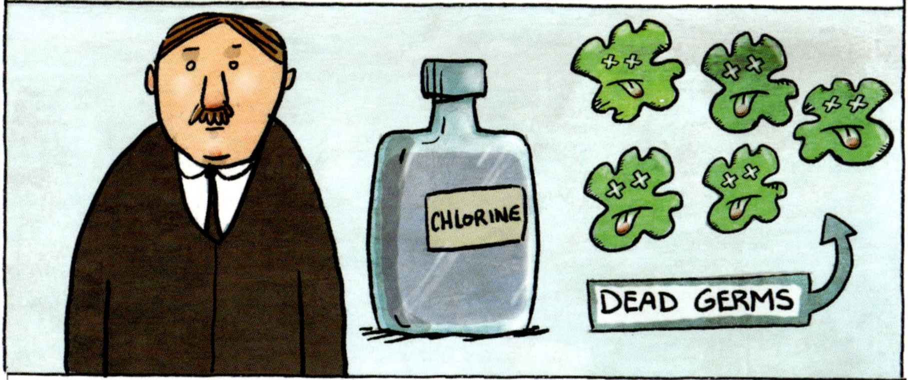
CHLORINE
DEAD GERMS

But many people had wrongheaded ideas.

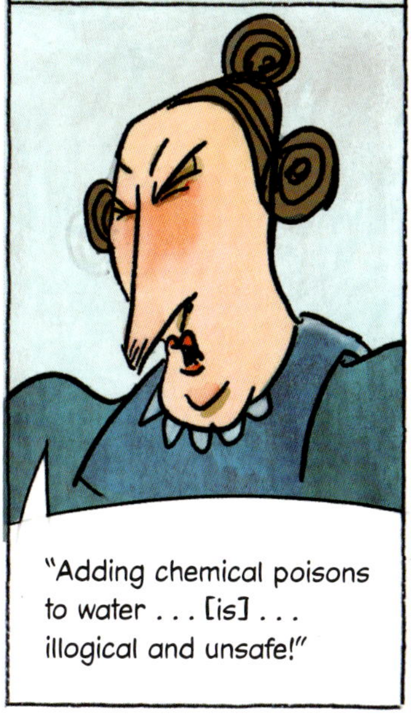
"Adding chemical poisons to water . . . [is] . . . illogical and unsafe!"

Dr. Leal eventually won the argument, and in 1908, Jersey City, New Jersey, became the first city with chlorinated water. Other cities followed, and outbreaks of waterborne diseases fell, health improved, and life expectancy increased.

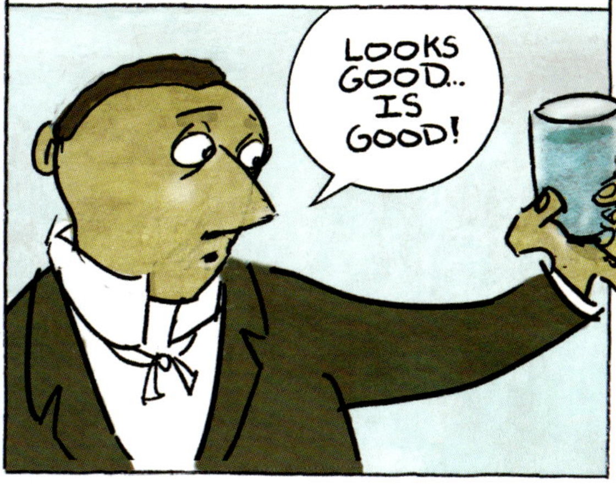
LOOKS GOOD.. IS GOOD!

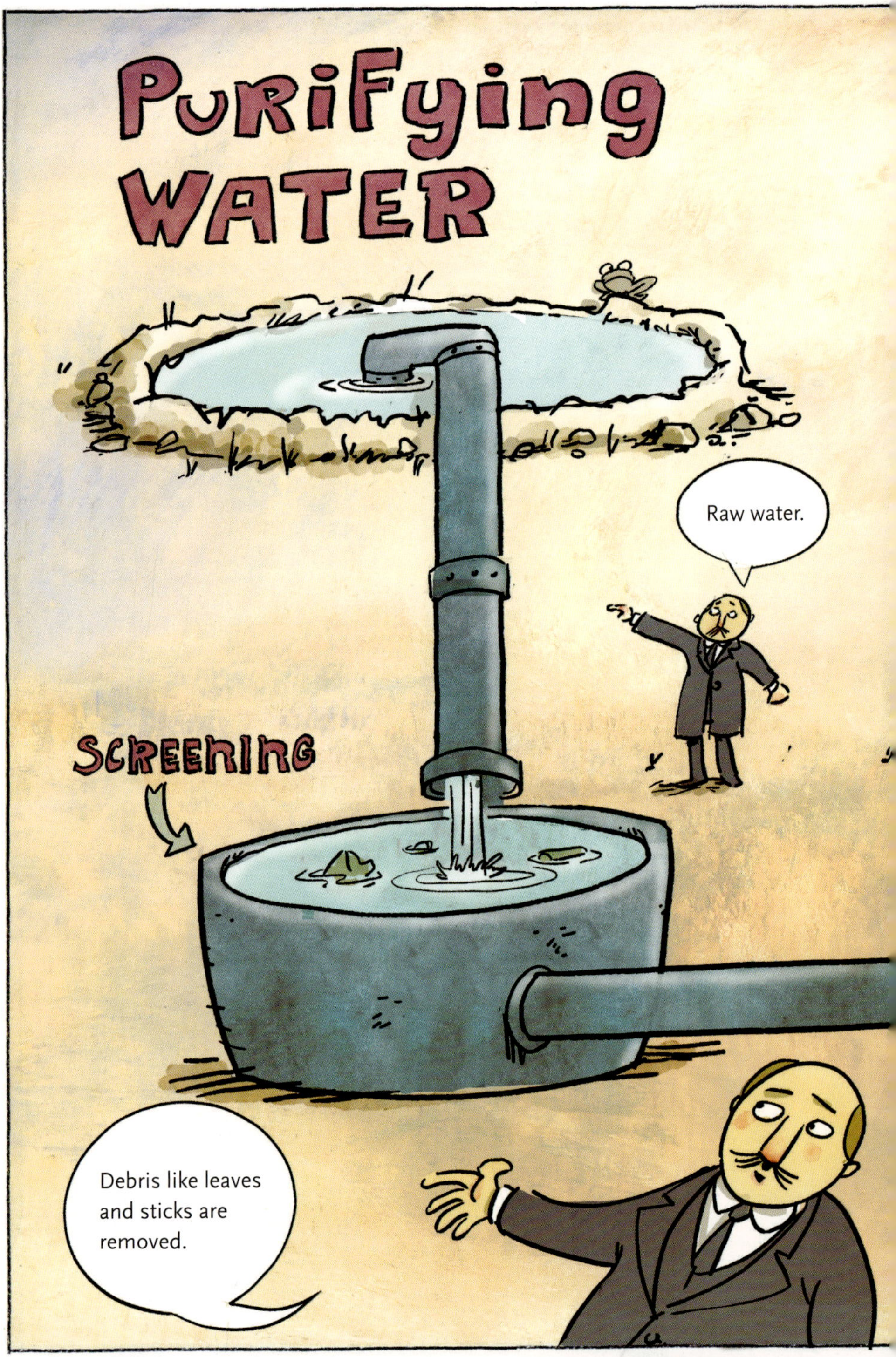
Purifying WATER
Raw water.
SCREENING
Debris like leaves and sticks are removed.

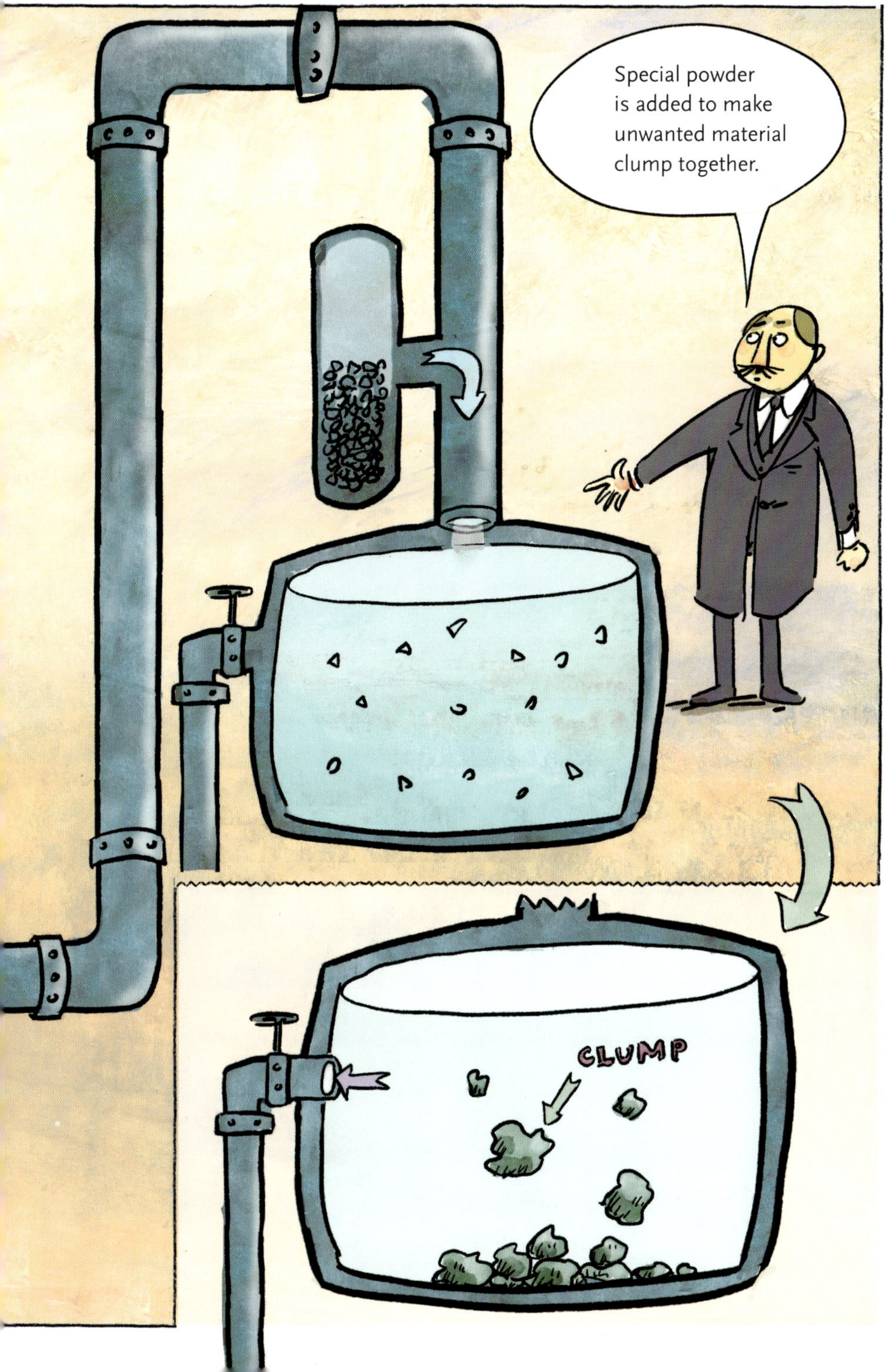
Special powder is added to make unwanted material clump together.
CLUMP

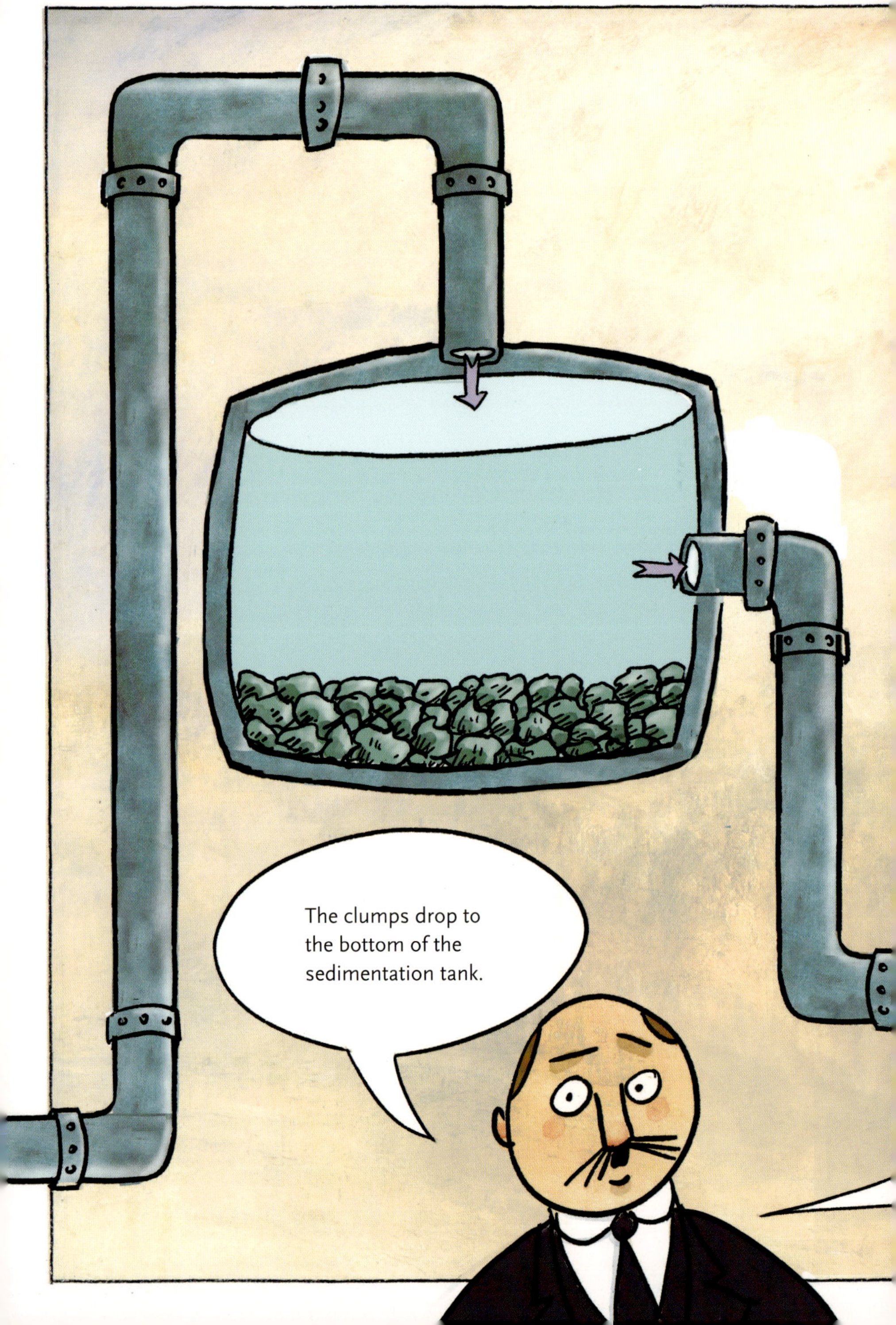
The clumps drop to the bottom of the sedimentation tank.

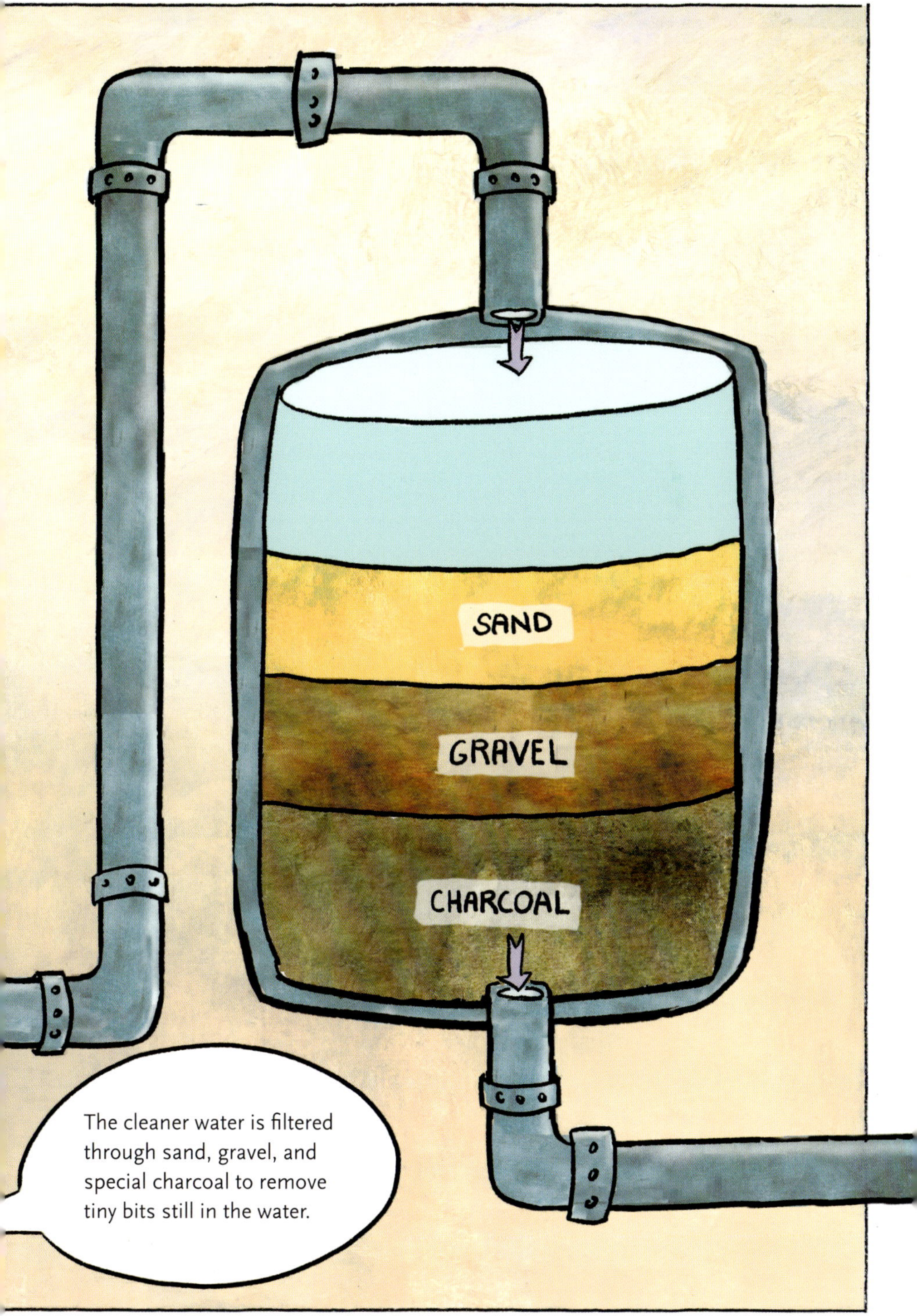
SAND
GRAVEL
CHARCOAL
The cleaner water is filtered through sand, gravel, and special charcoal to remove tiny bits still in the water.

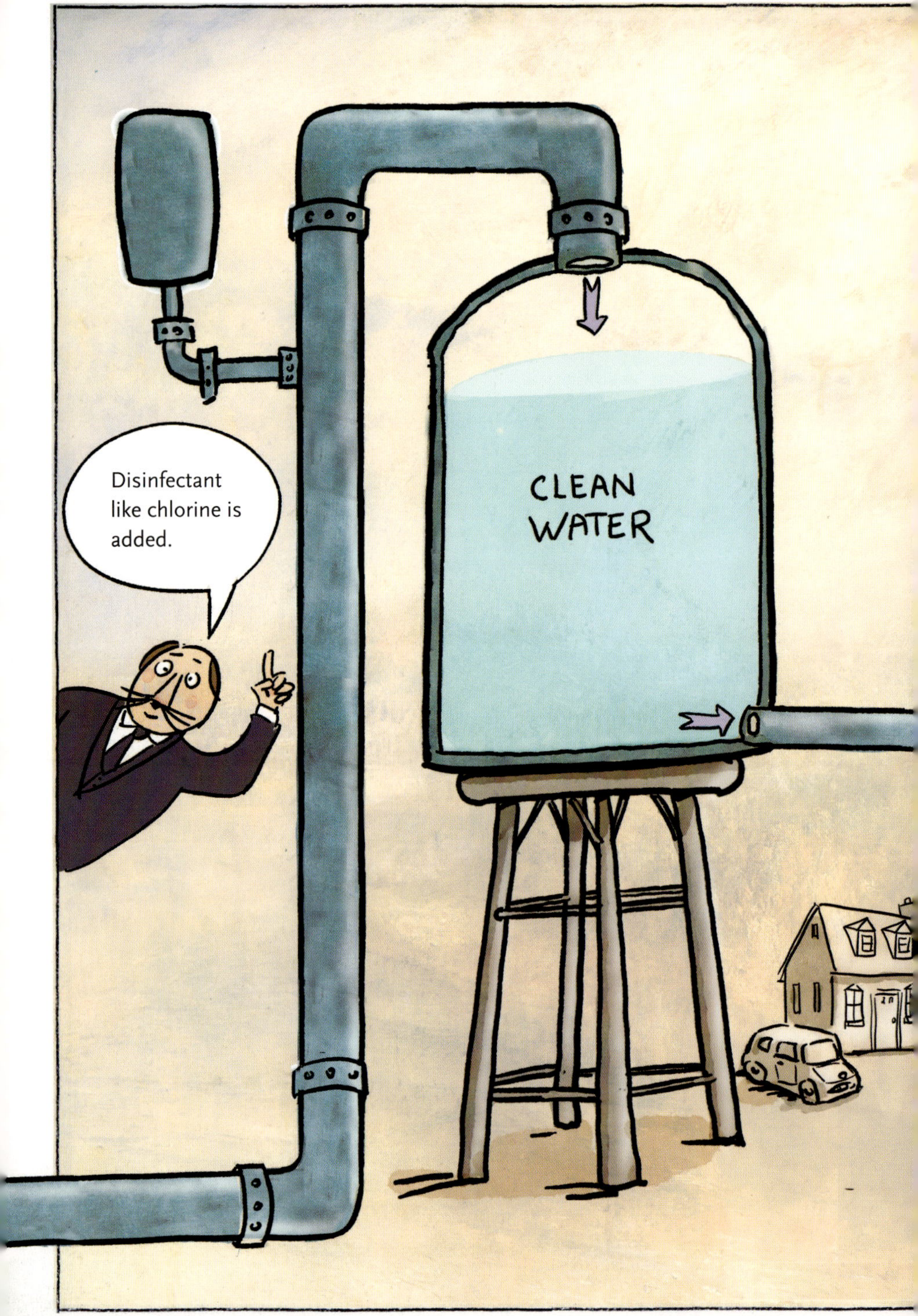
Disinfectant like chlorine is added.
CLEAN WATER

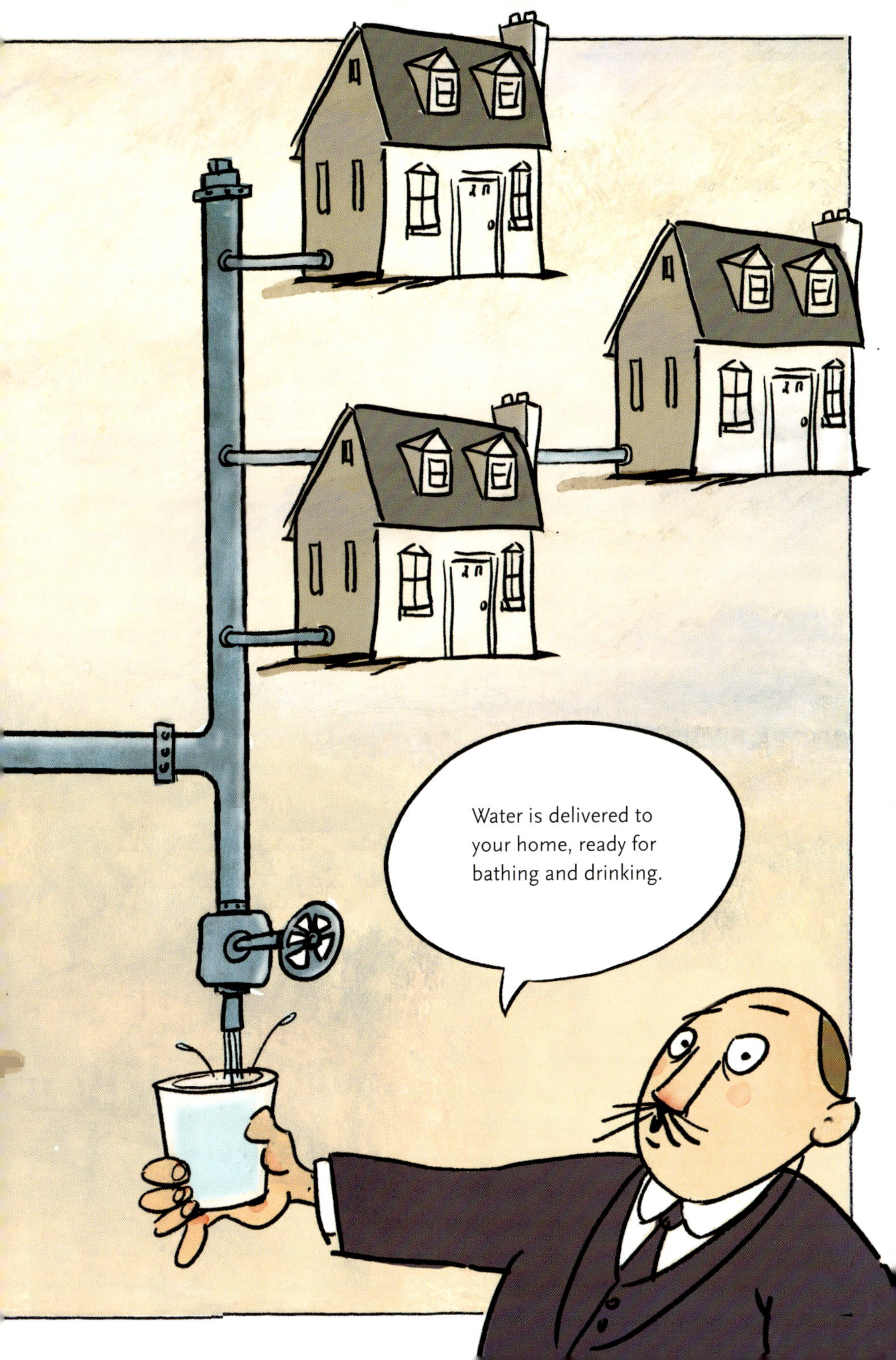
Water is delivered to your home, ready for bathing and drinking.

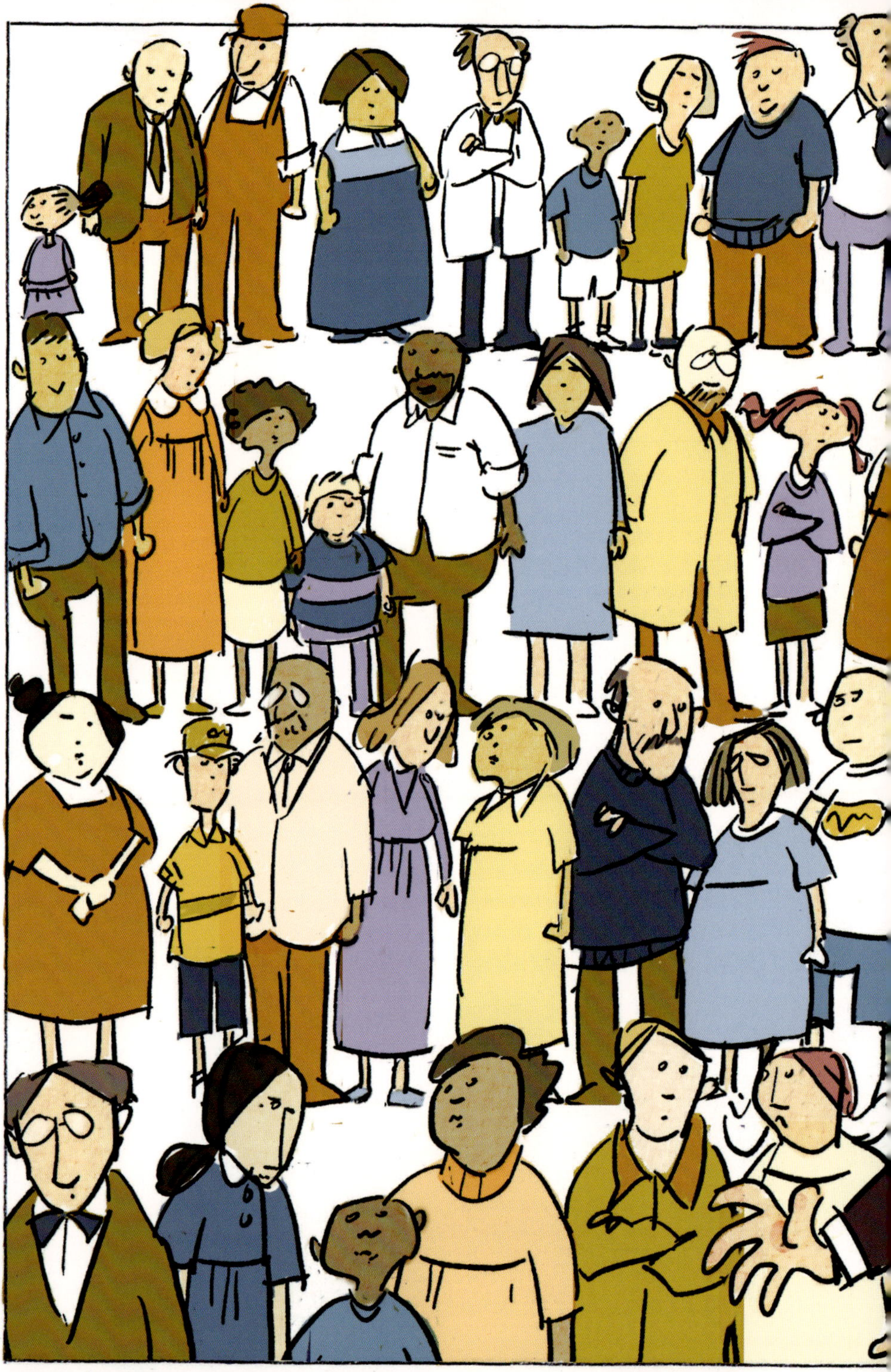

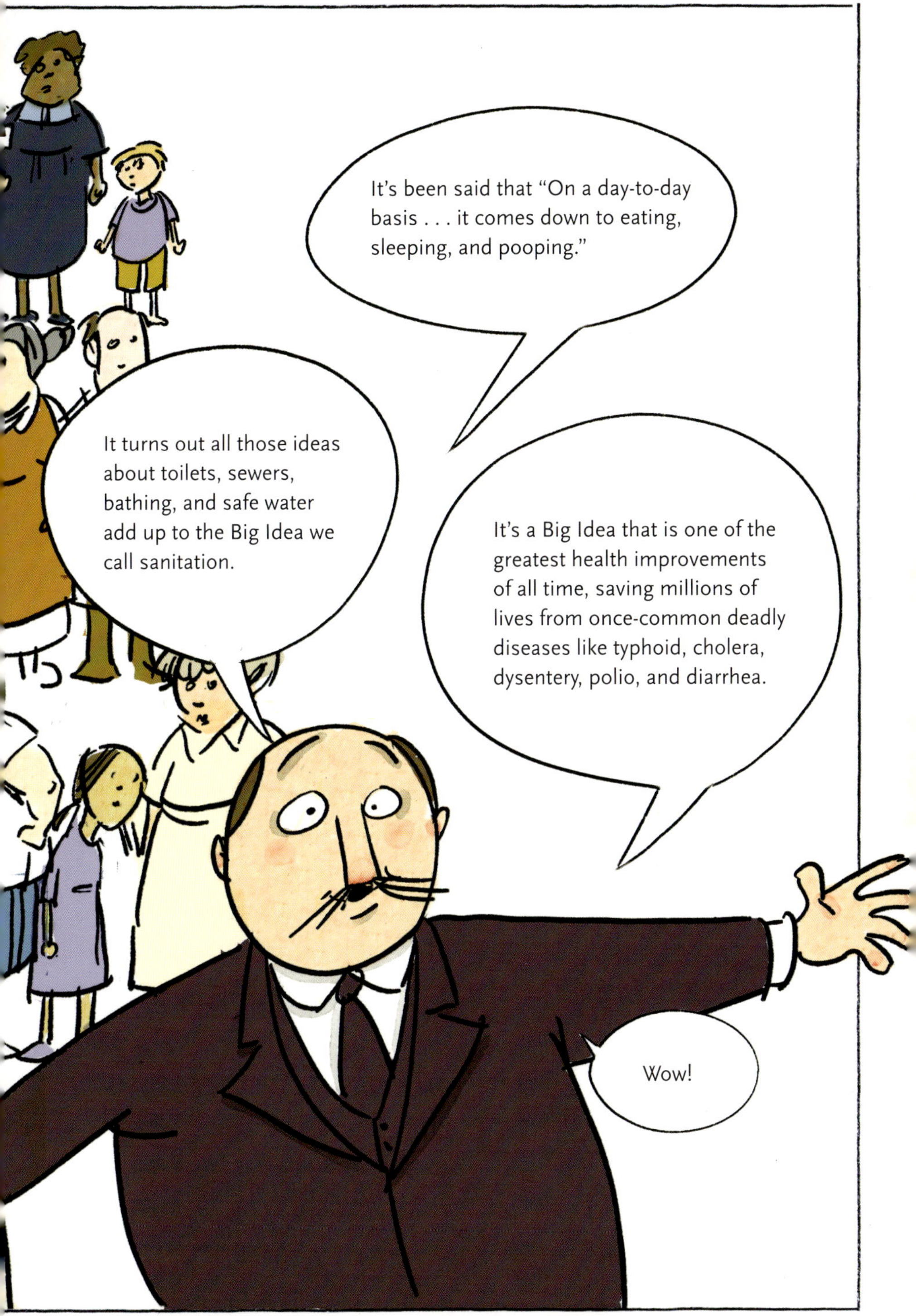
It's been said that "On a day-to-day basis . . . it comes down to eating, sleeping, and pooping."
It turns out all those ideas about toilets, sewers, bathing, and safe water add up to the Big Idea we call sanitation.
It's a Big Idea that is one of the greatest health improvements of all time, saving millions of lives from once-common deadly diseases like typhoid, cholera, dysentery, polio, and diarrhea.
Wow!

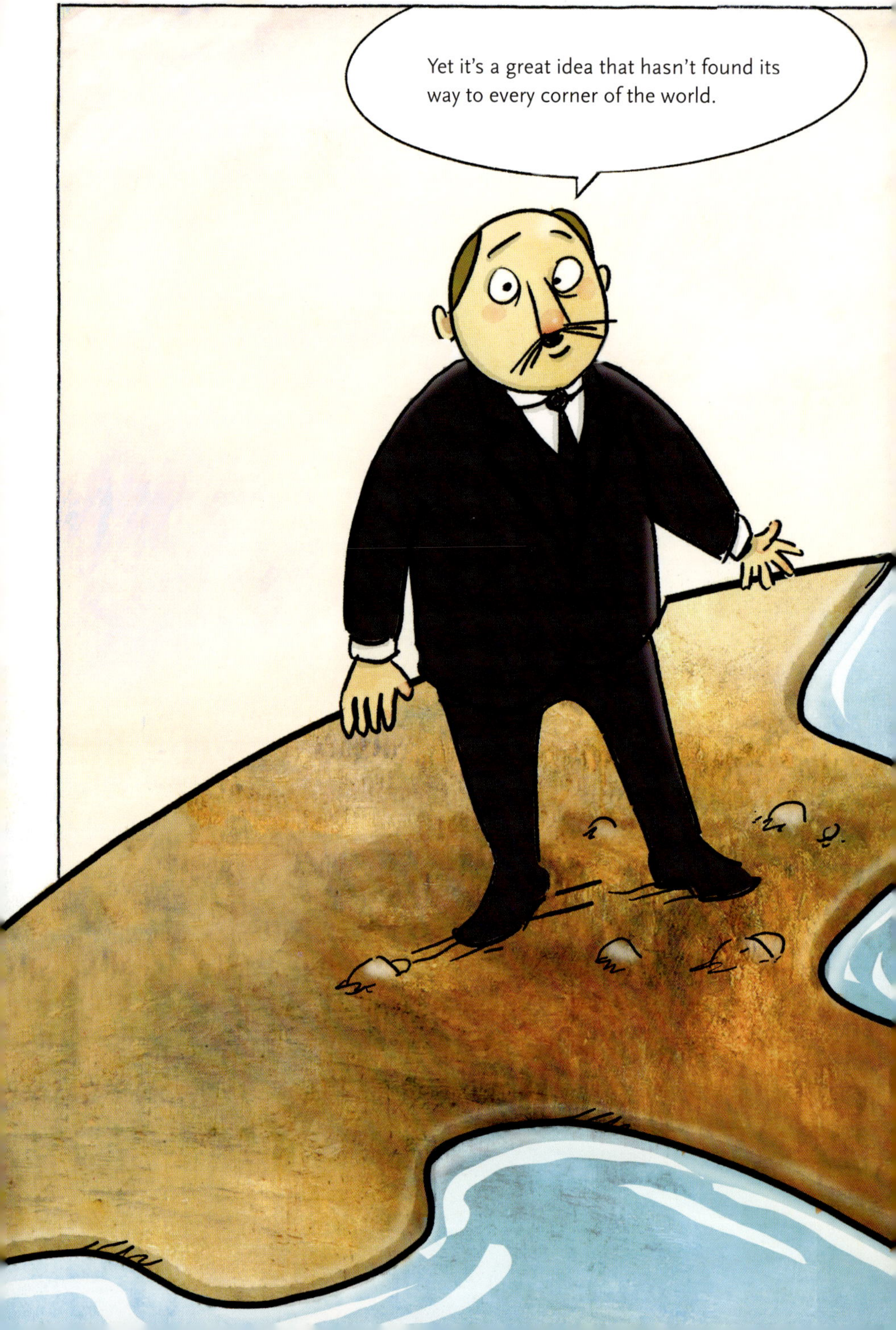
Yet it's a great idea that hasn't found its way to every corner of the world.

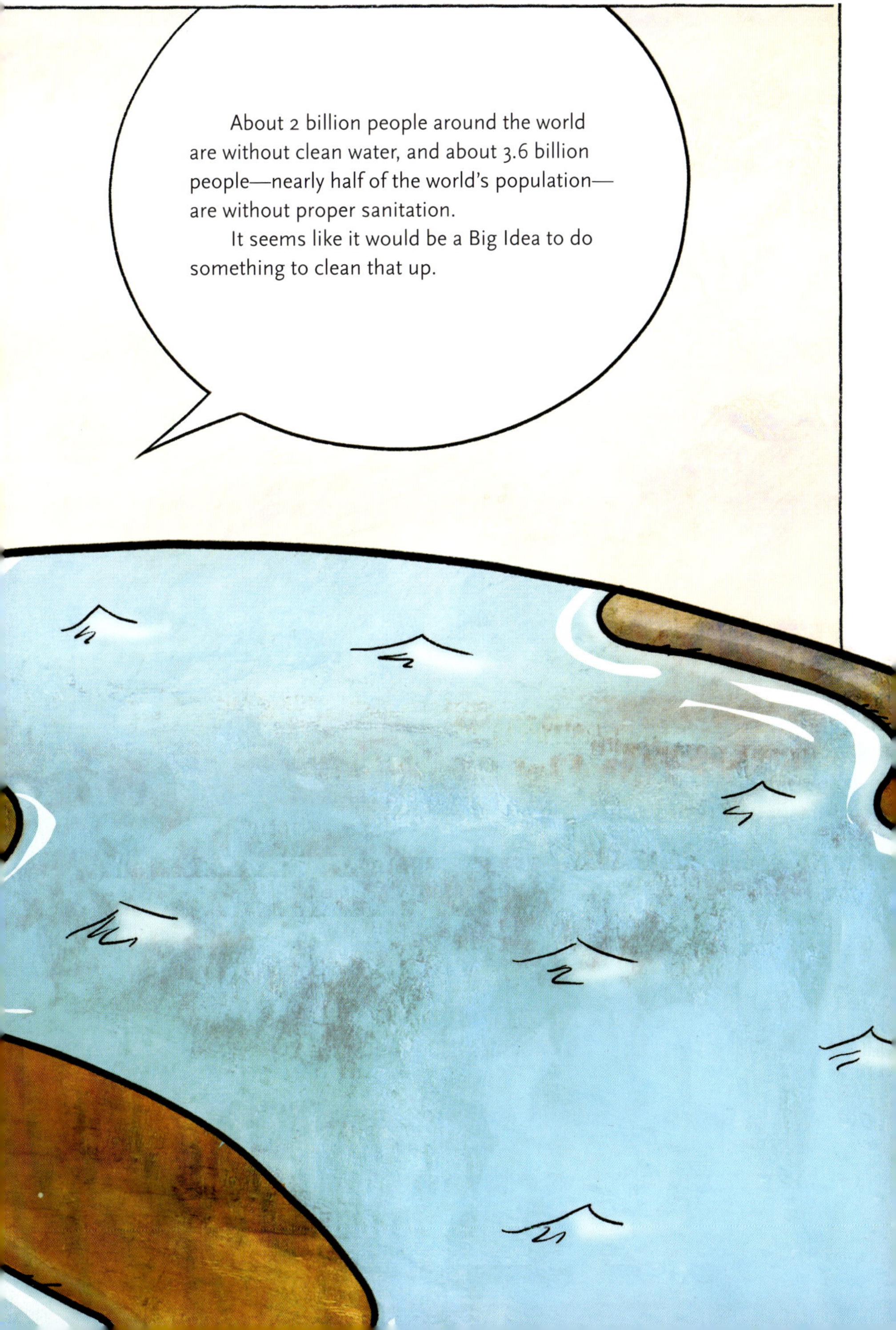
About 2 billion people around the world are without clean water, and about 3.6 billion people—nearly half of the world's population—are without proper sanitation.
It seems like it would be a Big Idea to do something to clean that up.

SELECTED TIMELINE

10,000 BCE
Early humans settle near rivers and lakes, recognizing the importance of sources of fresh water for survival.

5500 BCE (circa)
Stone huts in Scotland have toilets and drains.

Middle Eastern people use ceramic cylindrical tubes as toilets.

2700–1450 BCE
The Palace of Minos at Knossos on Crete uses toilets and a system of ceramic sewer pipes.

2500 BCE (circa)
Ancient Egyptians construct early water-distribution systems, such as canals and reservoirs along the Nile River, for agricultural and domestic use.

| 10,000 BCE | 5500 BCE | 4000 BCE | 3000 BCE | 2500 BCE | 2000 BCE | 1500 BCE |

4000 BCE (circa)
In ancient Mesopotamia (modern-day Iraq), civilizations like the Sumerians begin digging wells to access groundwater.

3000 BCE (circa)
The Indus Valley Civilization (in modern-day Pakistan and India) develops sophisticated water management systems, including public baths and drainage systems.

2000 BCE (circa)
Ancient Greeks and Romans build aqueducts to transport water over long distances, improving urban water supply and sanitation.

1500 BCE (circa)
The Indus Valley Civilization develops advanced sanitation systems, including public baths and covered drains in cities like Mohenjo-daro and Harappa.

500–400 BCE

Athens, Greece, employs a sewage system with clay pipes carrying waste to its outskirts.

Eighth to fourteenth centuries

Islamic civilization advances public sanitation with the construction of sophisticated water supply and sewage systems in cities like Baghdad and Cairo.

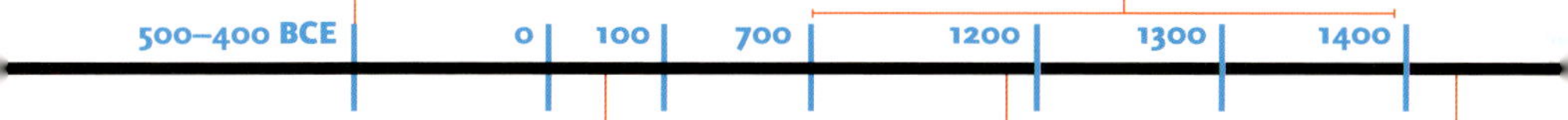

| 500–400 BCE | 0 | 100 | 700 | 1200 | 1300 | 1400 |

First century CE

The Roman Empire builds extensive aqueducts, public baths (thermae), and underground sewage systems (cloacae) in cities like Rome and Pompeii.

In China, people use toilets connected to pipes that empty into a pit.

1184

German King Henry VI hosts a gathering of fellow royals. The floor of his mansion collapses, and guests fall into the basement cesspit.

1423

The mayor of London builds a 128-seat toilet over the river Thames.

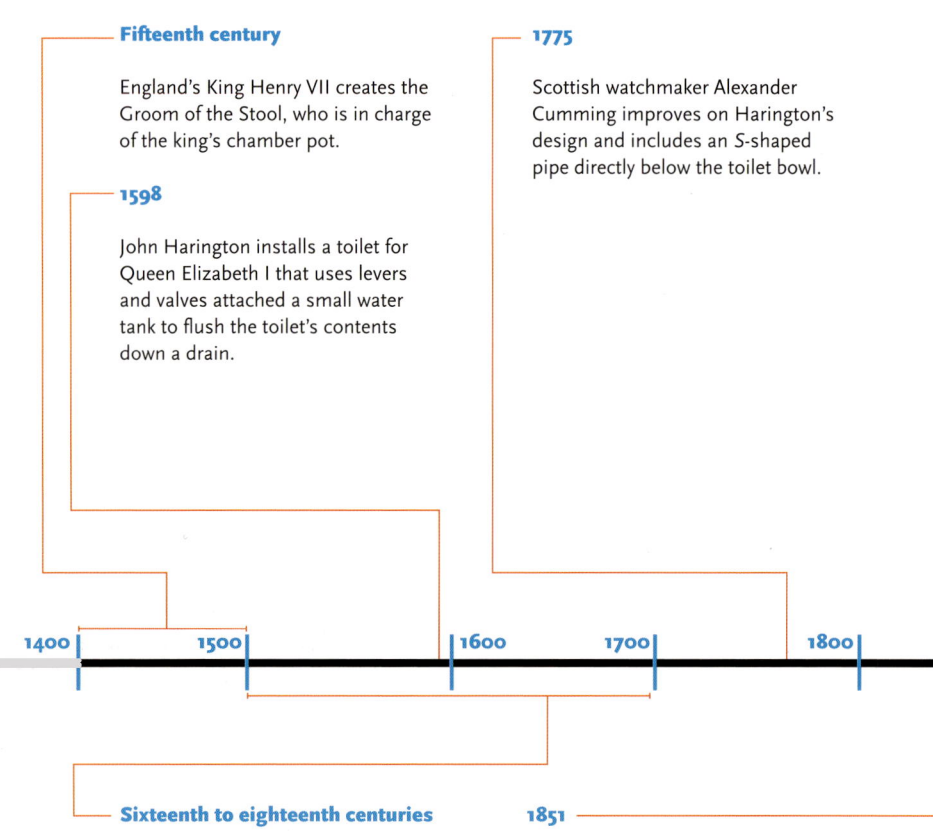

Fifteenth century

England's King Henry VII creates the Groom of the Stool, who is in charge of the king's chamber pot.

1598

John Harington installs a toilet for Queen Elizabeth I that uses levers and valves attached a small water tank to flush the toilet's contents down a drain.

1775

Scottish watchmaker Alexander Cumming improves on Harington's design and includes an S-shaped pipe directly below the toilet bowl.

Sixteenth to eighteenth centuries

European cities begin to address sanitation issues more systematically, with the construction of sewer systems and regulations for waste disposal.

1851

Public flush toilets based on Harington's and Cumming's designs are installed at the Great Exhibition.

1854

John Snow identifies the Broad Street pump as the source of a cholera outbreak in London, pioneering epidemiology and highlighting the importance of clean water in public health.

1858

The abominable smell of the polluted river Thames prompts the term the "Great Stink."

1861

Thomas Crapper opens his toilet business in London, to great success.

1865

In response to the "Great Stink," London's sewer system opens, although the whole project is not completed for another ten years.

1880s to 1890s

The development of municipal water treatment plants begins in Europe and North America, marking the start of systematic efforts to provide clean water to urban populations.

Late nineteenth century

The development of sanitary engineering leads to improvements in sewer systems, waste treatment, and water purification techniques in industrialized nations.

1895

The mayor of New York City appoints George E. Waring Jr. commissioner of the Department of Street Cleaning.

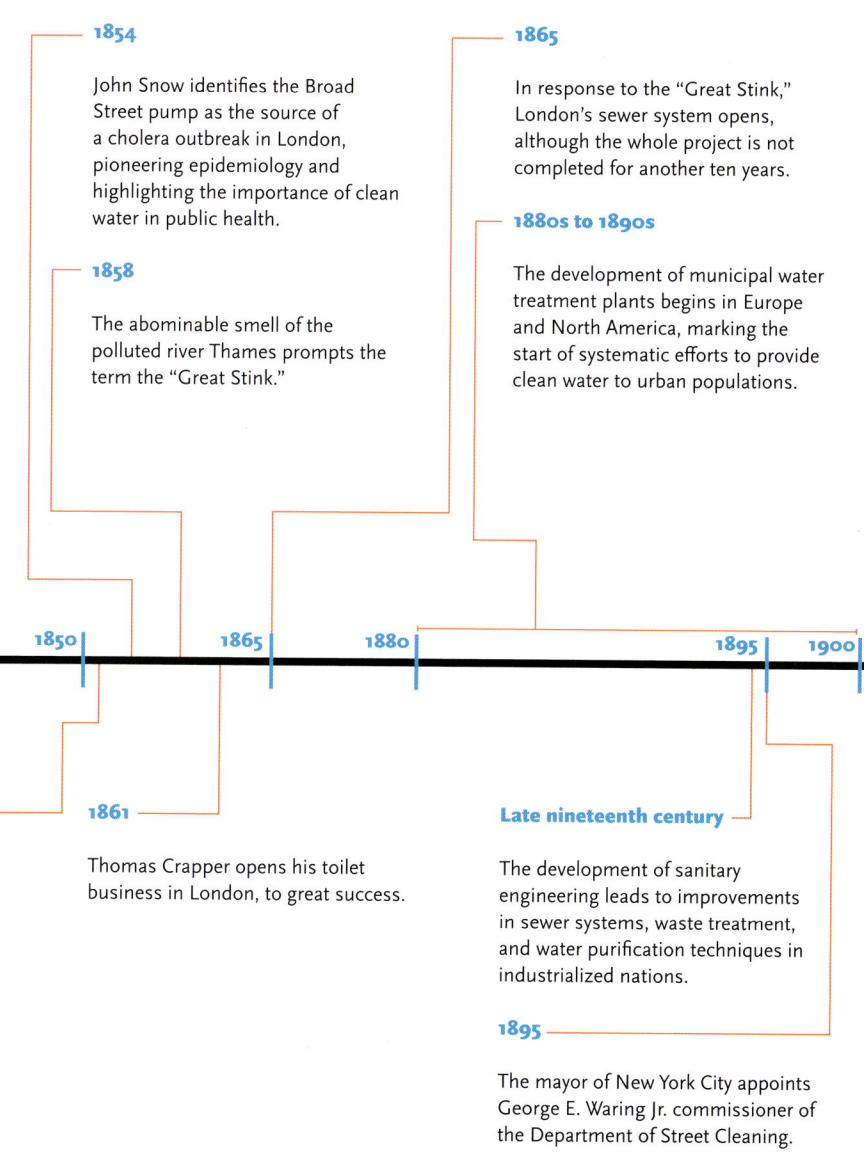

1906

The Pure Food and Drug Act is passed in the United States, establishing regulations for food safety and sanitation.

1950

A quarter of American households still do not have toilets.

1900

1950

1948

The World Health Organization (WHO) is established, emphasizing the importance of sanitation in promoting global health.

1972

The United Nations Conference on the Human Environment in Stockholm recognizes access to clean water as a basic human right.

1974

The Safe Drinking Water Act is passed in the United States, establishing regulations for drinking water quality and safety.

2010

The General Assembly of the United Nations (UN) declares access to clean water and sanitation a human right.

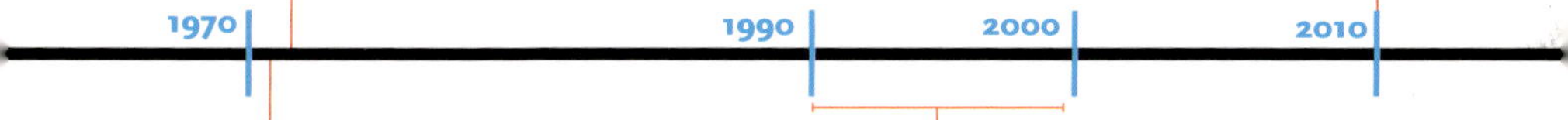
1970
1990
2000
2010

1990s

The WHO and United Nations Water (UN-Water) launch the Global Analysis and Assessment of Sanitation and Drinking-Water (GLAAS) to monitor global progress in water and sanitation.

WHO WAS GEORGE E. WARING JR.?

George E. Waring Jr., circa 1892

George E. Waring Jr. was an engineer with a knack for dealing with unwanted water. In 1857, he applied his expertise in drainage to a large park the city of New York was constructing in Manhattan, ensuring it was not a boggy mess. The playland of fields and meadows of fabled Central Park owes Waring a bit of a thank-you.

His work on the park was interrupted by the start of the Civil War. Waring fought battles and risked his life, rising to the rank of colonel, a title he carried over into his civilian life.

In the late 1870s, Memphis, Tennessee, battled yellow fever. Believing the disease was born of poor sanitation, the city called on Colonel Waring to clean things up. He provided the city with a new sewage plan, and yellow fever incidentally subsided; Memphis cheered Waring's success. The celebration was misplaced. People didn't know the disease was caused by the bite of an infected mosquito and not by bad sanitation. Why the disease ebbed with Colonel Waring's new sewage plan is unanswered.

In any case, Waring's apparent success in Memphis brought him to the attention of William Strong, the mayor of New York City. Determined to rid the filthy city of its garbage, manure, and rotting animal carcasses, Strong first turned to Teddy Roosevelt (who would later be elected president) to lead the Department of Street Cleaning. The then up-and-coming Roosevelt declined, choosing instead to run the city's police department, opening up the sanitation job for Colonel Waring.

Waring brought his experience from the Civil War to his position, demanding his sanitation workers adopt white uniforms, including a white pith helmet more likely seen on a jungle safari than on New York thoroughfares. He even paraded the workers in the streets. At first, it all seemed a bit comical to New Yorkers . . . until they saw the street cleaners' remarkable accomplishments.

"There is not a man or a woman or a child in New York who does not owe [Waring] gratitude for making New York in every part so much more fit to live than it was when he undertook the cleaning of the streets."

Although the hardworking street cleaners received the city residents' heartfelt appreciation, they were also saddled with expensive laundry bills to keep their white uniforms clean. And Waring callously cut their salary by 17 percent.

The colonel left the New York's Department of Street Cleaning in 1898, became a special commissioner for President William McKinley, and traveled to Cuba, which had fallen under American control after the Spanish-American War. Waring was tasked with eliminating yellow fever there and set out to clean the island up, still working under the false assumption that the disease was caused by poor sanitation. Tragically, he contracted the disease and died. He was sixty-five.

NOTES

Page 14—"Apollinaris pooped here": Zeldovich.

Page 26—". . . would make unsavory places sweet, noisome places wholesome, and filthy places cleanly": Hammond.

Page 36—". . . foul sewer, a river of pollution . . . festering and reeking with all abominable smells": Brigden.

Page 37—"Great Stink": Brigden.

Page 41—"All the streets are one mass of reeking, disgusting filth . . . the dirt prevails all over . . . in the thoroughfares, in the by-streets, the alleyways, the lanes": Larsen.

Page 54—"Get me a napkin quick. There's a turd floating in the air": NASA, "Apollo 10 Onboard Voice Transcription," 1969.

Page 55—"It's kinda like going to Camp Potty": Gannon.

Page 79—"I smell of armpits": Ashenburg, p. 99.

Page 80—"While Europeans rejected bathing, the rest of world kept at it. For example, in Turkey, bathing less than two or three times a week was thought 'nasty'": Ashenburg, p. 104.

Page 84—"without any clothes whatever, half an hour or an hour, according to the season": Worrall.

Page 86—"the great unwashed": Ashenburg, p. 170.

Page 87— "Social classes became divided not only by wealth and culture, but also by smell": Blakemore.

Page 95— "Adding chemical poisons to water . . . [is] . . . illogical and unsafe": American Chemistry Council Chlorine Panel.

Page 103—"On a day-to-day basis . . . it comes down to eating, sleeping, and pooping": Alex.

SELECT BIBLIOGRAPHY

Articles

"A Brief History of Toilets." *Five Minute History.* https://fiveminutehistory.com/a-brief-history-of-toilets/.

"Admit it, most of our best thinking is done while perched on the loo." *BBC Bitesize,* February 2019. www.bbc.co.uk/bitesize/articles/zfhmrj6.

Aicher, Peter. "Watering Ancient Rome." *NOVA/PBS,* February 22, 2000. https://www.pbs.org/wgbh/nova/article/roman-aqueducts/.

Ailes, Emma. "Scotland and the indoor toilet." *BBC,* April 19, 2013. www.bbc.com/news/uk-scotland-22214728.

Alex, Bridget. "What the Earliest Toilets Say About How Human Civilization Has Evolved." *Discover,* January 31, 2020. www.discovermagazine.com/planet-earth/what-the-earliest-toilets-say-about-how-human-civilization-has-evolved.

Apman, Sarah Bean. "Tenement House Act of 1901." *Village Preservation,* April 11, 2016. www.villagepreservation.org/2016/04/11/tenement-house-act-of-1901/.

"Apollo 10 Onboard Voice Transcription." National Aeronautics and Space Administration. https://www.jsc.nasa.gov/history/mission_trans/AS10_CM.PDF.

Ashenburg, Katherine. "Clean Aztecs, Dirty Spaniards." *Aztecs at Mexicolore,* September 21, 2008. www.mexicolore.co.uk/aztecs/home/clean-aztecs-dirty-spaniards.

Barksdale, Nate. "Who Invented the Flush Toilet?" *History,* April 17, 2020. www.history.com/news/who-invented-the-flush-toilet.

Barnett, Errol and Tim Hume. "The Himba: Namibia's iconic red women." *CNN,* May 18, 2012. https://www.cnn.com/2012/05/11/world/africa/himba-namibia-inside-africa/index.html.

"Baths." *PBS,* 2006. www.pbs.org/empires/romans/empire/baths.html.

Bayram, Seyma. "Billions of people lack access to clean drinking water, U.N. report finds." *NPR,* March 22, 2023. www.npr.org/2023/03/22/1165464857/billions-of-people-lack-access-to-clean-drinking-water-u-n-report-finds.

Bell, Bethan. "London's long-term lav affair: A history of public toilets in the capital." *BBC,* January 16, 2022. www.bbc.com/news/uk-england-london-59785477.

Berdy, Judith. "George Waring's Men In White." *New York Almanack,* January 24, 2021. https://www.newyorkalmanack.com/2021/01/george-warings-men-in-white/.

Blakemore, Erin. "Public Baths Were Meant to Uplift the Poor." *JSTOR Daily,* September 9, 2017. daily.jstor.org/public-baths-were-meant-to-uplift-the-poor/.

Bowden, Ebony. "Nightmarish 'fatbergs' are clogging New York's sewers." *New York Post,* April 22, 2019. nypost.com/2019/04/22/nightmarish-fatbergs-are-clogging-new-yorks-sewers/.

Braun, Adee. "The 19th-Century Night Soil Men Who Carted Away America's Waste." *Atlas Obscura,* March 15, 2016. www.atlasobscura.com/articles/when-american-cities-were-full-of-crap.

Brigden, James. "The Great Stink: London's Unbearable Summer of 1858." *History.* www.history.co.uk/articles/the-great-stink-londons-unbearable-summer-of-1858.

Cassidy, Cody. "Who Discovered Soap? What to Know About the Origins of the Life-Saving Substance." *Time*, May 5, 2020. time.com/5831828/soap-origins/.

Collinson, Alwyn. "How Bazalgette built London's first super-sewer." *Museum of London*, March 26, 2019. www.museumoflondon.org.uk/discover/how-bazalgette-built-londons-first-super-sewer.

Dowdeswell, Molly. "Hygiene Through History: How Filthy Were Our Ancient Ancestors?" *Ancient Origins*, November 7, 2022. https://www.ancient-origins.net/history-ancient-traditions/hygiene-0017494.

"Drinking-water." *WHO*, September 13, 2023. www.who.int/news-room/fact-sheets/detail/drinking-water.

Engelhaupt, Erika. "Huge Blobs of Fat and Trash Are Filling the World's Sewers." *National Geographic*, August 16, 2017. www.nationalgeographic.com/science/article/fatbergs-fat-cities-sewers-wet-wipes-science.

"Flushing out the truth: Jennings, Crapper and the public convenience." *London on the Ground*, September 2, 2022. www.londonontheground.com/post/flushing-out-the-truth-jennings-crapper-and-the-public-convenience.

Gannon, Megan. "The Scoop on Space Poop: How Astronauts Go Potty." *Space.com*, August 29, 2013. www.space.com/22597-space-poop-astronaut-toilet-explained.html.

"George Waring." *History*, August 21, 2018. www.history.com/topics/stories/george-waring.

Gill, N. S. "Roman Baths and Hygiene in Ancient Rome." *ThoughtCo.*, April 5, 2023. thoughtco.com/hygiene-in-ancient-rome-and-baths-119136.

Hammond, Alexander C. R. "Heroes of Progress, Sir John Harington." *Human Progress*, November 1, 2019. humanprogress.org/heroes-of-progress-pt-30-sir-john-harington/.

Harford, Tim. "How the humble S-bend made modern toilets possible." *BBC*, October 15, 2017. www.bbc.com/news/business-41188465.

Historical Census of Housing Tables: Sewage Disposal. U.S. Census Bureau. www.census.gov/data/tables/time-series/dec/coh-sewage.html.

History of Water Treatment. U.S. Environmental Protection Agency, February 2000. archive.epa.gov/water/archive/web/pdf/2001_11_15_consumer_hist.pdf.

Holzwarth, Larry. "The Unique Hygiene Habits of Our Founding Fathers." *History Collection*, November 15, 2020. historycollection.com/the-unique-hygiene-habits-of-our-founding-fathers/.

"How old is bathing?" *BBC History Revealed*, October 1, 2015. https://www.historyextra.com/period/prehistoric/when-did-humans-starting-bathing-having-baths-washing-personal-hygiene/.

"Inca Ritual Baths Studied In Peru." *Archaeology Magazine*, February 25, 2019. archaeology.org/news/2019/02/25/190225-peru-inca-baths/.

Ingraham, Christopher. "1.6 million Americans don't have indoor plumbing. Here's where they live." *Washington Post*, April 23, 2014. www.washingtonpost.com/news/wonk/wp/2014/04/23/1-6-million-americans-dont-have-indoor-plumbing-heres-where-they-live/.

Karki, Gaurab. "Steps of water purification process." *Online Biology Notes*, July 29, 2018. www.onlinebiologynotes.com/steps-of-water-purification-process/.

Katz, Leslie. "Neanderthals may have enjoyed hot baths at home in their caves." *CNET*, September 1, 2015. https://www.cnet.com/science/neanderthals-may-have-enjoyed-hot-baths-at-home-in-their-caves/.

Khoury, Walid, and Michael Stanley Gallisdorfer. "Journey through time: How ancient water systems inspired today's water technologies." *Smart Water Magazine*, September 12, 2020. smartwatermagazine.com/news/smart-water-magazine/a-journey-through-time-how-ancient-water-systems-inspired-todays-water.

Klotz, Irene. "NASA wants to save poop on the moon . . . for science." *NBC News*, October 24, 2011. www.nbcnews.com/id/wbna45021817.

Koeppel, Dan. "The Story of Soap." *New York Times*, April 15, 2020. www.nytimes.com/wirecutter/blog/history-of-soap/.

Lee, Jennifer. "He Cleaned the Streets, and Left the Presidency to Others." *New York Times*, October 1, 2009. archive.nytimes.com/cityroom.blogs.nytimes.com/2009/10/01/he-cleaned-the-streets-and-left-the-presidency-to-others/.

Leigh, Lex. "What's That Smell? Body Odor Through the Ages!" *Ancient Origins*, July 2022. www.ancient-origins.net/history-ancient-traditions/body-odor-0016979.

Little, Becky. "Why Pilgrims Arriving in America Resisted Bathing." *History*, August 23, 2023. www.history.com/news/american-colonists-pilgrims-puritans-bathing.

Margaritoff, Marco. "Who Invented The Toilet? Inside The Surprisingly Complicated History." *All Things Interesting*, March 7, 2022. allthatsinteresting.com/who-invented-the-toilet.

———. "Why Thomas Crapper's Name Is Synonymous With The Toilet Even Though He Didn't Actually Invent It." *All Things Interesting*, March 26, 2022. https://allthatsinteresting.com/thomas-crapper.

Martin, Andrew. "The Deadliest Toilet Accident In History- The Erfurt Latrine Disaster." *Medium*, November 21, 2021. historianandrew.medium.com/the-deadliest-toilet-accident-in-history-the-erfurst-latrine-disaster-cae1739630c2.

Mingren, Wu. "Groom of the Stool: Was The King's Toilet Guy The Worst Job Ever?" *Ancient Origins*, November 27, 2020. www.ancient-origins.net/history-ancient-traditions/groom-stool-0014596.

NYC Sewer System. NYC Department of Environmental Protection, March 1, 2021. storymaps.arcgis.com/stories/0d101320cceb46759335174b76fc4fd4.

Palumbo, Jacqui. "What history's bathing rituals reveal about status, purity and power." *CNN*, February 16, 2021. https://www.cnn.com/style/article/cultural-history-of-bathing-rituals/index.html.

"Pomander." Fashion Institute of Technology, August 15, 2018. fashionhistory.fitnyc.edu/pomander/.

Rowen, Karen. "Space Potty Training Secrets Revealed by Astronauts." *Space.com*, May 21, 2010. www.space.com/8465-space-potty-training-secrets-revealed-astronauts.html.

Rowley, Jim. "What Was Using The Bathroom Like In Ancient Rome?" *Ranker*, September 23, 2021. https://www.ranker.com/list/ancient-roman-toilets-history/jim-rowley.

"Sewage, the trace of our history." *We Are Water Foundation*, March 22, 2017. www.wearewater.org/en/insights/sewage-the-trace-of-our-history.

Srinivasan, Vivek. "Soap." *Medium*, January 12, 2024. medium.com/learning-by-proxy/soap-81016405a044.

Suddath, Claire. "A Brief History of Toilets." *Time*, November 19, 2009. content.time.com/time/health/article/0,8599,1940525,00.html.

"The History of Soap - When Soap Became Popular?" *Soap History*. www.soaphistory.net/soap-history/history-of-soap/#google_vignette.

Vickery, Amanda. "A brief history of human filth: how did people try to keep clean in the past?" *BBC History Magazine*, March 2, 2020. www.historyextra.com/period/general-history/history-human-dirt-how-people-keep-clean-bath/.

Water Treatment. Centers for Disease Control and Prevention. www.cdc.gov/healthywater/drinking/public/water_treatment.html.

Waters, Conny. "First Bathrooms Appeared Around 8,000 B.C In Scotland." *Ancient Pages*, December 11, 2016. www.ancientpages.com/2016/12/11/first-bathrooms-appeared-around-8000-b-c-in-scotland/#google_vignette.

"William Feetham." *Jane Austen's World*, November 11, 2010. janeaustensworld.com/tag/william-feetham/.

Worrall, Simon. "Ben Franklin Slept Here." *Smithsonian Magazine*, March 2006. www.smithsonianmag.com/travel/ben-franklin-slept-here-112338695.

Zeldovich, Lina. "How the Ancient Romans Went to the Bathroom." *Smithsonian Magazine*, November 15, 2021. https://www.smithsonianmag.com/history/how-the-ancient-romans-went-to-the-bathroom-180979056/.

Zhou, Nicole. "A City Built on Garbage: New York City's History As Told Through Its Trash." *Science Survey*, June 6, 2023. thesciencesurvey.com/features/2023/06/06/a-city-built-on-garbage-new-york-citys-history-as-told-through-its-trash/.

Books

Ashenburg, Katherine. *The Dirt on Clean: An Unsanitized History*. New York: North Point Press, 2007.

Jackson, Lee. *Dirty Old London*. New Haven: Yale University Press, 2014.

Muchembled, Robert. *Smells: A Cultural History of Odours in Early Modern Times*. Medford: Polity Press, 2020.

Smith, Virginia. *Clean: A History of Personal Hygiene and Purity*. New York: Oxford University Press, 2007.

Ward, Peter. *The Clean Body: A Modern History*. Montreal: McGill-Queen's University Press, 2019.

Journals

Butler, Lee. "'Washing off the Dust': Baths and Bathing in Late Medieval Japan." *Monumenta Nipponica* 60, no. 1 (2005): 1–41. http://www.jstor.org/stable/25066349.

De Feo, Giovanni, et. al. "The Historical Development of Sewers Worldwide." *Sustainability* 6, no. 6 (2014): 3936–3974. https://doi.org/10.3390/su6063936.

Jahn, Samia Al Azharia. "From Clarifying Pearls and Gems to Water Coagulation with Alum. History, Surviving Practices, and Technical Assessment." *Anthropos* 94, no. 4/6 (1999): 419–30. http://www.jstor.org/stable/40465012.

Larsen, Lawrence H. "Nineteenth-Century Street Sanitation: A Study of Filth and Frustration." *Wisconsin Magazine of History* 52, no. 3 (1969): 239–47. http://www.jstor.org/stable/4634439.

Schafer, Edward H. "The Development of Bathing Customs in Ancient and Medieval China and the History of the Floriate Clear Palace." *Journal of the American Oriental Society* 76, no. 2 (1956): 57–82. https://doi.org/10.2307/595074.

"Ten Great Public Health Achievements." *JAMA* 306, no. 5 (2011): 484–487. jamanetwork.com/journals/jama/fullarticle/201339.

Wald, Chelsea. "The secret history of ancient toilets." *Nature* 533 (2016): 456–458. doi.org/10.1038/533456a.

Ward, Roy Bowen. "Women in Roman Baths." *Harvard Theological Review* 85, no. 2 (1992): 125–47. http://www.jstor.org/stable/1509900.

Video

American Chemistry Council Chlorine Panel. "Celebrate Drinking Water Chlorination." American Chemistry Council. September 24, 2018. YouTube video, 1:50. www.youtube.com/watch?v=wccG-bhBqjU&t=95s.

AUTHOR'S NOTE

Some Big Ideas grab our attention more than others. Things like machines that think, rockets to the moon, and the electric world grab our attention with the brilliance of fireworks. Every mention of them seems to demand to be punctuated with an exclamation point. Other Big Ideas, though, are not so well received, and it is in this category that the Big Ideas of sanitation and clean water find themselves. Flushing a toilet or opening the tap for a glass of water are such ordinary actions that they fly past with utterly no thought . . . that is, until the toilet fails to flush, or the tap water spills out of the faucet cloudy with dirt. Then the mind focuses completely on their loss.

For many people, the absence of sanitation and clean water are temporary events, the results of natural disaster or momentary equipment failure, afflictions mostly remedied within days. But the blessings of sanitation and clean water are not the case for huge numbers of others around the globe. It is sad to note that more people have mobile phones than access to a toilet. The numbers tell the story: Over 2 billion people lack access to clean water. About 1.5 billion people lack private toilets and latrines, of which about 400 million defecate in the open: in street gutters, behind bushes, or in bodies of water. The lack of basic sanitation brings diseases like cholera, dysentery, and diarrhea, the last killing hundreds of thousands of children every year.

Adequate sanitation and clean water—along with vaccines—are the pillars of public health, and their impact is measured in untold millions of saved lives. They provide a foundation on which cultures and societies can thrive . . . and offering the chance for the people of those cultures and societies to dream up their own new Big Ideas.

And remember that Big Ideas are not an end point but just one stop on a continuum of ideas—big *and* small—that stretch across time. Whether an inspired success or a tragic failure, the ideas are a trail I'll follow in this series. And, like other trips, the pleasure will not be in the destination but in the journey.

INDEX

A
Africa, 80
air baths, 84
American Revolution, 82
Ancient Greeks, 12
animals. *See also* horses
    in public toilets, 13, 15
Apollo 10, 54, 58
aqueducts, 65, 80, 106, 107
Arab soap makers, 89
Aztecs, aqueducts built by, 80

B
bathhouses, 71, 76. *See also* public baths
bathrooms, 53
baths, 81. *See also* public baths
    air, 84
    aqueducts for, 65, 80, 106, 107
    bubonic plague influence on, 74–76
    class systems and, 86, 87
    Founding Fathers and, 82–84
    fresh water, 61, 62
    steam, 80
    washbasin, 82
bathtubs, 83, 84, 86
    wooden, 70–71
bathwater, 65, 75
Big Sewer, 38–39, 50
body, cleanliness of, 77
body odor, 78–79, 81
    pastes for, 63, 80
    soap for, 67, 87, 88–89, 90
bubonic plague, 74–76

C
castle toilets, 20–22
ceramic sewer pipes, 9, 106
cesspools. *See* pits, for poop and pee
chamber pots, 9, 15, 17, 24, 108
China
    poop and pee pits in, 18, 19, 107

water filtration in, 92
chlorine, 95, 100
cholera outbreak, in London, 109
Civil War, 113
class systems, baths and, 86, 87
clean water, 6, 28, 94, 105, 109, 110
    chlorine added, 100
    filter for, 99
    Safe Drinking Water Act, 111
cloacae. See sewage
cold water, 67, 82, 83, 85
Crapper, Thomas, 33, 109
Cumming, Alexander, 28, 29, 30, 108

D
death, poop and pee causing, 23
Department of Street Cleaning (1895), 6, 42, 109, 114
dirty water, 85, 90–91
    boiling of, 92
disease-causing microbes, in water, 94, 95, 103
drains, 26, 106, 108, 113
    S-shaped pipe for, 28, 29
    U-shaped pipes for, 33

E
Egyptians, 62, 63, 106
Elizabeth I (queen), 26, 108
enclosed toilets, 11
epidemiology, 109
Europe
    bubonic plague, 74–76
    castle toilets in, 20–22
    municipal water treatment plants in, 109
    public baths in, 72–73
explosive gases, from waste, 15

F
fatbergs, 51
Feetham, William, 85
fertilizer, sewage as, 17

filtration, of water, 92–93, 96–99
flush toilet, 30, 33, 34, 108
Founding Fathers, 82–84
fragrance, for body odor, 79
Franklin, Benjamin, 84
fresh water, 61, 62

G
General Assembly, of United Nations, 111
germs, 17, 94, 95
Global Analysis and Assessment of Sanitation and Drinking-Water (GLAAS), 111
graffiti, 14
Great Exhibition, 30–31, 108
"Great Stink," 35, 36, 37, 109
Greece, 10, 92, 107
    palace toilet in, 11
    public baths in, 65
Groom of the Stool, 24, 25, 108

H
Hancock, John, 83
Harington, John, 26, 27, 28, 29, 30, 108
Henry VI (king), 22, 23, 107
Henry VII (king), 24, 25
Himba people, Africa, 80
home toilets, 16
horses, 1, 2, 3, 5
    poop and pee of, 4, 40–41
hot water, 70, 85

I
indoor toilets, 8, 52
Indus Valley, 10, 62, 106, 109
International Space Station, 55, 56

J
Japan, wooden bathtubs in, 70–71
Jefferson, Thomas, 83

K
Koch, Robert, 94

L
laws, for toilets, 52
Leal, John L., 95
London
    cholera outbreak in, 109
    fatbergs in, 51
    "Great Stink," 35, 36, 37, 109
    Thames river, 24, 34–37, 39, 84, 107

M
Machu Picchu, Peru, 81
McKinley, William, 114
Memphis, Tennessee, 113
Middle East, 9, 62, 92, 106
    soap created in, 88, 89
municipal water treatment plants, 109

N
New Jersey, 49, 95
New York City, 40
    Department of Street Cleaning, 6, 42, 109, 114
    fatbergs in, 51
    street cleaners, 43–47, 114
    toilet laws in, 52
Nile River, 106

O
odor. *See* body odor
128-seat toilet, over Thames river, 24, 107
otijize, 80
outhouses, 41, 52, 53

P
pastes, for body odor, 63, 80
Pasteur, Louis, 94
Peru, 81
pipes
    ceramic sewer, 9, 106
    indoor water, 34
    S-shaped, 28, 29, 108
    U-shaped, 33

pits, for poop and pee, 16, 17, 52
    in China, 18, 19, 107
poop and pee, 6, 7. *See also* waste
    basement full of, 22, 23
    chamber pots for, 9, 15, 17, 24, 107, 108
    horses, 4, 40–41
    pit of, 16, 17, 18, 19, 52
    sewage, 6, 17, 34–37, 39, 106, 107, 113
    on spacecrafts, 56–59
    street cleaners, 43–47
public baths, 67, 71, 72, 76, 106, 107
    in Europe, 72–73
    gender and, 68–69
    in Greece, 65
    for Romans, 65, 66
public toilets, 12, 13, 14, 15
    at Great Exhibition, 30–31
    in the home, 32
Pure Food and Drug Act (1906), 110
purification of water, 96–101

R

raw water, 96
Romans
    aqueducts and, 65, 106, 107
    home toilets of, 16
    public baths and, 65, 66
    toilet construction and, 12–13
Roosevelt, Teddy, 42, 113

S

Safe Drinking Water Act (1974), 111
sanitation, 103, 105, 108, 113, 114
    General Assembly of United Nations, 111
    GLASS, 111
    WHO, 110
sea, waste in, 45, 48, 49
sedimentation tank, 98
sewage, 6, 113
    as fertilizer, 17
    systems for, 106, 107
    Thames river, 34–37, 39
sewers
    Big Sewer, 38–39, 50
    clogged, 15
    dirty water and, 90–91
    water, 11, 13
showers, 85
size, of bathrooms, 53
skinny-dipping, 84
Snow, John, 109
soap, 67, 87, 88–89
    dirty water and, 90
spacecrafts
    International Space Station, 55, 56
    poop and pee disposal on, 56–59
    toilets on, 54–55
Spanish-American War, 114
S-shaped pipe, 28, 29, 108
standing water, 29
steam baths, 80
Stockholm, United Nations Conference in, 110
stone huts, in Scotland, 8, 106
street cleaners, 43–47, 114
strigil, 67
Strong, William, 113

T

Thames river, London
    Franklin in, 84
    128-seat toilet over, 24, 107
    sewage in, 34–37, 39
thermae. See public baths
timeline, for toilets, 106–11
toilets, 10, 60, 110
    castle, 20–22
    chamber pots as, 9, 15, 17, 24, 108
    construction of, 12–13
    drains for, 26, 28, 29, 106, 108, 113
    enclosed, 11
    flush, 30, 33, 34, 108
    home, 16
    indoor, 8, 52
    outhouses, 41, 52, 53
    public, 12, 13, 14, 15, 30–31, 32
    on spacecrafts, 54–55

timeline for, 106–11
trough, 8, 11
Turkey, bathing in, 80

U

United Nations
    Conference on the Human Environment, 110
    General Assembly of the, 111
United Nations Water (UN-Water), 111
United States, 81
    municipal water treatment plants in, 109
    Pure Food and Drug Act, 110
    Safe Drinking Water Act, 111
UN-Water. *See* United Nations Water
U-shaped pipes, 33

W

Waring, George E., Jr., 112, 113
    Department of Street Cleaning, 6, 42, 109, 114
    street cleaners, 43–47, 114
wars
    Civil War, 113
    Spanish-American War, 114
washbasin, 82
Washington, George, 82
waste
    discarding of, 8, 10, 19, 38
    explosive gases from, 15
    in the sea, 45, 48, 49
water, 10, 19. *See also* clean water
    chlorine added to, 95, 100
    cold, 67, 82, 83, 85
    dirty, 85, 90–91
    disease-causing microbes in, 94, 95, 103
    filtration of, 92–93, 96–99
    fresh, 61, 62
    hot, 70, 85
    purification of, 96–101
    raw, 86
    sewer, 11, 13
    standing, 29
water closet, 53

water-distribution systems, 106
wells, 106
wooden bathtubs, 70–71
World Health Organization (WHO), 110
    United Nations Water and, 111

Y

yellow fever, 113, 114

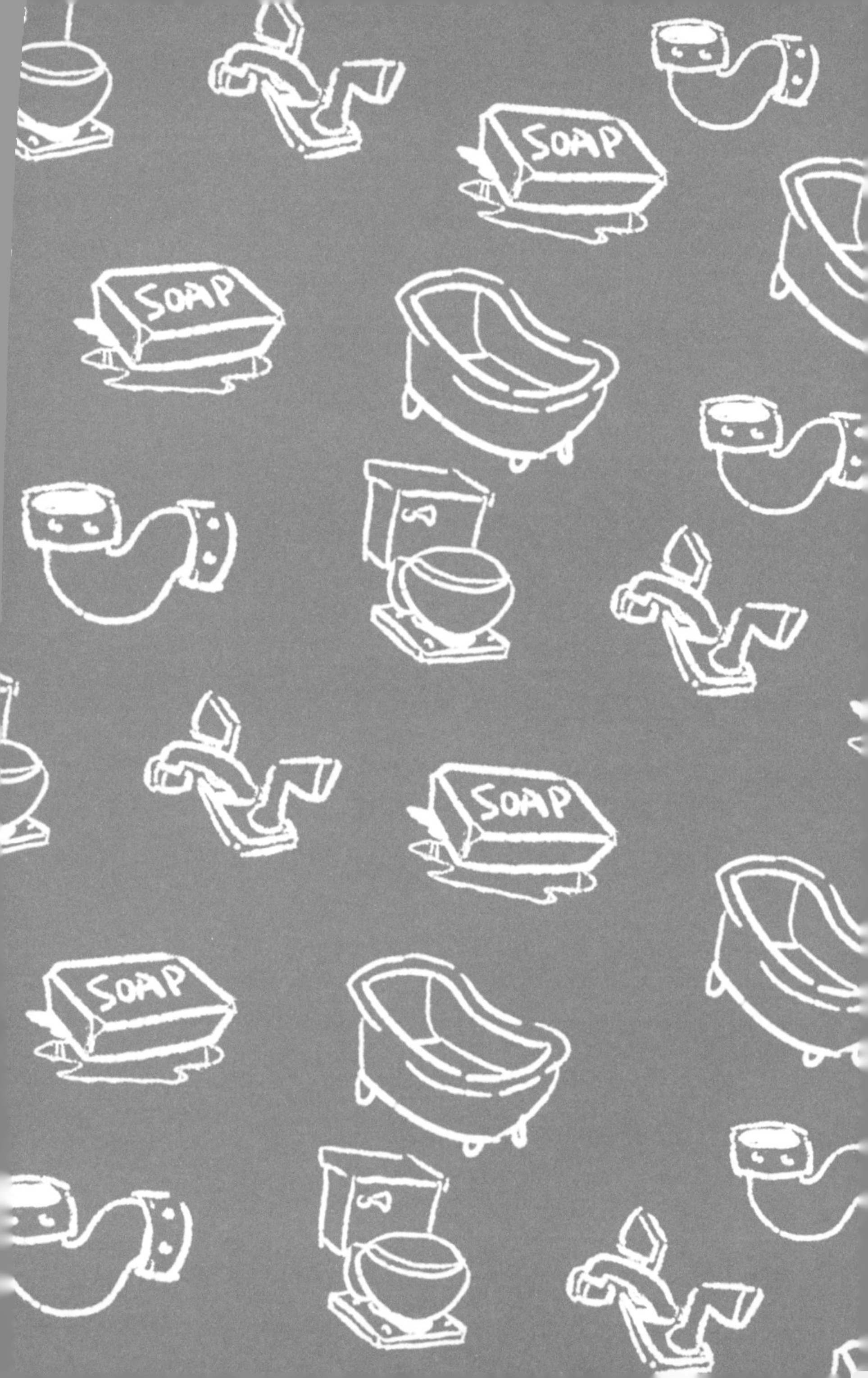
SOAP
SOAP
SOAP
SOAP

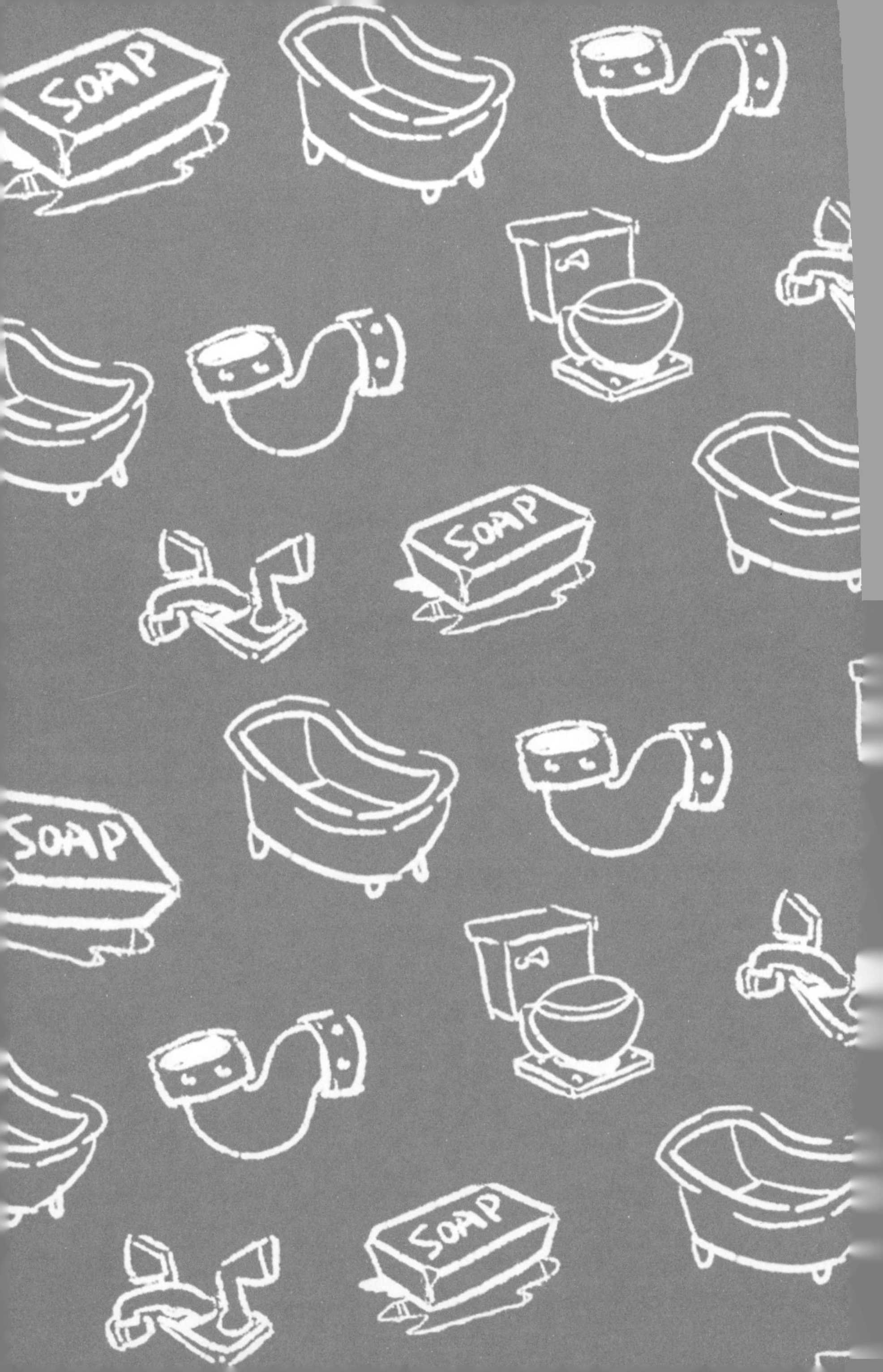
SOAP
SOAP
SOAP
SOAP